AGENCY, PARTNERSHIP, AND THE LLC

IN A NUTSHELL

THIRD EDITION

By

J. DENNIS HYNES

Nicholas A. Rosenbaum Professor of Law, Emeritus
University of Colorado School of Law

and

MARK J. LOEWENSTEIN

Nicholas A. Rosenbaum Professor of Law
University of Colorado School of Law

THOMSON

WEST

Mat #40333590

COPYRIGHT © 1997 WEST PUBLISHING CO.

© West, a Thomson business, 2001

© 2005 Thomson/West

      610 Opperman Drive

      P.O. Box 64526

      St. Paul, MN 55164–0526

      1–800–328–9352

Printed in the United States of America

ISBN 0–314–15894–4

TEXT IS PRINTED ON 10% POST CONSUMER RECYCLED PAPER

I dedicate this third edition to my colleague, mentor and friend, Professor of Law Emeritus J. Dennis Hynes, the author of the first two editions of this Nutshell.

Mark J. Loewenstein

*

PREFACE

This Nutshell seeks to describe, succinctly, the law as it relates to agency and unincorporated business entities. These areas, particularly agency law, have ancient origins, yet are constantly being reexamined. Indeed, the law of agency has just been restated for a third time by the American Law Institute, and that has been one of the developments that prompted the preparation of this third edition of the Nutshell. Unincorporated business entities–partnerships (general and limited), business trusts and limited liability companies—have been the subject of considerable legislation at the state level in recent years, due in part to changes in federal tax laws. Uniform acts in these areas that once stood unchanged for decades are now being revised frequently. These developments, too, prompted this third edition.

Another development that prompted this edition relates to the philosophy that now characterizes statutes relating to unincorporated business entities. Although, traditionally, the rights and liabilities of the owners of such entities were often statutory questions, increasingly they have become matters of contract (except, perhaps, in those general partnerships where the partners have not bothered to enter into an agreement). The statutes have thus largely become default rules when the parties have not agreed otherwise. The drafters of these statutes are taking this trend to its logical extreme, even permitting the waiver of fundamental fiduciary duties in the agreements of the owners. This edition of the Nutshell seeks to capture developments on this front as well.

Despite these legal developments, this third edition follows the excellent organization of the prior editions, with the principles of agency law set forth first, followed by an examination of the various forms of unincorporated business entities. This is a logical sequence, as agency law is a powerful influence on the law as it relates to unincorporated business entities, and explains why, in many law schools, the two subjects are taught together in a single course.

I am indebted to my colleague, mentor and friend, J. Dennis Hynes, who has provided me with the opportunity to assume the authorship of this Nutshell. I have benefited greatly from the thoroughness and attention to detail embodied in the earlier editions of this Nutshell, a standard that I have sought to meet.

MARK J. LOEWENSTEIN
Nicholas A. Rosenbaum Professor of Law

Boulder, Colorado
October 2005

OUTLINE

PART III.   EXTERNAL MATTERS; RIGHTS OF THIRD PARTIES

OUTLINE

TABLE OF CASES

References are to Pages

XVII

TABLE OF CASES

*

AGENCY, PARTNERSHIP, AND THE LLC

IN A NUTSHELL

THIRD EDITION

*

INTRODUCTION

This book is organized as follows. The basic terminology used in the law of agency, partnership, the LLC, and other unincorporated business enterprises will be defined in a Glossary at the beginning of Part I, followed by a brief essay on the basic elements of the agency relationship and the differences between agency and other relationships that appear similar to it. The internal rights and liabilities of the parties to an agency relationship will be described in Part II. External rights and liabilities, including those of parties who are strangers to the relationship, will be explained in Part III. The partnership, the limited partnership, and the LLC will be the main focus in Part IV, which will cover creation of the business entity, ownership status, management rights and agency powers of owners, limitations on distributions, transfer of ownership interests, dissolution, and liquidation or sale of the business.

*

PART I
BASIC TERMINOLOGY

GLOSSARY

Definitions of the most frequently used terms and concepts in agency, partnership, the LLC, and other unincorporated business enterprises are set forth below. Of course, no definition is final because the law continually is responding to changing notions of social and economic policy. Nevertheless, there is considerable agreement among lawyers and judges with regard to the basic terminology and principles in this area of the law, making a description of the basic terminology useful to the reader.

Agency—The agency relationship is a consensual relationship created when one person (the agent) acts on behalf of and subject to the control of another (the principal).

Agent—An agent is a person (which can include an entity, like a corporation, partnership, or LLC) who acts on behalf of and subject to the control of another.

3

Agent's agent—This sometimes confusing phrase describes a person who acts on behalf of and subject to the control of an agent for another (the agent's principal), but who is not responsible to and does not have the power to create liability for the agent's principal, usually because the agent did not have authority to delegate duties. The phrase is confusing because a subagent (see below) also is an agent of an agent. (The difference is that the subagent is also the agent of, and thus possesses the power to create liability for, the agent's principal as a result of authorized delegation by the agent.) The confusion can be dispelled only by seeing the language in context. Although sometimes ambiguous, the phrase can serve the useful purpose, once a situation is analyzed, of sharply delineating the relationship of the parties in just a few words. Section 37 C of this book develops these concepts.

Apparent authority—Apparent authority is the power of an agent to bind the principal to unauthorized contracts. The power is created by manifestations, which can be subtle and indirect, of the principal to the third party that are reasonably relied upon by the third party.

Borrowed employee/Borrowed servant—An employee (servant) is borrowed when exposure to vicarious liability for the torts of the employee is shifted from the lending employer to the borrowing employer. The standards for determining when an employee is borrowed are in conflict and confusion in the law of many states. The majority rule appears to require both a transfer of the allegiance of the employee and control by the borrowing employer before vicarious liability is shifted from the lending employer to the borrowing employer.

Business trust—The business trust is a form of doing business through use of a trust. The business trust recently has received significant statutory treatment in some states. At the present time it is infrequently used except in specialized security transactions. It is covered in the Introduction to unincorporated business enterprises in Part IV of this book.

Co-agent—A co-agent is one of two or more agents of a principal. Co-agents can be in a hierarchical relationship, such as a president of a corporation and her secretary. Hierarchical co-agency appears confusingly like subagency because the secretary functions throughout the working day under the direction and control of the president and may even have been hired by the president. Yet the secretary is a co-agent, not the president's agent, because both the president and the secretary work on behalf of their common employer.

Control—Control means to exercise authority over; to dominate; to direct; to regulate. This word has different meanings in the law of agency depending upon context. If, for example, the issue being pursued is liability for the physical torts of another, a special kind of control, over physical conduct and over the details of the activity involved, is required. If instead the issue being pursued involves liability for nonphysical torts like fraud, or contractual liability, the requirement of control does not include control over the physical conduct of the purported agent.

Disclosed principal—A principal is disclosed when a party entering into a contract arranged by an agent has notice of the principal's existence and identity. Under such circumstances, the agent acting in the transaction is not a party to the contract in the absence of special facts, like guaranteeing the contract.

Employee—The term employee is a defined term in the Restatement (Third) of Agency, § 7.07 (T.D. No. 5, 2004) and is used to describe an agent for whose torts the principal is vicariously liable. Thus, an employee is "an agent whose principal controls or has the right to control the manner and means of the agent's performance of work." It replaces the term "servant," used in earlier Restatements of Agency and in many common law cases. The new definition makes clear that the term is not limited to traditional, compensated employees, as the definition goes on to provide that "the fact that work is performed gratuitously does not relieve a principal of liability." The term might also exclude an agent who is an employee for purposes of federal and state laws, but whose principal lacks the right to control the manner and means of the agent's performance of work.

Employer—This term is used in the Restatement (Third) of Agency to describe a principal who is vicariously liable for the torts of its "employee" agent. See the definition of "employee." The term "employer" replaces the term "master," used in earlier Restatements of Agency and in many common law cases. As used in the Restatement (Third) of Agency, the term "employer" includes principals who, for other purposes (such as coverage under various federal and state laws regulating the employment relationship), are not "employers."

Fiduciary—A fiduciary is a person who has a duty to act primarily for the benefit of another in matters connected with his undertaking. The fiduciary concept is central to the law of agency because an agent acts on behalf of another (the principal) and thus occupies a position of trust.

General agent—A general agent is an agent authorized by the principal to conduct a series of transactions involving continuity of service, like a manager of a business. A general agent does not require fresh authorization for each transaction.

Independent contractor—"Independent contractor" is an ambiguous phrase in the law of agency. It can refer to a nonagent, such as a building contractor who contracts to build something for an owner but who is not subject to control over the physical conduct of the work and who does not act on the owner's behalf, instead merely benefiting the owner as a result of performance under an ordinary contract. It can also refer to a nonemployee agent, such as a real estate broker or a lawyer, who acts as agent for another but who is not subject to control by the principal over the manner and means of the agent's performance of the work. A principal is not liable for the physical torts of a nonemployee agent (independent contractor). The Restatement (Third) abandons this term. To determine whether a principal is vicariously liable for the tortious conduct of its agent, the Restatement (Third) has a special definition of the term "employee." If the agent falls within this definition (which focuses on the degree of control that the principal has over the agent), the agent is an employee and the principal has respondeat superior liability for the employee's tortious conduct. The Restatement (Third) also uses the term "nonagent service provider" in some comments to capture one of the meanings of "independent contractor" set forth here.

Inherent agency power—The doctrine of inherent agency power states that a general agent has the power to bind the principal to unauthorized acts beyond the reach of the traditional doctrines of apparent authority and estoppel if the acts done "usually accompany or are incidental to" authorized transactions. It is a controversial doctrine in the literature of agency and has been abandoned in the Restatement (Third) of Agency.

LLC—The acronym "LLC" stands for "limited liability company." The LLC is a relatively new form of doing business in an unincorporated capacity. Upon proper filing, the owners of the business enjoy full liability protection from the debts of the business. The LLC is described in the Introduction to Part IV and is covered in detail in Chapter 15. All states allow the creation of LLCs.

LLLP—The acronym "LLLP" stands for "limited liability limited partnership." It refers to a limited partnership in which not only the limited partners but also the general partners have full liability protection from the debts of the business. This very new form of doing business is described in the Introduction to part IV and is covered in Chapter 14. To date (June 2005) at least 16 states have legislation providing for the LLLP.

LLP—The acronym "LLP" stands for "limited liability partnership." It is a recent innovation in the law of partnership, following the widespread adoption of statutes authorizing the LLC. It refers to a general partnership in which the partners acquire liability protection from the debts of the business through the proper filing of a statement of qualification. This new form of doing business is described in the Introduction to Part IV and is covered in Chapter 11. All states have legislation providing for the LLP.

Master—The word "master" is a term of art in the law of agency. It identifies a principal who employs an agent to perform services and who controls or has the right to control the manner and means of the agent's performance of the service. A master is vicariously liable for the torts of its servant under the doctrine of respondeat superior. This term has been abandoned by the Restatement (Third) of Agency which, instead, uses the term "employer." See that definition, *supra*.

Member—The word "member" is used to describe a person with an ownership interest in an LLC. Nearly all state statutes on the LLC refer to owners as "members."

On behalf of—The phrase "on behalf of" describes an essential element of the agency relationship. It means acting *primarily* for the benefit of another, not merely benefiting another by one's actions. A person who acts on behalf of another ordinarily is a fiduciary of the other, due to the trust being placed in the actor under such circumstance.

Operating agreement—An operating agreement is an agreement of all the members of an LLC relating to the affairs of the LLC and the conduct of its business. It is analogous to a partnership agreement.

Partially disclosed principal—A principal is partially disclosed when a party to a contract arranged by an agent has notice that the agent is acting on behalf of someone but does not know the identity of the principal. Under this circumstance it is inferred, subject to agreement otherwise, that the agent is a party to the contract, as is the principal. The Restatement (Third) of Agency does not use this term, employing in its place the term "unidentified principal."

Partnership—A partnership is an association of two or more persons to carry on as co-owners a business for profit. It can be formed without any papers being prepared or filed and without the owners even realizing that they are creating a partnership. The partnership is described more fully in the Introduction to part IV and is covered in detail in Chapters 11–13.

Principal—A principal is the one for whom action is taken by an agent. The action is taken on behalf of and subject to the principal's control.

Respondeat superior—This Latin phrase means, "let the master answer." It is a shorthand and classic expression for the doctrine that a master/employer is vicariously liable for the torts of its servant/employee committed within the scope of employment.

Servant—The word "servant" is a term of art in the law of agency. It has been replaced by the term "employee," as defined in Restatement (Third) of Agency § 7.07 (T.D. No. 5, 2004). See the definition of "employee." A servant is an agent who is employed to perform a service. The manner and means that the agent uses to perform the service is subject to the right of control of the master.

Sole proprietorship—A sole proprietorship occurs when a person carries on a business as its sole owner. No forms need to be prepared or filed with the state in order to create a sole proprietorship. The proprietor is personally liable for the debts of the business and pays income taxes on the net income of the business. The sole proprietorship is covered in the Introduction to part IV.

Special agent—A special agent is an agent who is authorized to conduct a single transaction or a series of transactions not involving continuity of service, such as a real estate broker. In general, a special agent requires fresh authorization for each separate transaction. A general agent can be a special agent for a particular transaction, such as the manager of a business who is instructed to buy a vacation home for the owner of the business.

Subagent—Subagency exists when an agent (A) is authorized expressly or (more commonly) implicitly by the principal (P) to appoint another person (B) to perform all or part of the actions A has agreed to take on behalf of P. If A remains responsible to P for the actions taken, B is a subagent and A is both an agent (to P) and a principal (to B). B is an agent of P as well as A, which underscores the importance of P's express or implied consent to this relationship. See "agent's agent" for the distinction between that concept and "subagent."

Undisclosed principal—A principal is undisclosed when a party to a contract arranged by an agent is unaware that the agent is acting for a principal and thus assumes that the agent is contracting on its own behalf. Under these circumstances the agent is a party to the contract (as is the undisclosed principal, assuming the agent is authorized or has the power to bind the principal).

Unidentified principal—The phrase "unidentified principal" is a synonym for "partially disclosed principal" and is the term preferred by the Restatement (Third) of Agency. As noted under the definition of partially disclosed principal, this status exists when a party to a contract arranged by an agent has notice that the agent is acting on behalf of another but does not know the identity of the principal.

Vicarious liability—Vicarious liability exists when one person is held liable for the wrongs of another.

CHAPTER 1

THE AGENCY RELATIONSHIP

§ 1. Defining the Agency Relationship

An agency relationship is created when one person (the agent) consents to act on behalf of and subject to the control of another (the principal). As developed below, this seemingly simple arrangement can have serious consequences, not all of them positive, for one or both of the parties to it and for third parties who come into contact with the agent.

A. The Restatement of Agency

The Restatement of Agency is published by the American Law Institute ("ALI"), a voluntary, non-official association of judges, lawyers, and law professors. One of the main activities of the ALI is preparing and publishing restatements of the law, which describe the law in a particular area by black letter text with comments and illustrations. One of the goals of the ALI is to restate the common law in an organized and reasonably clear way. The Restatement of Agency (Second) (1958) ("R2d") is one of the most respected and influential of the many restatements published by the ALI, in large part because of the careful and competent analytical and taxonomical work of its authors. It is heavily used by courts as a source of agency law. The ALI has just completed preparation of the Restatement (Third)of Agency (2005) ("R3d"), which, subject to minor editorial changes, was approved at the 2005 annual meeting of the ALI. Because the final version of the Restatement of Agency (Third) was not available at the time of the publication of this Nutshell, references are furnished to the various tentative drafts (T.D.) where the cited sections may be found.

A definition of the agency relationship is set forth in R3d § 1.02 (T.D. No. 2, 2001). That definition, quoted below, enjoys nearly universal usage by courts and commentators.

Agency is the fiduciary relation that arises when one person (a "principal") manifests assent to another person (an "agent") that the agent shall act on the principal's behalf and subject to the principal's control, and the agent manifests assent or otherwise consents so to act.

An example of an agency relationship is provided in comment b to R2d § 1: "Thus, when one asks a friend to do a slight service for him, such as to return for credit goods recently purchased from a store, neither one may have any realization that they are creating an agency relation or be aware of the legal obligations which would result from performance of the service."

As the example indicates, the relationship of principal and agent can be created without any awareness of the consequences to the parties. In fact, an agency relationship can be created even when the parties expressly deny the existence of an agency relationship between them. A great deal turns on whether an agency relationship exists because this legal relationship can generate costs as well as benefits for both the agent and the principal. The finding of an agency relationship usually is made by the jury as trier of fact. If the facts are not in dispute and inference of agency or nonagency is clear, however, the decision will be made by the court as a matter of law on the reasoning that a question of law exists whenever the court determines that reasonable people could not differ on a matter.

B.　The Elements of an Agency Relationship

The agency relationship involves three basic elements: assent, control, and acting on behalf of. Each of these elements will be discussed below.

Assent. Both parties must assent to an agency relationship. It is important to be alert to the factual subtleties of implied assent, where conduct manifests assent even when no words are exchanged. A nod of the head or a failure to object when action taken previously in an agency capacity is again proposed can constitute implied assent under certain circumstances. The principal-agent relationship need not be based on contract, although it usually is. A gratuitous agent is as much an agent as any other. Thus the law of agency is not simply one aspect of the law of contracts. Instead, it spreads across and touches nearly all areas of the law.

Control. The meaning of the word "control" seems obvious and is readily presumed in ordinary conversation. At a minimum it means that the agent must respond to the directions of the principal. A useful judicial description of control is that it involves "an element of subservience." Ahn v. Rooney, Pace, Inc. (S.D.N.Y. 1985). But, as the comments to R3d § 1.01 make clear, it is not just the ability to dominate or control that defines the relationship between a principal and an agent; rather an agency relationship exists when the person subject to the dominance or influence of another consents to act on behalf of the other and the other has the right of control.

When applied to the myriad situations in which agency is at issue, however, "control" turns out to be ambiguous and its meaning easy to manipulate. Also, as mentioned in the Glossary, control is defined in different ways depending on the nature of the liability being asserted against the principal. A different kind of control is required for liability based on a physical tort (see § 16) than for liability based on the claimant's expectations: see § 28 (fraud) and § 38 (contractual liability based on apparent authority).

One cannot legitimately infer that control exists solely from an unrestricted right to terminate a relationship. See, e.g., Lavazzi v. McDonald's Corp.

(Ill. App. 1992), stating: "A right to rescind a contract or to call off the work is generally insufficient to establish control and impose liability."

On behalf of. The acting party must be acting "on behalf of" (or, as some courts say, "primarily" for the benefit of) the principal in order to create the special powers and liabilities that accompany the agency relationship. If the acting party is acting on its own behalf, it is not a fiduciary nor is it fair, in the eyes of many courts, to subject the other party to the special burdens (to be developed throughout this book) of being a principal.

It is true that a paid agent is motivated by the prospect of receiving compensation and thus has a personal stake in the situation. But compensation is earned by acting in a manner that advances the interests of the principal and thus the paid agent is considered to be *primarily* acting for the benefit of another. Merely acting in a way that benefits another, even when there is control, does not establish agency.

For example, a subscriber benefits from the delivery of a newspaper to her home. Also, she may exercise some control over the carrier, such as specifying where to throw the paper, when to suspend delivery, and so forth. Yet the relationship between subscriber and carrier clearly is not an agency relationship. To hold otherwise would expose her to liability for the negligence of the carrier while delivering a paper to her home. Instead, the carrier is considered to be acting primarily for the benefit of the newspaper or for his own benefit, depending on the relationship he has with the newspaper.

Another example is that of a plumber who installs a new hot water heater in a home. Again, this action benefits the homeowner and again she is in a position to exercise some control, such as when to install the hot water heater, what door to bring it in, requiring the plumber to clean his muddy boots before walking on her carpet, and so forth. Yet no court would characterize the relationship as an agency relationship, making the homeowner liable, say, for the plumber's negligence while driving directly to her home to install the water heater or liable for the bill the plumber owes for tools and equipment used in the installation. Absent special facts, the plumber is considered to be primarily acting for his own benefit when delivering and installing the water heater, largely because he sets the price and profits from the sale. In no sense would one expect loyalty, a fundamental feature of an agency relationship, from a plumber to a customer.

The distinction between actions taken "on behalf of" and actions that merely "benefit" another is sometimes difficult to draw, however. Also, although the "on behalf of" element is fundamental to the agency relationship, occasionally a court will minimize or even ignore it, possibly with a particular result in mind.

The fiduciary nature of the agency relationship "signified that an agent must act in the principal's interest as well as on the principal's behalf." R3d, § 1.01, comment e. Sections 13–15 of this book describe the responsibilities that attach to one who agrees to act in the interests of and on behalf of another and thus becomes a fiduciary.

Proof of agency. As noted above, the resolution of the issue whether an agency relationship exists is ordinarily one of fact. The burden of proof is on the one asserting the existence of an agency relationship.

It will sometimes be the case that the relationship in question cannot easily be characterized. Elements of several distinct legal relationships may be combined in a confusing way. When this is so, it may be that the consequences of characterizing a relationship as one of agency will as a practical matter carry substantial weight in the determination of the court.

C. Uses of Agency; Ambiguity of the Word "Agency"

A person can do many things through an agent. Although one thinks of agency as primarily a commercial subject, agency is used in personal and governmental situations as well. With regard to when one can act through an agent, see *Mays v. Brighton Bank* (Tenn.App.1992): "Unless prevented by public policy, a statute, or a contract requiring personal performance, what a person can lawfully do himself, he can do through an agent."

The words "agency" and "agent" are ambiguous because they sometimes are used in settings outside of the law of agency. It thus is necessary to look at context when determining the meaning of those words. See *Ex Parte Charter Retreat Hosp., Inc.* (Ala.1989): "The term 'agency' is frequently used to describe an arrangement which does not rise to the level of a principal/agent relationship.... Indeed, that term is also often used in statutes or constitutional provisions in a more restricted sense than that commonly given it and, where so used, its significance must generally be determined by a study of the context."

(i) The Electronic Agent. An example of the ambiguity of the word "agent" is contained in § 2–103(*l*)(g) of Article Two of the Uniform Commercial Code, where the phrase "electronic agent" is introduced and defined as follows: " 'Electronic agent' means a computer program or an electronic or other automated means used independently to initiate an action or respond to electronic records or performances in whole or in part, without review by an individual." There is no consent between principal and agent in this context, of course. The Uniform Commercial Code is a statute, however, and can give the word "agent" whatever meaning its drafters desire.

(ii) The Escrow Agent. The phrase "escrow agent" is another example of the ambiguous use of the word "agent." An escrow "is a deed, money or chattel delivered to a person, the holder, by another and which the holder contracts to retain until the happening or nonhappening of an event; if the event happens, or fails to happen, before a specified time, the escrow is to be delivered to a third person; otherwise [the holder] is to return it to the depositor." R2d § 14 D. Escrow is widely used when closing a home sale. Conventionally, the seller delivers a deed and the buyer a check into escrow, with the escrow holder usually a title insurance company, and those items are exchanged at the closing.

Until the specified event does or does not occur, the holder is not truly an agent of either party because neither party can direct the holder to do any act that is inconsistent with the agreement among the parties. Without control, there is no agency. Thus, the description in R2d § 14 D of the party holding the property as "holder" is more accurate than the commonly used phrase "escrow agent." Nevertheless, the phrase "escrow agent" is widely used. Once the event has or has not occurred, however, true agency surfaces. The holder becomes the agent for delivery to the appropriate party of the subject matter of the escrow.

With regard to risk of loss (embezzlement by the escrow holder, for example), it is placed on the person who holds title to the property at the time of the loss, which almost always would be the party contributing the property to the escrow. Perhaps the rationale underlying this allocation of loss is that such party would be the one most likely to have the property insured at the time of loss.

§ 2. The Principal

A principal is the one for whom the agent acts. The action is taken on behalf of and subject to the control of the principal. Although it is natural to think of a principal as a sole proprietor of a business, the concept of principal applies well beyond that. Among others, it includes the homeowner who employs a gardener or a chauffeur and it includes a corporation that employs thousands of agents.

§ 3. Introduction to the Liabilities of a Principal

The status of having a person act on your behalf and subject to your control carries the obvious benefits of being able to accomplish more through the work of others than one could by working alone. Modern enterprise depends heavily on the use of agents. Our economy would be vastly different and far more primitive if everyone has to accomplish all transactions on an individual, personal basis. Benefits generate burdens as well, however, and this truism applies to the law of agency. At a minimum, common sense dictates that a person should be liable, in tort or contract, for his or her directed acts. O.W. Holmes regarded this as the true meaning of the maxim, *qui facit per alium, facit per se* (he who acts through another acts himself). (O.W. Holmes, Agency, 5 Harv. L. Rev. 1 (1891)).

A principal's liability extends beyond commanded acts, however, to include liability under certain circumstances for acts that the principal did not intend or desire and even for acts that the agent was expressly forbidden to do, as developed in § 25. Thus the liability of a principal includes strict liability because it can exist regardless of the degree of care exercised over the selection and supervision of the agent. One well-known illustration of strict liability, the doctrine of respondeat superior, will be discussed in § 16.

It is the combination of control and action "on behalf of" that creates the strict liability imposed on a principal for the acts of its agent within the scope of the relationship. Control over another does not, by itself, account for strict liability. Instead, the law of torts has for centuries created a duty of due care based on control, exposing the person in control to liability for negligence. And action "on behalf of" also does not alone account for strict liability. If it did, trust beneficiaries would be liable for the acts of their trustees, as would those benefiting from guardianship and conservatorship. (Trustees, guardians, and conservators clearly act on behalf of their beneficiaries but are not subject to control by the beneficiaries, and thus are not agents.) Instead, it is the privilege of having a person act both on one's behalf and subject to one's control that creates the special status of a principal and subjects the principal to strict liability.

Agency costs. Principals run risks and incur unintended costs when they use the services of agents, as developed throughout this book. These costs are referred to as "agency costs" in much of today's literature on the risks of enterprise. The phrase "agency costs" is usually defined to include "the costs to the principal of obtaining faithful and effective performance by his agents." Posner, Economic Analysis of the Law 392 (4th ed. 1992). For elaboration, see Brody, 40 N.Y.L.Sch.L.Rev. 462 (1996): "Agency costs are at the heart of the maxim: 'If you want something done right, you have to do it yourself.' To an economist, agency costs arise because the agent simply does not have the same incentives as the principal. Agency costs include, among other things, the principal's costs of monitoring the agent (against misunderstandings, shirking, and even theft)."

§ 4. The Agent

An agent is a person who acts on behalf of and subject to the control of another. The word "agent" is derived from the Latin word *agens*, the present participle of *agere*, to drive, act, do. Ordinarily an agent acts only in a representative capacity, binding his principal to a contract but not himself (see Chapter 7). Thus it is said that anyone can be an agent, even one who has no capacity to enter into a contract, such as a minor.

Although it is natural to think of an agent as an individual, an entity also can be an agent. As stated in R2d § 14 M, "It is an accepted principle of agency that the term 'agent' includes both natural persons and corporations, notwithstanding the anthropomorphic sound of the titles. It follows that a corporation can be an agent for another corporation."

§ 5. Distinguishing the Agency Relationship From Other Relationships

These materials will distinguish the agency relationship from several other common legal relationships that contain elements that overlap or appear to overlap with agency. Distinguishing among these relationships may reinforce an understanding of the conceptual nature of agency and help to define boundaries between different kinds of distinct legal relationships that sometimes appear close to agency.

A. Agent or Seller

An agent sells goods on behalf of another. A seller sells on its own behalf. Disputes sometimes arise when one party transfers an asset to another and contracts for control over some of the actions of the other party. Is the transaction one of sale or agency? For example, a manufacturer markets its products in a defined territory through a distributor. The distributor buys the goods and then resells them to retailers at a price it sets. The manufacturer requires in its agreement with the distributor that it approve the retailers selected by the distributor, that its contract forms be used, that it can give directions to the retailers, and that the distributor maintain a certain level of inventory of the goods and replacement parts. Is this a sale with strings attached or is the distributor an agent by virtue of the substantial amount of control reserved by the manufacturer?

In the fact situation described above, which is closely patterned on *Stansifer v. Chrysler Motors Corp.* (9th Cir.1973), the fact that the distributor (Fisher) held title to the goods and could set its own price with the retailers supported a characterization of the relationship as one of buyer-seller, not agency. The court relied on § 14 J of R2d, which states in part, "[W]hether [distributor] is an agent or is himself a buyer depends on whether . . . his duty is to act primarily for the benefit of the one delivering the goods to him or to act primarily for his own benefit." Although Chrysler exercised considerable control over Fisher's operation, Fisher was setting prices for its own profit and thus pursuing its self-interest in this relationship. An essential element of the agency relationship, the "on behalf of" element, was missing from this arrangement. (It should be noted that sometimes a distributor under such an arrangement will be an agent with regard to a limited matter, such as extending the manufacturer's warranty to the ultimate customer.)

The above situation contrasts with the ordinary consignment arrangement, in which the owner retains title over the goods, sets the prices, and gives the person selling the goods (called a consignee) return privileges for unsold goods. This arrangement usually is classified as one of agency. The consignee is not setting prices for its own profit but instead responds to the price set by the owner, receiving a commission upon sale, and thus is deemed to be acting "primarily" for the benefit of the owner when marketing the goods.

Although who holds title to the goods plays a role in both of the above situations, this does not mean that where title lies always provides a clear answer to the agency question. Other facts can influence a court's characterization of a relationship. See *Owensboro v. Dark Tobacco Growers' Ass'n* (Ky.1927)(growers of tobacco transferred title of their tobacco to nonprofit Association, which marketed it; Association paid all net proceeds of sale to the growers; the court held that Association had "mere naked title" and was the agent of the growers).

Historically an agent employed to sell goods entrusted to his possession by consignment was called a *factor*. He sold the goods in his own name and was paid by commission (today this type of agent is sometimes called "commercial agent" or "commission merchant" and the word "factor" is commonly used to describe financial intermediaries who supply funds to businesses, taking back accounts receivable). A *broker* is an agent paid by commission who ordinarily acts as an intermediary between buyer and seller, does not have possession of the property, and does not sell in her own name. These definitions are not always used consistently. The meaning of "broker" can be greatly varied by trade usage or by statute, for example.

B. Agent or Bailee

Ann lends her watch to Betty for the day. Several hours later Betty sells the watch to Chris, pocketing the proceeds. Chris in good faith thought that Betty was the owner of the watch. Is Ann bound by the sale? No, if it was merely a loan. Perhaps yes, if Betty was given authority to deal with the watch in some way, such as soliciting offers of sale. If it was merely a loan, the transaction was one of bailment. A bailment is the rightful possession of goods by one (the bailee) who is not the owner.

A bailee is not an agent and has no power to deal with the goods by virtue of the bailment, despite the good faith of the innocent purchaser. (The Uniform Commercial Code § 2–403(2) constitutes a statutory exception to the bailment rule for merchants who deal in goods of the kind bailed with them. They have the power to transfer all rights to such goods to a buyer in the ordinary course of business, whether or not given authority to do so by the owner who entrusted them with possession of the goods. For example, if an owner leaves her watch with a retail jewelry store for repair only, she would be bound by a sale of the watch to an innocent customer of the store. This power of merchants is not an agency power.)

If instead consent is given to sell or mortgage the goods, for example, then the bailee is also an agent, authorized to deal with the goods on behalf of another. The agent-bailee has the power to bind the owner even beyond the authority given, committing the owner to different terms or with different persons than those authorized. There is no power, however, to commit the owner to a different kind of transaction than that authorized (for example, if the agent-bailee was authorized only to mortgage the goods, a sale of them would not bind the principal).

C. Agent or Trustee

As defined in the Restatement of Trusts § 2, "A trust is a fiduciary relationship with respect to property, subjecting the person by whom the title to the property is held to equitable duties to deal with the property for the benefit of another person, which arises as a result of a manifestation of an intention to create it." Although trustees and agents both are fiduciaries, a trustee ordinarily derives guidance from the terms of the trust and is not subject to the control of either the creator or the beneficiary of the trust. This distinguishes a trustee from an agent because, as noted above, one of the distinctive features of agency is the continuous subjection of the agent to the will of the principal. If a trustee is subject to control by the creator or the beneficiary of the trust, however, then the relationship of agent-trustee arises. Under such circumstance, the law of agency controls resolution of disputes.

D. Principal or Creditor

A controlling creditor runs certain risks under the law of agency in some jurisdictions, particularly if the creditor (often referred to as a trade creditor) engages in trade with the debtor and bargains for a stronger trade position as part of the consideration for the loan. If its control over a debtor's business is substantial, particularly if it is affirmative in nature and includes the right to initiate transactions, the creditor may be classified as a principal with the debtor its agent, exposing it to liability for losses incurred by the debtor's business.

The ability of a creditor to initiate transactions (which surely must be a rare situation in the business world, with the possible exception of debtor insolvency, where creditors are attempting to salvage a failing business) is deemed by some authority to be incompatible with creditor status. See R2d § 14 0. The law of agency is invoked to characterize the creditor-debtor relationship, apparently on the reasoning that the creditor both benefits from the transaction and controls the debtor. The use of agency doctrine in this setting is doubtful, however, because it focuses exclusively on control without considering the equally important "on behalf of" element, an element that seems hard to satisfy in this context where the debtor is generating profits in its own interest.

A few courts take this reasoning a step further, finding liability for a controlling creditor even absent the power to initiate transactions. See *A. Gay Jenson Farms v. Cargill* (Minn.1981). The Cargill case involved 86 farmers who had not been paid for their crops by Warren, a local grain elevator company that had promised to pay for the crops but became insolvent. The farmers sued Cargill, a large international trader of grain products, claiming that Cargill was Warren's principal. Cargill had loaned money to Warren in return for a right of first refusal on Warren's grain in addition to interest. In the loan agreement Cargill was granted the right to inspect and audit Warren's books, to give its consent prior to significant expenditures of capital and indebtedness by Warren, plus other minor items of passive control.

The court held Cargill liable for Warren's $2 million debt to the farmers on the reasoning that Cargill was Warren's principal, based on its right of control and the benefits it received as trade creditor, including obtaining a source of grain. The court's finding of agency seems false. The court appears to read control too broadly and to confuse mere benefit with acting on behalf of, since Warren was generating profits for its own use in its own business. Perhaps this case is an example of a court manipulating agency principles to reach a deep pocket.

E. Agency and the Corporate Board of Directors

Defining the corporation. A brief explanation of the corporation might prove useful for the reader who has not yet taken the course on corporations. A corporation is a legal entity formed under a state statute by filing articles of incorporation with the proper state office. The articles designate, among other things, the number of shares and kinds of stock the corporation is authorized to issue. Stockholders are the owners of a corporation. As a legal entity a corporation can sue and be sued, own property, and pays taxes on its income. A board of directors, which is elected (usually annually) by the stockholders, sets policy and makes the major decisions for the corporation. The board in turn appoints officers, who are employees and run the day to day business of the corporation.

A corporation can act only through its employees. The board of directors acts only as a group. Individual directors have no authority to establish policy nor can they run the operations of the business unless they also are officers.

Debts of a corporation are satisfied out of its assets. Thus, the stockholders, members of the board, and officers all enjoy limited liability in the sense that they are not personally liable for the debts of the business.

Corporations are required to file reports, usually annually, with the state and to operate with a certain degree of formality. A corporation may be established with a perpetual life.

As noted above, a corporation pays taxes on its income. Shareholders also are taxed when the corporation distributes profits to them, usually in the form of dividends. (In contrast, partnership income is taxed only at the individual partner level. The partnership itself pays no tax. The double taxation in the corporate form makes it unattractive to some investors, inspiring a search for forms that offer both protection from liability for the obligations of the business and the attractiveness of partnership taxation. See Part IV, discussing the LLP, the LLLP, and the LLC, all forms of doing business that satisfy these concerns.)

Agency status of directors of a corporation. Although a board of directors is elected by the shareholders, the board uses its own business judgment in managing the affairs of the corporation, making the control by the shareholders too remote to constitute agency. As noted in R3d § 1.01, comment f(2) (T.D. No. 2, 2001): "Directors' powers originate as the legal consequence of their election and are not conferred or delegated by shareholders." In addition, an individual director has no power on his own to act on the corporation's behalf, unless the director is also an employee of the corporation.

Officers and other employees. Corporate officers are appointed by the board to operate the corporation. They, as well as the employees they hire, act on behalf of the corporation and are subject to the control of the board, and thus are agents.

§ **6.** Complex Agency Relationships

The ambiguous principal. This topic does not involve distinguishing agency from other relationships but instead deals briefly with the difficulties raised when it is unclear on whose behalf an agent is acting in a particular transaction. Sometimes it is not obvious whether the person who is the active party in a transaction between two others is the agent of both of them or the agent of only one of them, or the agent of one for part of the transaction and the agent of the other for another part of the transaction. Under some circumstances this uncertainty is referred to as the ambiguous principal problem. As a practical matter, the underlying equities of a case will sometimes influence a court in characterizing the relationships.

One situation that has been litigated a number of times involves problems that can arise when an employer both arranges for group insurance for its employees and administers the program. One day the employer commits an error while handling insurance paperwork for an employee. Who bears the burden of this error? That question is answered in many courts by asking who is the principal of the employer, the insurance company or the employee on whose behalf the employer was acting at the time the error was committed?

A fairly substantial line of cases holds that the employer is the agent of its employee on the reasoning that the interests of the employer and employee are congruent and are adverse to the insurance company. This reasoning seems dubious because the insurance company impliedly consents to this conflict of interest upon entering its relationship with the employer (of course, collusion between employer and employee would constitute a defense for the insurance company). A contrasting line of authority classifies the employer as the agent of the insurance company on the reasoning that, although the "on behalf of" element applies to both parties and thus is neutral, the control element realistically applies only to the insurance company because it establishes the procedures used by the employer in administering the group policy. This is the better reasoning because it gives equal weight to all of the elements of the agency relationship.

The nature of the work being done by the employer at the time of the error is significant. In *Madden v. Kaiser Found. Hosp.* (Cal.1976), the court held that when *negotiating* a group medical plan for state employees the board of administration acted as agent of the employees. In its opinion the court cited an earlier case holding that when *administering* a group plan the employer was the agent of the insurance company. The court expressly approved this distinction in legal status based on different activities.

Some useful language addressed to this problem is contained in R2d § 14 L, comments a and c. It reads in relevant part as follows:

a. A person who is employed by two others to conduct a transaction between them, all the facts being known to both parties, is normally the agent of both and owes a duty to each to deal with them fairly. On the other hand, a person may be in the general employment of one principal and nevertheless be employed by another to conduct a transaction between himself and the person in whose general employment he is. ...The ultimate question is whether it is understood that the agent owes primary allegiance to the general employer or to the other party. *In answering this question, there is an inference that the general employment continues.* (Emphasis added.)

   c.   The situations which call for application of the rule stated in this Subsection are varied and the facts of each must be examined to determine to which of two parties the agent owes the duty of loyalty, which is the ultimate fact to be decided. A statement in the contract of the parties that he is the agent of one of them is not conclusive (see §§ 1 and 220), nor is the fact that he receives his compensation from one of them.

The subagency, co-agency, and agent's agent relationships can also be classified as complex agency relationships, involving difficult issues of characterization, indemnity, and compensation. These relationships are defined in the Glossary and covered in more detail in § 7 (compensation), § 8 (indemnity), and especially § 37C.

The dual agency rule. The dual agency rule states that an agent cannot act on behalf of the adverse party to a transaction connected with the agency without the permission, express or implied, of the principal. If the two principals are unaware of the double employment, the transaction between them is voidable. If one principal secretly employs the agent to act on its account knowing the second principal is unaware of the double employment, the second principal can rescind or choose to affirm the transaction and recover damages from the first principal or the knowing agent. Although the dual agency rule appears at first glance to be related to the ambiguous principal problem, it ordinarily does not play a role in that context because the agent usually acts with the consent of all parties in the ambiguous principal setting, as in the employer-administered group insurance problem addressed at the beginning of this section.

QUESTIONS AND ANSWERS

In view of the difficulties sometimes posed when trying to identify agency relationships, it seemed appropriate to conclude this chapter with several problems drawn from actual cases involving identification of agency relationships. The problems are structured as questions and answers.

Question 1. Franchisor, Inc. ("FR"), a well-known name in the restaurant business, and Franchisee, Inc. ("FE"), have a contractual relationship that grants FE the exclusive right to use FR's name in a certain territory. In return, FR is granted 5% of the gross sales of FE, the right to specify the items and products that FE can sell, to require FE to purchase all flour and pancake mixes from FR, and to promulgate a standard operations manual binding upon FE covering quality control, record keeping, hours of operation, employees' appearance and demeanor, and training of managers. Plaintiff claims that FE is an agent of FR because FR both has extensive control over FE and benefits from its relationship with FE, and thus plaintiff is able to serve process on FE for a claim it has against FR. Is plaintiff's claim valid?

Answer. Plaintiff's claim that an agency relationship exists between FR and FE is not valid. Although FR clearly exercises substantial control over FE's business and benefits from the relationship, the other equally important element of an agency relationship, "on behalf of," is not satisfied. FE is generating profits from its business *primarily* for its own benefit, not for FR, which receives only a percentage of profits as compensation for allowing FE to use FR's name. See *Stanford v. Dairy Queen Prods.* (Tex. Ct. App. 1981) ("The parties simply had *different* purposes and objects.... [T]he typical restaurant operator did not *act for* [FR] and *in its behalf*").

It is important to note that plaintiff's claim depends on establishing a genuine agency relationship between FR and FE. Plaintiff's claim would have more substance if instead it were based on estoppel due to the misleading appearance of ownership of the business. See § 30 of this book.

Question 2. Jones shipped an expensive and heavy piece of industrial equipment, a precision-grinding machine, via railroad to his plant. Upon arrival, Jones discovered that the machine was badly damaged during shipment. He refused to pay the freight charge until Able, the railroad's station agent, wrote on the freight bill, "Damage on this shipment, C.D. Able." One year later Jones filed a written claim with the railroad for damage to his machine. The railroad refused to pay on the ground that the written claim was not made within nine months, as required by a term of the bill of lading for the shipment. Jones argues that the signature by Able satisfied the writing requirement. The railroad responds arguing that the written claim must be made by Jones, not by Able, who is the agent of the railroad. Does Jones have an effective rebuttal to this argument?

Answer. Yes, Jones has a rebuttal that was found effective in *Thayer v. Pacific Elec. Rwy.* (Cal. 1961). Jones argues that Able was his agent, not the railroad's, when he made the above writing noting damage to the shipment, which was received by the railroad. Thus, the railroad received notice from Jones (through his agent) well within the nine-month period. The railroad will rebut by claiming that Able was its agent because it had a continuing relationship with him, paid him, he was acting throughout on its behalf, and it is impossible for the same person to both give and receive notice.

Jones will respond by claiming that Able was his agent only for the brief period involved in making the writing. At that time Able was acting on behalf of and subject to the control of Jones, by implication. Also, this act was ministerial in nature. It did not involve judgment or discretion and thus, even though railroad did not consent to this temporary agency, consent was not necessary. The decision of *Thayer* is consistent with this analysis. In addition, the strong equities underlying the claimant's case doubtless played a major role in the court's decision to find a special agency relationship in *Thayer*.

Question 3. Wholesale Company contracts with Retail, Inc., to lend a substantial sum of money to Retail. In addition to promising to repay the loan with interest, Retail promises to stock goods supplied by Wholesale in advantageous places in its store, readily noticeable by and accessible to its customers. Also, Retail grants Wholesale the right to inspect its books, to veto any guarantees by Retail over $5000, and to veto any cash withdrawals over $2500 by its owners. Wholesale is sued by a creditor of Retail who claims that Wholesale is Retail's principal because of its control and the benefits it receives in its trade relationship with Retail as a result of the contract, and thus is responsible for the debt. Is the claim sound?

Answer. No, the claim is not sound. Retail is not the agent of Wholesale. Retail is not conducting its business on Wholesale's behalf. Instead, Retail retains the profits generated by its business and thus is not acting *primarily* for the benefit of Wholesale. Any claim brought against Wholesale as a result of its relationship with Retail would have to be based on negligence stemming from Wholesale's exercise of its control, assuming any such facts could be established.

PART II

INTERNAL MATTERS: RIGHTS AND DUTIES BETWEEN PRINCIPAL AND AGENT

CHAPTER 2

DUTIES OF PRINCIPAL TO AGENT

The primary common law duties a principal owes its agent are: (i) to pay compensation for services rendered when compensation is reasonably expected, (ii) to reimburse for expenses reasonably incurred during the course of the agency, (iii) to indemnify for losses and liabilities resulting from authorized, good faith performance of the agency, (iv) to act with due care toward the agent; and (v) to deal with the agent fairly and in good faith. Most of these duties can be characterized as implied terms of the principal-agent contract or as inherent in the agency relationship, which is not always contractual. All of them can be altered or negated by express agreement between principal and agent with the possible exception of the duties of good faith and care, which probably cannot be completely negated.

Many agency relationships involve full time employment of the agent, which introduces the complexities of modern employment law in addition to the common law principles summarized above. There is considerable regulation of the employment relationship at both the state and federal level. Much of employment law is statutory in nature and is sufficiently comprehensive and complex to support a separate course in law school. Legislation covers, among other things, unemployment compensation, worker's compensation, sexual harassment, age and racial discrimination, safety regulations, minimum wage, disability, and labor laws. Some of the legislation, especially federal legislation, covers only employers of a certain size. These materials will not attempt to cover the field of employment law, instead concentrating on the fundamental common law principles of agency.

§ 7. Duty to Pay Compensation

Most agency arrangements include an express agreement by the principal to pay for work performed. This does not resolve all issues, however. Even with an express contract, litigation is frequent in, for example, the sales commission context over the meaning or application of phrases like "exclusive agency," "exclusive right to sell," "exclusive representative," and "procuring cause," among others. See *Roberts Assoc. v. Blazer Int'l Corp.* (E.D. Mich. 1990), an opinion that discusses at length the meaning of these phrases. The court rejects an agent's argument that he was entitled to commissions on all future sales made to customers he had brought to the principal even though he had not made the particular sale involved. The court held that, in the absence of specific language in the contract supporting the agent's broad claim, he must be the "procuring cause" of the particular sale for which a commission is claimed. Also, the court defined "exclusive agency" to allow the principal to itself make sales without commission liability to the agent (although the agent is entitled to commissions if other agents make the sale) and "exclusive right to sell" to confer commission rights on the agent regardless of who made the sale, even the principal.

A duty to pay also can arise by implication. "Unless an agreement between a principal and an agent indicates otherwise, a principal has a duty to pay compensation to an agent for services that the agent provides." R3d § 8.13, comment d (T.D. No. 6, 2005). Sometimes, however, the circumstances (such as the minor nature of the services involved) will destroy any inference of an implied promise to pay. Also, courts have stated that the law will presume that services rendered by members of a family "were gratuitous favors merely, prompted by friendship, kindness and the relationship between them." *Hartley v. Bohrer* (Idaho 1932). This presumption can be rebutted, but to do so in a family setting would ordinarily require fairly clear evidence of intent to pay.

Some useful language on implied compensation is contained in *McCollum v. Clothier* (Utah 1952):

> [T]his rule should not be applied to bind one under implied contract who merely permits services to be rendered to him, or accepts benefits from another, under such circumstances that he may reasonably assume they are given gratuitously. The law should not require everyone to keep on guard against such possibilities by warning persons offering services that no pay is to be expected. It is, therefore, essential that the court should exercise caution in imposing obligations of implied contract.

The *McCollum* court stated that the test to apply is "[W]ere the circumstances such that the plaintiff [agent] could reasonably assume that he was to be paid and that the defendant [principal] should have reasonably expected to pay for such services."

The agent's lien. Subject to agreement otherwise, an unpaid agent rightfully in possession of property of the principal has a lien upon the property for the amount due from the principal. In general, the lien consists of a right to retain possession of the property, including documents, until the amount due the agent is paid.

Subagents. P hires A to collect a claim in a distant state, promising to pay A $3,000. A engages B, who lives in the distant state, to do some work on the matter, promising to pay her $1,000. One can argue that B is a subagent on the assumption that P impliedly consented to that relationship, based on the understanding that A would not do the work personally in view of the distance involved and thus would delegate the job. Also, ordinarily P would assume that A would be responsible for whomever he hires to do the distant work. (Of course, the parties are free to agree otherwise. A would want to make B a co-agent, not a subagent, and thus avoid the burdens of being B's principal. A could accomplish this by clarifying this understanding with P and obtaining P's consent. P, on the other hand, would want B to be an agent's agent— see Glossary and § 37 C. The parties would have to resolve this by negotiation.)

B performs the work she agreed to do but is not paid as promised by A, her immediate principal, who has become insolvent. Can B collect the amount due her from P, the remote principal? Although, as we will see below, a subagent has a right of indemnity against the remote principal, it is well settled that a subagent does not have a right to compensation against the remote principal in the absence of a promise from P (to guaranty A's debt to B, for example). R3d, § 8.13 (T.D. No. 6, 2005). This rule applies because a compensation claim is based in contract and there is no contract between the subagent and the remote principal. Courts consider it unfair to subject the remote principal to liability for breach of a contract that it did not make. The claim for indemnity, on the other hand, rests on general principles of agency law, as noted below.

§ 8. Duty of Reimbursement, Indemnity, and Exoneration

Indemnity. An agent is entitled to be reimbursed by the principal for expenses reasonably incurred in the performance of the agency (for example, P directs A to pay a debt owed by P and supplies A with no money) and to be indemnified (that is, to be made whole) for any losses suffered during the course of the agency, but not for losses caused solely by his or her fault. R3d § 8.14 (T.D. No. 6, 2005). The policy underlying this right is well explained by Judge Learned Hand in *Admiral Oriental v. United States* (2d Cir.1936). In upholding a grant of indemnity to an agent for litigation expenses incurred in successfully defending a suit arising out of proper performance of the agency, Judge Hand stated:

> The doctrine stands upon the fact that the venture is the principal's, and that, as the profits will be his, so should be the expenses. Since by hypothesis the agent's outlay is not due to his mismanagement, it should be regarded only as a loss, unexpected it is true, but inextricably interwoven with the enterprise. . . . No doubt the amount of its expenditures is always open to

contest, but their necessity is undoubted and it is that which imposes the liability.

The agent's right to indemnity, unless expressly agreed to, depends on reasonable inferences drawn from the circumstances. The customs of the business and the nature of the relationship play a role in drawing an inference with regard to the existence of an agent's right to indemnity. For example, a real estate broker operating in an agency capacity would ordinarily be expected to bear certain expenses, like advertising costs, in carrying out the agency. Such expense would be regarded as part of the real estate business, not of selling one's home.

A subagent is entitled to indemnity from both the immediate principal (the person who hired the subagent) and the remote principal (the one for whom the immediate principal works), on the reasoning expressed above. If the subagent obtains indemnity from the immediate principal, the immediate principal can in turn obtain indemnity from the remote principal, again on the theory that it is the remote principal's business that is being done and "as the profits will be his, so should be the expenses." This situation was involved in *Admiral Oriental*. (In litigation matters, the agent should notify the principal and attempt to put the financial burden upon it, thus avoiding the risk of unknown defenses or a claim by the principal that the agent's defense was ineffective or litigation costs too high.)

Exoneration. Exoneration is an equitable remedy that is available to an agent. It can be used to avoid the expenditure of personal resources under circumstances in which the principal should bear the loss. As Judge Hand stated in *Admiral Oriental*, in addressing the issue whether an agent may sue before he has suffered loss, "In an action at law, such a petition would be premature; the plaintiff having paid nothing, may not yet call for indemnity. In equity, however, the rule is otherwise; before paying the debt a surety may call upon the principal to exonerate him by discharging it; he is not obligated to make inroads into his own resources when the loss must in the end fall upon the principal."

§ 9. Duty of Care

An employer is subject to a common law duty of care toward its employees arising from its control over the work environment. This duty includes using due care in the construction, repair, or inspection of the premises where employees work, in the selection of fellow employees, and in the management of the work. The duty to provide a safe place to work is nondelegable, which means that the employer cannot absolve itself of liability by hiring an outside business to make repairs. If the work is done negligently, the employer will be vicariously liable even in the absence of control over the physical conduct of the contractor (see § 23 B).

A. The Fellow Servant Rule

Although the duty of care is nondelegable with regard to providing a safe place to work and in that limited sense involves strict liability for employers to their employees under the common law, courts declined to extend the doctrine of respondeat superior (see Glossary and § 16) to employees who are injured by the negligence of fellow employees. The fellow servant rule holds that unless a negligence case can be proven against the employer, an injured employee's recourse under the common law is limited to the personal liability of the tortfeasor plus whatever medical and disability insurance the employee has purchased. The policy underlying the fellow servant rule relies primarily on the contractual nature of the relationship between employee and employer, as explained below.

Farwell v. Boston & W.R. (Mass.1842), the case which originated the fellow servant rule in this country, explained the rule as follows:

> The general rule is that he who engages in the employment of another for performance of specified duties for compensation takes upon himself the natural and ordinary risks and perils incident to the performance of such services, and in legal presumption the compensation is adjusted accordingly.... Each [employee] is an observer of the conduct of the others, can give notice of any misconduct and leave the service, if the common employer will not take precautions. By these means, the safety of each will be more effectually secured than could be done by a resort to the common employer for indemnity.

As explained below, the fellow servant rule, while still a part of the common law, has little practical effect today in most states due to statutory changes in the employment relationship. Its remaining impact is primarily in domestic and farm employment situations in some states.

B. Worker's Compensation

The fellow servant rule, which requires proof of employer fault, and includes the standard defenses to a negligence suit of contributory or comparative negligence and assumption of risk, meant that most industrial injuries went uncompensated. The response to this problem was legislative in nature, invoking the advantage the legislative process has over the common law, which exists to resolve disputes and cannot design a complex administrative system to address a particular social problem. Worker's compensation legislation was passed in every state in the early part of the twentieth century.

Although there is diversity among the states with regard to detail, all states require employers to compensate employees for injuries on the job. An administrative agency promulgates regulations, grants awards to workers according to a detailed schedule of recoveries for injuries, and resolves disputes relating to coverage and other matters. Medical care is paid for and cash payments are made to employees or dependents reflecting income loss, calculated as a fraction (usually two-thirds) of the employee's weekly earnings at the time of injury, subject to a maximum amount. There is no recovery for pain and suffering.

An employee is entitled to compensation even if the injury was not caused by the fault of the employer and, more controversial, even though it was caused solely by the employee's own negligence. Employees who are covered by worker's compensation do not retain their common law rights against the employer, resulting in a trade-off of a more certain recovery for less damages (usually) as against the opposite condition under the common law.

§ 10. Duty to Deal Fairly and in Good Faith

An implied duty is imposed by courts on the principal to deal fairly and in good faith with the agent. This duty is broad and largely undefined, with the potential to cover many different situations. As one example of its application in a fairly broad but understandable context, the principal is required to maintain a standard of conduct that will not harm the agent's business reputation or reasonable self-respect. Breach by the principal allows the agent to terminate the relationship and to sue for breach of contract, assuming the relationship is not at will.

The case of *Taylor v. Cordis Corp.* (S.D.Miss. 1986), provides an example of a claim based on the duty of good faith. Taylor was an agent who attempted to nullify a noncompete covenant (see § 15 B(ii)) he had signed with Cordis, his employer, by alleging that Cordis had committed a material breach of their contract, enabling Taylor to cancel the contract. The alleged breach was failing to inform Taylor of a battery-depletion problem in the heart pacemakers he was selling on behalf of Cordis. Taylor argued that Cordis was under a duty to inform its sales staff as soon as it learned there might be a problem. Instead, Cordis waited until after it had taken time to investigate and verify complaints, a period of over a year, before informing Taylor and others. This delay damaged his reputation by diminishing the confidence physicians had in him, Taylor argued.

The court held that Cordis was under a duty to inform its sales staff of defects but only after, in the exercise of reasonable diligence, it had fairly concluded that a specific product presented a threat of harm to others. After a careful analysis of the facts, the court found that Cordis's notification of Taylor had been timely, thus in effect granting an employer reasonable time to investigate and verify the validity of complaints before being under a duty to inform its agents.

CHAPTER 3

DUTIES OF AGENT
TO PRINCIPAL

The following list of duties an agent owes the principal is longer and more complex than the list of duties the principal owes the agent. If this seems odd, recall that the agent is the acting party in the relationship, the person in whom trust is placed. Also, it is the agent who engages with third parties, creating for the principal the risk of liability as well as the prospect of gain.

A useful summary of many of the duties of an agent is contained in Seavey, Law of Agency 236 (1964). It is quoted immediately below. It does not describe all of an agent's duties (it does not include the duty of obedience and the duty to indemnify for losses caused by wrongful conduct, for example), but it nevertheless constitutes a helpful summary of much of an agent's duties.

[An agent] has a duty to account for money or property received on account of the principal [and to keep the principal's assets separate from his own]. In his dealings with the principal, he has a duty of full disclosure; in acting for the principal he must not prefer his own [or others'] interests, he cannot compete with the principal nor, without disclosure of his interest, sell his own property to the principal. In carrying out the directions of the principal, he has the duty to use normal care.

§ 11. Duty of Good Conduct; Duty to Obey

An agent is subject to a duty not to act in a manner that makes continued friendly relations with the principal impossible. Also, the agent must not bring disrepute to the principal. This limitation has been invoked in cases involving an agent who made disparaging remarks at a social function about the quality of merchandise sold by his employer and an employee who was discharged after committing a serious crime involving sexual misconduct with a minor. In another example, a church was justified in firing an employee (its music director) after the employee, a body builder, illegally received a shipment of anabolic steroids on church property. McGarry v. St. Anthony of Padua Roman Catholic Church (N.J. 1998). Many such cases arise in the context of a claim for unemployment compensation benefits.

An agent must obey all reasonable directions of the principal. This rule holds true even if the principal had promised not to limit or terminate the agent's authority and commits a breach of contract with the agent by doing so. "If the principal does not have this kind of control over the conduct of the agent, the relation is not an agency." W. Seavey, Law of Agency 240 (1964).

The duty to obey in a commercial setting is unique to agency and distinguishes the agent from all other fiduciaries. There are limits, however. An agent does not have to obey orders that are illegal or unethical. See *Ford v. Wisconsin Real Estate Bd.* (Wis.1970)(real estate broker has no duty to obey principal's instruction to engage in racial discrimination in showing principal's property).

§ 12. Duty to Indemnify Principal for Loss Caused by Misconduct

A principal has a right of indemnity against an agent for losses caused by wrongful behavior. Wrongful behavior in this context includes an agent's negligent or intentional damage to the principal's property or to the property or persons of others for which the principal is held liable; it also includes losses caused by the agent's departure from instructions. This duty of indemnity is distinguishable from the duty of indemnity described in § 8, which runs from principal to agent and is activated by a loss incurred by the agent while reasonably discharging the task assigned by the principal. The duty being addressed in this section involves wrongful behavior of the agent, runs from agent to principal, and involves redressing a loss to the principal.

Some courts base the agent's duty to indemnify the principal on the law of restitution, applying the policy that an active wrongdoer should ultimately bear liability for the losses he or she causes, not an innocent party held vicariously liable because of a relationship with the wrongdoer. Other courts characterize the duty as an implied term in the contract between principal and agent to act with reasonable care or, if the relationship is noncontractual, as inherent in the agency relationship. The parties to the agency relationship can by agreement alter or abrogate this duty.

A frequently debated application of the above principle is the duty of an employee to indemnify the employer for damages the employer has to pay resulting from the employee's negligence while acting within the scope of employment. The debate focuses on the appropriateness of holding employees liable for ordinary negligence. Those who disagree with this application of the duty of indemnity argue that the cost of mere negligence (as contrasted with gross negligence or intentional misconduct, which they concede fall within the duty of indemnity) belongs on the business and should be reflected in the price of the product or service offered by the business, thus spreading the loss and making the product bear its full cost.

In assessing the persuasiveness of this argument, it may be useful to recall that vicarious liability reaches beyond employment relationships to include voluntary, nonemployment, nonbusiness principal-agent relationships (see § 16), which undermines the "spreading the loss" and "true cost of the product" arguments. This may in part account for the fact that the overwhelming weight of authority recognizes the employer's right of indemnity whenever the employee wrongfully causes the employer a loss, through negligence or otherwise.

As a practical matter, employers rarely invoke their right to indemnity, in part for reasons of employee morale and in part because most employees do not have the resources to make it worthwhile. Almost all modern indemnity cases involve employees negligently driving their own cars while on the employer's business, which means that the litigation usually is between two insurance companies, with the employee's insurance company making the above arguments about exceptions to the duty to indemnify.

§ 13. Duty to Account

As noted in § 1, an agent is a fiduciary, a status created by the agent's consent to act on behalf of the principal. The responsibilities attached to the agent's status as fiduciary include a duty to account for money or property received as agent for the principal. An account is usually defined as a detailed statement in writing of debts and credits or of receipts and payments, covering monetary transactions engaged in by the agent while acting on behalf of the principal, although it sometimes can be more informal. Whenever a principal has trusted an agent to handle its money or property the principal is entitled to an explanation, in the form of an accounting, of the existence, location, and status of such assets upon demand by the principal or at times specified by agreement or custom, and upon termination of the agency.

§ 14. Duty of Care and Full Disclosure

Subject to agreement, the duty of care includes the duty of a paid agent to act with the "care, competence, and diligence normally exercised by agents in similar circumstances." R3d § 8.08 (T.D. No. 6, 2005). If an agent purports to have even greater skill, he is held to that higher level. The duty of care and other fiduciary duties do not differ significantly if the agency is gratuitous, although as a practical matter a court may not be as demanding in applying the standard of care to a gratuitous agent.

The duty of full disclosure includes a duty to inform the principal of all facts relevant to a transaction that the agent reasonably believes the principal would want to know. In one respect full disclosure is related to the duty of care. In *Lindland v. United Business Investments* (Ore.1984), for example, the court held that a broker engaged in listing and selling businesses was required by its duty of care to inform a seller who hired the broker about the financial weakness of the buyer of the business.

In another respect the duty of full disclosure is a specific application of the duty of loyalty (see § 15) and includes a duty to deal fairly with the principal. It is most frequently litigated in this context, usually involving a claim of conflict of interest. The phrase "conflict of interest" is well defined by the *Lindland* court as follows:

"Conflict of interest" encompasses situations in which the agent is acting entirely or substantially for the agent's own benefit and situations in which the agent is acting on behalf of a third party whose interest is adverse to that of the principal. [W]e refer to the former situation as "self-dealing" and the latter as "conflict of interest." The mere fact that [a] broker stands to earn a commission for his efforts on behalf of a principal does not, without more, establish that the broker is engaged in self-dealing or has a conflict of interest with the principal.

The practical importance of distinguishing the circumstance that gives rise to the duty of full disclosure relates to burden of proof. If the fact situation involves a conflict of interest (broadly defined to include self-dealing), the burden of proving full disclosure is placed on the agent. This is because the very existence of an undisclosed conflict of interest raises a prima facie case of breach of the duty of loyalty. If the facts do not raise an issue of conflict of interest, the burden of proof of lack of disclosure is on the principal.

As noted above, an agent is required to deal fairly and make full disclosure of all facts that the agent should know would reasonably affect the principal's judgment. This is true even when the agent is openly acting as an adverse party to the principal, with regard to a matter initially entrusted to him. If the principal naturally relies on the agent for advice, the agent's adverse interest does not relieve the agent from giving impartial advice. If the agent cannot do so, the agent should see to it that the principal secures the advice of an impartial third party.

§ 15. Duty of Loyalty

It is the agent's obligation as a fiduciary to keep the principal's interest foremost in mind when acting on the matter entrusted to him. Abnegation of self can be difficult but the agent has been put in the position he is, and entrusted with the powers he has, in order to advance the interests of the principal. Many of the complex problems addressed in fiduciary law arise because an agent has lost sight of that perspective. Sometimes courts seem to reach far in punishing an agent or in defining the scope of fiduciary duties broadly in an ambiguous situation, but it is important to remember that the courts see themselves as protecting a relationship of trust and confidence. (There are limits to this duty, as to all duties. For example, despite the duty of loyalty, an agent is privileged to report criminal misbehavior of his principal. R3d § 8.05, comment c (T.D. No. 6, 2005)).

The duties described in this chapter exist in the absence of specific agreement between the principal and agent. The Restatement of Agency (Third) includes a section describing how a principal may consent to an agent's conduct that would otherwise constitute a breach of the agent's duty of loyalty. R3d § 8.06 (T.D. No. 6, 2005).

Remedies of the principal. A clear breach of loyalty occurs when an agent takes a bribe from a third party while acting for the principal. The agent forfeits not only the bribe but also any compensation he would receive growing out of the transaction, on the equitable principle that a fiduciary is not to profit from his own wrong. Also, if the agent has made it possible for others to profit from his breach of loyalty, he can be held accountable for those profits whether or not he receives any part of them. The policy behind this rule is deterrence of breach of loyalty. The principle of deterrence is so strong that a principal does not need to prove that any loss was caused by the fiduciary's misconduct. A knowing third party also is liable to the principal for committing the tort of encouraging a fiduciary to breach his duty. Hayes–Albion Corp. v. Kuberski (Mich. 1984).

A useful, brief comment on the remedies of the principal is contained in W. Seavey, Law of Agency 252. It is quoted below:

> Almost any dereliction by an agent who has contracted with the principal is a breach of contract, but the principal may have a cause of action which will give greater returns than one for breach of contract. A principal whose agent has improperly used property for his own advantage would have, at his option, an action for breach of contract, an action in tort for the harm done, an action [in restitution] for the value of the benefit received by the agent, and an action to require the transfer to him [by constructive trust] of any specific property received by the agent. The use of

one remedy rather than another may be of great importance.

A. Loyalty During the Relationship

(i) Scope of fiduciary duty. The breadth and scope of fiduciary duty varies with the position held by the agent. The more trust that is placed in an agent and the greater the discretion an agent has, the more demanding a court will be about loyalty. But in most jurisdictions the duty of loyalty applies to all employees, even though the occasion for violation of a duty may be rare with an employee who has a routine, nondiscretionary job. An argument was made and rejected in *Graphic Directions v. Bush* (Colo.App.1993) that an hourly employee with no management or administrative authority is not a fiduciary and thus has no duty of loyalty to his employer. The case involved a suit against an employee who was a technical artist and who, prior to leaving his employment, had solicited customers of his employer for his future business. The employee was held liable to his employer.

(ii) Misusing information. The duty of loyalty includes a duty not to compete with the principal in the absence of his knowledge and consent. This includes not using confidential information in competition with or to the injury of the principal. As noted in R2d § 395, comment a, an agent "has a duty not to use information acquired by him as agent or by means of opportunities which he has as agent to acquire it, or acquired by him through a breach of duty to the principal, for any purpose likely to cause his principal harm or to interfere with his business, although it is information not connected with the subject matter of his agency." This limitation would include, for example, information the agent learns from secretly examining the files and memoranda of his employer or by eavesdropping on conversations in the workplace.

This duty applies not only to information expressly stated to be confidential "but also to information which the agent should know his principal would not care to have revealed to others or used in competition with him." Id., Comment b. It does not include matters of common knowledge in the community or special skills the agent has acquired because of his employment. The prohibition against using confidential information applies even after the agency relationship terminates, as developed below.

B. Post–Termination Competition

One of the most frequently litigated issues involves post-termination competition by a former employee. The common law historically has encouraged competition, so long as it is fair. Among other things, this means that an employee is entitled to make full use of skills developed on the job. For a general discussion of a former employee's common law right to solicit past customers, see Seavey, Law of Agency 250–51 (1964):

In the absence of a restrictive covenant, an agent whose agency is terminated without breach by him is entitled freely to compete with his former principal in the solicitation of former customers, acting for himself or another principal, except by use of confidential information which it is improper for him to use for any purpose. If an agent wrongfully terminates his employment before the time contracted for, any competition by him until the end of that time is doubly wrong and may be enjoined.

Also, an employee is entitled while still employed to plan for post-termination competition by renting office space, filing papers to create a business entity, preparing advertisements, and so forth. An employee is not, however, free to "feather his own nest at the expense of his employer while he is still on the payroll" by soliciting customers of his employer prior to leaving the employment. *Biever, Drees & Nordell v. Coutts* (N.D.1981). This restriction may also apply to pre-termination solicitation of key employees. These rules exist in the absence of an agreement on post-termination competition, a topic that will be covered below.

(i) Trade secrets. A trade secret, broadly defined, consists of confidential information used in the employer's business that gives the employer an advantage over competitors. Restatement (Third) Unfair Competition § 39. A customer list is an example of a trade secret, assuming that, as stated in *Town & Country House & Home Service v. Newbery* (N.Y.1958), the list was compiled by "business effort and the expenditure of time and money, constituting a part of the good-will of a business which enterprise and foresight have built up."

Although, as noted above, an employee ordinarily is free to compete upon termination of the employment, the competition must be fair. It is everywhere considered unfair for an employee to use confidential information, including trade secrets, against the employer after terminating the relationship. The employee is given access to the customer list or other trade secrets while in a position of trust. Subsequent use of that list or other secret without consent is an abuse of trust. Also, a trade secret is an asset of the employer. It is unfair to let an employee appropriate that asset without agreement and compensation. This is true whether the employee misappropriates the information in physical form or commits it to memory. R3d § 8.05 (T.D. No. 6, 2005).

An employer is entitled to pursue an injunction against unconsented use of a trade secret and to seek damages for losses sustained by the misuse. These remedies are part of a common law restraint that applies even in the absence of a contractual agreement not to use trade secrets. A contractual agreement can be useful, however, both in defining what is a trade secret and in drawing lines with regard to post-termination conduct, as noted below.

(ii) Covenants not to compete. A noncompetition covenant can be of considerable assistance to an employer when attempting to prevent misuse of a trade secret or invasion of the goodwill of the business. The employer can by contractual agreement define the trade secret and obtain the employee's consent to that definition and agreement not to use or disclose the trade secret after terminating the employment. Also, limits can be set on post-employment competition, defined in part by the nature of the business and of the work the employee was doing.

Noncompete covenants cannot be used simply to stifle competition. Such use would violate the common law's long-standing policy against unreasonable restraints on competition. In order for a noncompete covenant to be enforceable it must rest upon a protectable interest and must be reasonable in time and geographic scope. The interests entitled to be protected by a covenant include "trade secrets, the goodwill of the business, and an extraordinary investment in the training or education of the employee." *Robbins v. Finlay* (Utah 1982). In this context goodwill usually means protection of the employer-customer relationship. The reason for protecting this relationship apparently is that the employee, upon joining the business, acquires knowledge of and access to the employer's customers as part of a relationship of trust. It is considered wrong for the employee to appropriate some or all of those customers upon leaving the business, at least when he has agreed not to do so.

Sometimes a court will "blue pencil" an overly broad covenant if enforceable language grammatically can be severed from the unenforceable portion. Other courts will issue an injunction that reduces the overly broad area or time covered by the covenant even though the precise language cannot be pencilled out, thus taking a more flexible approach.

In general, covenants not to compete are not favored in the law, which means that the party seeking to enforce them must draft them in a careful, measured way, with an explanation of the need for restrictions and as much clarity as possible. In some jurisdictions there exist statutory restrictions on covenants not to compete. Also, special rules exist with regard to lawyers and noncompete covenants. Ethical rules place restrictions on the enforceability of such covenants, in part to enhance client choice of counsel.

C. Pre-Empting Business Opportunities

One area of frequent litigation concerning the duty of loyalty involves disputes over whether a business opportunity belonging to a principal has been pre-empted by an employee or other fiduciary. A pre-emptive business opportunity is one that is so closely related to the business that it is fairly considered an incident of it. An employee or other fiduciary can take personal advantage of a pre-emptive opportunity only if the employer knows and consents. This concept was involved in one of the most famous cases involving fiduciary duties, *Meinhard v. Salmon* (N.Y.1928) (per Cardozo, J.).

Meinhard involved a joint venture between Meinhard and Salmon to lease a hotel for 20 years, with the understanding that it would be remodeled into an office building. The venture proved successful. Four months before the end of the 20 year term the owner of the property and five lots adjacent to it offered to Salmon, who had managed the venture, a much larger development project. The project involved destruction of the buildings on all of the lots, including the remodeled hotel, and construction of a skyscraper in their place, under lease terms that could extend to 80 years. Salmon agreed to the project, taking it for himself without informing Meinhard. Upon discovering the new project, Meinhard demanded a half-interest, suing Salmon for breach of fiduciary duty.

Judge Cardozo, writing for the majority, found that Salmon had breached his duty of loyalty to Meinhard. In resolving this issue, Cardozo stated that there must be a "nexus of relation" between "the business conducted by the manager and the opportunity brought to him as an incident of management. For this problem, as for most, there are distinctions of degree. Here the subject-matter of the new lease was an extension and enlargement of the subject-matter of the old one." (There was a vigorous dissent, arguing that the venture was limited in scope, designed "to exploit a particular lease," and that the vast new project was something "distinct and different.")

The following sentences, taken from Judge Cardozo's opinion, are among the most quoted in the law:

Many forms of conduct permissible in a workaday world for those acting at arm's length, are forbidden to those bound by fiduciary ties. A trustee is bound by something stricter than the morals of the market place. Not honesty alone, but the punctilio of an honor the most sensitive, is then the standard of behavior. As to this there has been a tradition that is unbending and inveterate. Uncompromising rigidity has been the attitude of courts of equity when petitioned to undermine the rule of undivided loyalty by the "disintegrating erosion" of particular exceptions. Only thus has the level of conduct for fiduciaries been kept at a level higher than that trodden by the crowd. It will not consciously be lowered by any judgment of this court.

Although these sentences were written in the context of a joint venture, courts have often quoted them in cases involving the fiduciary obligations of an agent.

It is not always easy to decide whether a particular opportunity is an incident of an enterprise. In *Fuqua v. Taylor* (Tex.App.1984), the court held that a joint venturer was under a duty to inform fellow venturers of an opportunity to reacquire a lapsed well but had no duty to inform them of a lease two miles away from the lapsed well. The court stated: "Appellees have not cited, nor have we discovered, any authority holding that mere proximity is sufficient to extend a fiduciary duty from property within the scope of a fiduciary relationship to other property." In *Dixon v. Trinity Joint Venture* (Md. App.1981), a general partner was held to have breached a fiduciary duty to inform the limited partners of an opportunity to buy ten acres of land adjacent to land the partnership was developing.

PART III

EXTERNAL MATTERS; RIGHTS OF THIRD PARTIES

CHAPTER 4

VICARIOUS TORT LIABILITY

---

§ 16. Respondeat Superior

The Latin phrase *respondeat superior* ("let the master answer") is a shorthand and widely used means of describing the vicarious liability of a principal for the torts of an agent. It is not a form of substitute liability, however. Vicarious liability is liability *in addition* to the liability of the person committing the tort, who remains personally liable for the tortious conduct.

A principal is not invariably liable for the torts of his or her agent; rather, the principal is only liable if, among other things, the principal has a certain degree of control over the agent. When that degree of physical control was present, the common law described the principal as a "master" and the agent as the principal's "servant."

As noted in the Glossary, the Restatement (Third) of Agency abandons the terms "master" and "servant." In their place, the new Restatement uses the terms employer and employee. It is important to note, however, that the terms employer and employee are specially defined terms for purposes of vicarious liability. R3d § 7.07 defines such an employee as "an agent whose principal controls or has the right to control the manner and means of the agent's performance of work." The section goes on to provide that "the fact that work is performed gratuitously does not relieve a principal of liability." Thus, it is clear that a principal may be vicariously liable for the torts of its agent even if the agent is not, *for other purposes,* an "employee" of the principal. For example, in *Heims v. Hanke* (Wis.1958), the court upheld a finding that an uncle was vicariously liable for the acts of his 16–year-old nephew who negligently created a dangerous condition for a passerby while gratuitously helping his adult uncle wash the uncle's car. The court reasoned that because the nephew responded to his uncle's directions, the nephew was a servant. Under the new Restatement, the nephew would be the uncle's employee for purposes of the uncle's vicarious liability.

The definition of "servant" in the Second Restatement was substantially the same as the new definition of employee. The shift from servant to employee has the advantage of removing from the legal discourse a term (servant) that carries some unwanted implications. However, its replacement (employee) is less than ideal because employee is a well-accepted term that suggests a compensated relationship with certain responsibilities accruing the employer (such as paying employment taxes, providing worker's compensation insurance, etc.). In addition to the problem of uncompensated agents, there are some cases in which employers are not liable for the torts of their employees because the employer lacks the necessary control over the employee. (See *Cooke v. E.F. Drew & Co.* (2d Cir.1963), rejecting an argument that an agent is a servant as a matter of law "merely because he devoted his full-time to the business of Drew [his employer] or because there was a written contract of employment with Drew and the company deducted social security and withholding taxes." The Cooke court thus sees the word "employee" as overinclusive when used as a substitute for "servant.")

Nevertheless, as a matter of fact, in most cases in which a principal has the necessary degree of control over its agent to result in vicarious liability, the agent will be an employee for all purposes. And the instances in which a true employer lacks the necessary control over its employees to result in vicarious liability will be rare. Indeed, many courts today classify an employee as a servant even when the employer does not actually exercise control over physical conduct due to the specialized nature of the work of the employee, like lawyers or doctors working full-time for one employer. Those courts seem to be creating a conclusive presumption that full-time employment creates a *right* of control over physical conduct, which satisfies the test for respondeat superior liability. Whether the courts will embrace this new terminology, however, remains to be seen. In this book, we will use the terms employer-employee in lieu of master-servant, but will not substitute terms when the courts have used the older terminology.

§ 17. The Policy Behind Respondeat Superior

The strict liability of respondeat superior has proven difficult to explain in our common law system of torts, which is based largely on the fault principle. The liability of respondeat superior is strict because employers are held liable no matter how careful they have been in selecting, training, and supervising their employees. Evidence offered concerning the care taken by an employer in the operation of its business would be stricken as irrelevant in a respondeat superior case.

Numerous efforts have been made to justify this form of strict liability. It has been argued that employers should be responsible for the negligence of persons working on their behalf because they initiate the activity, profit by it, and have the power to closely supervise the work of their employees and thus can take steps to minimize their exposure to liability. Because an employer has a right of indemnity against a wrongdoing employee (see § 12), as a formal matter the employer is being required only to bear the risk of insolvency of the negligent actor. Also, it has been argued that vicarious liability, by taking away the defense of due care, provides an added incentive for employers to exercise the considerable degree of control they have over their employees and to discipline them for misconduct, thus reducing the risk of loss.

Another argument is that economically the loss belongs on the employer because in reality most employers are businesses and sell products or services. It is economically sound to place the cost onto the business, which will adjust its price accordingly. This has two benefits. First, it spreads the loss among the users of the product or service rather than leaving it on the victim (it is true that frequently the victim has accident, disability, and health insurance, and that social welfare programs often assist those who do not have insurance, so that the "loss spreading" argument, standing alone, is sometimes artificial). Second, to place the cost onto the business facilitates accident reduction through "general deterrence." That is, placing such costs onto businesses that cause losses may reduce accidents overall by making accident prone or carelessly run businesses more expensive than competing businesses or industries, thus making substitute products or services that are less costly attractive to the purchaser. This theoretically would reduce the incidence of loss by reducing or eliminating businesses that impose heavy costs on others, through operation of the competitive marketplace.

A skeptic might say that the above arguments are window dressing and do not fairly apply to all respondeat superior situations, particularly those involving charitable activities and personal relationships of a nonbusiness nature. Instead, the deep pocket theory explains what is really going on. The employer almost always has more resources than the employee and thus has the deeper pocket and is held liable for actions taken within the scope of employment. The deep pocket theory, unexpressed by courts, may explain the origins of respondeat superior, which was created at a time when social insurance did not exist and most employees truly were servants of aristocratic, wealthy households or businesses that usually could afford to pay for damages done. The deep pocket theory understandably offends many as unprincipled because it uses wealth as the basis for liability, but there may be an element of truth to the skeptic's position.

These arguments, or some combination of them, have proved persuasive to courts. Respondeat superior liability is universally accepted in the common law. The only issues that remain alive today focus on the scope of liability, a matter that will be addressed below.

§ 18. Limitation to Losses Caused by Tortious Behavior

Liability in respondeat superior is vicarious in nature, stemming from the faultworthy conduct of an employee. It sometimes has been argued, on general deterrence and loss spreading grounds, that an employer should be liable for all losses caused by an employee, even those not resulting from tortious behavior. This argument has been rejected on the reasoning that an employer does not always have a better risk-bearing capacity than the injured party (consider the small plumbing shop whose employee without negligence causes damage to equipment owned by a multi-national, billion-dollar oil company). When one combines this lack of superior risk-bearing capacity with the fact that the incentive to discipline employees for misconduct is not present when the behavior of the employee is not wrongful, liability has not been extended to such circumstances.

§ **19.** Imputed Contributory Negligence

Assume that Pam, an employer, is sitting in the passenger seat of a car being driven by Ed, her employee, on the way to a conference related to work. Ed negligently causes an accident with Tom, another driver, who also is driving negligently. Pam is injured and her car is damaged. She wants to sue Tom for these losses. Can she successfully do so? Granted, she is vicariously liable for the damages caused by Ed, but in this suit she is a plaintiff, not a defendant. Surprisingly, it is the general rule even today that if an employee's negligence is imputed to an employer, so is his contributory negligence. The effect of this rule is to destroy or reduce (if comparative negligence is adopted in the jurisdiction) the recovery of the employer for loss caused by the negligence of the other party to the accident.

This rule is called the "both ways" test, based on the fact that an employee's negligence is imputed both ways: to create vicarious liability for the employer and to destroy or weaken the employer's cause of action against a negligent stranger. The both ways test recently has been rejected by some states, sometimes in reliance on the deep pocket theory, noting that the theory of making a solvent defendant available does not apply to the employer's suit for injury to herself.

§ 20. Direct Tort Liability of an Employer

Direct tort liability as against an employer is frequently an alternative claim for liability in the typical respondeat superior case, especially cases involving intentional torts. The typical claim against an employer alleges lack of due care in hiring or supervising an employee.

Williams v. Feather Sound, Inc. (Fla.App.1980) is a frequently cited case. It involved a suit against a condominium developer by a homeowner who was assaulted in her home by an employee of the developer. She sued the developer for negligent hiring. The court discussed the scope of an employer's duty to check into the character of applicants for employment. It differentiated between an employee hired to do only outside work (no duty to inquire beyond information supplied by the applicant) and an employee who will have access to the inside of homes (a duty exists to make an independent inquiry). The court held that an employer is chargeable with such information as it could have obtained upon making reasonable inquiry into the more trusted employee's background. This concept is reflected in R3d § 7.05 (T.D. No. 5, 2004).

§ 21. Liability of the Employee

An agent is personally liable for affirmative acts of wrongdoing committed while acting on behalf of another. Acting as agent does not somehow confer personal immunity on the acting party. To find otherwise would be to take the fiction of identification of principal and agent (that the agent is simply the alter ego of the principal) to an extreme that no court or commentator has recognized.

A more troubling issue involves the personal liability of an agent for a failure to act (nonfeasance), where the agent fails to perform a duty owed to the principal. An example of this is the failure of an agent to repair the principal's property contrary to instructions, and a person is injured. Courts are divided on this. Many courts hold the agent not liable. One of the classic statements of this approach is from *Delaney v. Rochereau* (La.1882): "At common law, an agent is personally responsible to third parties for doing something which he ought not to have done, but not for not doing something which he ought to have done, the agent, in the latter case, being liable to his principal only. No man increases or diminishes his obligations to strangers by becoming an agent." Contrasting authority stresses the control an agent may have under some circumstances because of the agency status (such as being in control of property), which should create a duty to act with care. See Seavey, Studies in Agency 5 (1949). The Restatment reflects these cases by stating that "an agent is subject to tort liability to a third party harmed by the agent's conduct only when the agent's conduct breaches a duty that the agent owes to a third party." R3d § 7.02 (T.D. No. 5, 2004).

§ 22. The Independent Contractor Exception of the Second Restatement

In addition to the concept of master-servant, the Restatement (Second) of Agency employed the term "independent contractor" and set forth a definition in R2d § 2 as follows:

(3) An independent contractor is a person who contracts with another to do something for him but who is not controlled by the other nor subject to the other's right to control with respect to his physical conduct in the performance of the undertaking. He may or may not be an agent.

As the above quotation indicates, the phrase "independent contractor" is ambiguous, including within its scope both agents and nonagents. The term was intended to provide an alternative to the term "servant," which contemplates control by the principal. Because the independent contractor, or acting party, by definition is not controlled by the party who retained him, the retaining party ordinarily is not responsible for the torts of the acting party, with certain exceptions covered in § 23. With a non-agent, no agency relationship exists upon which to pin vicarious tort liability. With the agent that is not subject to the control of the principal, there is no basis for imposing vicarious liability because the principal, having no control over details, is unable effectively to increase the amount of care taken during performance of the activity.

The Restatement (Third) has abandoned the use of the term "independent contractor." Instead, it uses the term "employee" (see § 16 above) to describe those agents with respect to whom the principal (or employer) bears vicarious liability. In comment f to R3d § 7.07 (T.D. No. 5, 2004), the drafters have set forth the "indicia" that are relevant to determining whether an agent is an employee. These include: "the extent of control that the agent and the principal have agreed the principal may exercise over the details of the work; whether the agent is engaged in a distinct occupation or business; whether the type of work done by the agent is customarily done under a principal's supervision; the skill required in the agent's occupation; whether the agent or the principal supplies the tools or other instrumentalities required for the work and the place in which to perform it; the length of time during which the agent is engaged by a principal; whether the agent is paid by the job or by the time worked; whether the principal and the agent believe they are creating an employment relationship; and whether the principal is or is not in business." Resolution of this question usually is by the trier of fact.

The key element of control over details is satisfied not only by actual control but also by the right of control. The above factors help in drawing an inference of right of control. With regard to the significance of the manner of payment, see *Cooke v. E.F.Drew & Co.* (2d Cir.1963), drawing an inference of right of control when an employee was paid by salary since "his time belonged to his employer and he was entitled to be paid irrespective of results."

Most courts hold that reserving the right to inspect the work being done to ensure that the contract is performed according to its terms, and to see that the contractor operates in a safe manner, does not in itself constitute the kind of control necessary to create an employer-employee relationship. See *Noonan v. Texaco* (Wyo.1986)("an owner who undertakes to see that an independent contractor operates in a safe manner ought not to be penalized") and *Eden v. Spaulding* (Neb.1984)("the employer of an independent contractor may, without changing the status, exercise such control as is necessary to assure performance of the contract in accordance with its terms").

Non-employee agents. A real estate broker is an example of an agent who is not an employee of the principal who retains him. A homeowner who lists her home for sale with a real estate broker is not liable for the negligent driving of the broker when bringing a potential purchaser to the home despite the existence of an agency relationship between the homeowner and the broker. There is no control over the manner and means of driving and hence no fair inference that the homeowner could, through the exercise of control, attempt to ensure that the work (that is, the agent's driving) is done more safely. Also, the costs of negligent driving seem more appropriately assessed onto the broker's business, not added to the expenses of a homeowner when trying to sell her home.

As noted above, the common law and the Restatement (Second) of Agency referred to such agents as "independent contractors," although such agents might more accurately have been referred to as "nonservant agents." This less ambiguous phrase does not enjoy widespread usage in the law of agency. Perhaps this is because historically the phrase "independent contractor" was first used to distinguish between kinds of agents in this context and it has dominated usage ever since. Whether the courts will abandon the term independent contractor as have the drafters of the Restatement (Third) only time will tell. For the sake of consistency, if not clarity, this book will refer to agents who are not employees as non-employee agents.

Non-agent Service Providers. A building contractor is an example of the other kind of independent contractor, one who is not an agent. It is true that the building contractor's work benefits the owner. But it cannot fairly be inferred that the contractor is working on the owner's behalf or that the owner has any control over the details of the work. Instead, the contractor is conducting its own business and reaping its own profit. It orders materials for the job in its own name and pays for them, and is in control over the manner and means of accomplishing the construction work involved in the job.

A taxi driver is another common example of a nonagent service provider or, in the terms of Restatement (Second), an independent contractor. The passenger benefits from the driving and exercises some control, including initiating the activity, specifying where the driver is to go, and so forth. Yet clearly there is no command relationship (contrast the relationship of taxi driver and passenger with that of chauffeur-employee and employer), nor is the taxi driver acting primarily for the passenger's benefit, but instead is either working for a taxi company or is driving on his own, with the goal of maximizing personal income. When this book uses the term "independent contractor," it means a nonagent service provider. A service provider who is an agent, such as a real estate broker, is referred to as a non-employee agent.

§ 23. When a Principal is Liable for the Torts of an Independent Contractor (Non-Agent Service Provider)

Some of the cases addressing the limitations described below involve the non-agent service provider and thus the matter is one of general tort law. The concepts are closely related to agency issues, however. Sometimes, for example, a case will involve a plaintiff arguing in the alternative that a negligent actor was the defendant's employee or, if not, defendant is liable under an exception to the doctrine that a person is not vicariously liable for the conduct of one who is not his agent.

A. The Inherently Dangerous Activity Exception

A person who engages another to do inherently dangerous work is vicariously liable for the negligence of the contractor. "Inherently dangerous" work is defined as work "which, in its nature, will create some peculiar risk of injury to others unless special precautions are taken—as, for example, excavations in or near a public highway." Prosser and Keeton on Torts 472 (5th ed. 1984). The policy underlying this exception apparently is that special responsibilities go along with initiating an activity that is inherently dangerous to the community, even when the employer does not have control over details.

B. The Nondelegable Duty Exception

A nondelegable duty is one that "requires the person upon whom it is imposed to answer for it that care is exercised by anyone, even though he be an independent contractor, to whom performance of the duty is entrusted." Restatement of Torts 394. A duty is characterized as nondelegable when "the responsibility is so important to the community that the employer should not be permitted to transfer it to another." Prosser and Keeton on Torts 512 (5th ed. 1984). The inherently dangerous activity exception can be characterized as one kind of nondelegable duty.

The nondelegable duty concept often is invoked when a duty originates in a contract, statute or administrative regulation, or under circumstances where defendant has extended an invitation to plaintiff, such as opening premises to the public. A recent case involving nondelegable duty is *Kleeman v. Rheingold* (N.Y.1993), which held that an attorney's duty of care in the service of process for a client cannot be delegated to a process serving company.

There is a danger in a sweeping application of the nondelegable duty concept. Broadly read, it could swallow the principle of non-liability for the conduct of independent contractors by, for example, declaring all duties of care nondelegable. This would mean that a homeowner who hired an independent, professional tree service to trim her trees would be vicariously liable for the negligence of a tree trimmer employed by the service in dropping a limb onto a neighbor's car. This would result in imposing liability when the party employing the non-agent service provider, or independent contractor, has no means to protect herself by exerting detailed control over the activity. Such extraordinary strict liability instead should be confined to narrow and unusual circumstances.

Also, a broad application of the nondelegable duty exception can lead to a misallocation of the burdens and costs of doing business by placing the costs of doing business on the customers of the independent contractor's business rather on the business itself. It is true that indemnity can be sought against the independent contractor, as explained below, but litigation costs, among others, would be unfairly imposed on the party that engaged the independent contractor.

C. Negligence in Selection of Contractor

The party hiring an independent contractor is under a duty to use care in choosing that contractor. The more dangerous the activity, the more care must be taken. But liability stems directly from the lack of care, not vicariously from the relationship. In general, a person hiring a contractor who will not be an agent does not need to inquire into the contractor's solvency or insurance coverage, nor into the adequacy of its equipment or personnel. As stated in the Restatement (Second) of Torts § 411:

> [O]ne who employs a carpenter to repair the ceilings of his shop or [a plumber] to install plumbing in his hotel is entitled to assume that a carpenter or plumber of good reputation is competent to do such work safely. ...Indeed, there is no duty to take any great pains to ascertain whether his reputation is or is not good. The fact that he is a carpenter or plumber is sufficient, unless the employer knows that the contractor's reputation is bad or knows of facts which should lead him to realize that the contractor is not competent.

§ 24. The Borrowed Employee

There are occasions when one employer (the "general employer") loans one of its employees to another employer (the "borrowing employer" or the "special employer"), usually along with rental of equipment, to do a particular job. If the employee is found to be a borrowed employee, or in the terminology of the Restatement (Second), a borrowed servant, the special employer, not the general employer, is vicariously liable for the employee's wrongdoing.

The law of borrowed servant thus bears some relationship to the independent contractor concept. If an employee is found not to be borrowed, "the general employer is an independent contractor providing a man to do the job." Seavey, Reuschlein and Hall, Agency and Partnership 23 (1962). Many cases involve the operation of cranes on construction sites. The general employer (the crane service company) ordinarily continues paying the wages of the employee (the crane operator) and the borrowing employer (the general contractor) necessarily has control over the work of the employee while on the job site. An issue is raised when the employee commits a tort while working under the orders of the borrowing employer. Suppose, for example, the crane operator negligently injures someone while working pursuant to the hand signals of the general contractor's foreman. The crane operator is employed and being paid by the crane service company but was under the direction and control of the general contractor at the time of the accident. Which employer is responsible for the injury?

The law in this area is confused, in part because the employee is doing the work of both employers and is, in one sense, under the control of both employers. Who is the principal? (In that respect the law of borrowed employee provides a further example of the ambiguous principal problem described in § 6.) As noted above, the significance of this special category of agency law is that if an employee is classified as a borrowed employee, respondeat superior liability is shifted from the general employer to the borrowing employer.

But when is an employee regarded as "borrowed"? The test in many jurisdictions is whether it can reasonably be inferred that the employee's allegiance has been transferred to the borrowing employer. As stated in one of the most famous cases in this area, *Charles v. Barrett* (N.Y.1922), "[A]s long as the employee is furthering the business of his general employer by the service rendered to another, there will be no inference of a new relation unless command has been surrendered, and no inference of its surrender from the mere fact of its division." Under this test, called the transfer of allegiance test, relatively few employees would be borrowed. Usually the employee is furthering the business of his employer and command rarely is completely surrendered by the general employer. This approach is consistent with the basic definition of the agency relationship because the court is looking to see to whom the agent gives his loyalty. Usually an employee will give his allegiance to the person who pays him, the general employer.

Not all jurisdictions use the transfer of allegiance test. Some focus on the precise act causing injury and ask who was exercising control at that time, a natural inquiry. This line of authority, however, seems to lose sight of the "on behalf of" element of agency by focusing exclusively on control. Yet control alone cannot create respondeat superior liability. If that were true, the foreman of a construction crew would be vicariously liable for the negligence of the workers in the crew, based on his indisputable control over the physical conduct of the workers. Such a result would ignore the fact that the foreman and the workers are joint employees (co-agents). The workers are working on behalf of the company that employs them, not the foreman. The foreman is subject only to direct (not vicarious) liability for negligently exercising control, a standard that could usefully be applied to the borrowing employer.

A few jurisdictions ignore both the issue of allegiance and the fact of control at the time of the wrongful act. These courts instead hold both employers jointly and severally liable, as if they were partners or joint venturers, reasoning that the employee is doing the work of both. This approach is rejected by the great majority of courts on the reasoning that, as expressed in the frequently quoted language of *Atwood v. Chicago R.I. & P. Ry.* (W.D.Mo.1896), "A man cannot serve two masters at the same time; he will obey the one and betray the other." If the interests of the two employers conflict (regarding exposing the rented equipment to a risk of damage, for example), the employee will have to choose whose orders to obey. This makes it necessary, in the view of most courts, to confine respondeat superior liability to one employer. This problem would not arise if the employers were in a partnership or joint venture or if they jointly hired the employee, but that is not the situation being addressed in the borrowed employee context. The temptation to bend doctrine and hold both employers jointly and severally liable is minimal in the eyes of most courts, perhaps because the injured party already has two defendants available: the wrongdoer and the wrongdoer's employer.

§ 25. The Scope of Employment Limitation

A. Negligence

All authorities agree that there must be some connection with the principal's business before the tortious act of an agent will create vicarious liability for the principal. No one argues that a trucking company should be liable for the negligence of one of its drivers committed while driving to a family picnic on a day off.

The scope of employment defense to a respondeat superior claim addresses this issue. *Joel v. Morison* (Eng.1834) originated the widely used "frolic" versus "detour" distinction. If employees are on a frolic, the employer is not liable for harm they negligently cause. If they are on a mere detour, the scope of employment defense is not available to their employer. When is an activity a frolic and when is it a detour? The Restatement of Agency has crafted a test that seeks to capture the many judicial opinions in this area. The test of R3d § 7.07 (T.D. No. 5, 2004) is as follows:

> An employee acts within the scope of employment when performing work assigned by the employer or engaging in a course of conduct subject to the employer's control. An employee's act is not within the scope of employment when it occurs within an independent course of conduct not intended by the employee to serve any purpose of the employer.

This test leaves many difficult questions of fact, of course. The court in *Fiocco v. Carver* (N.Y.1922) provides a procedural assist to the fact-finding process: if an employee is using a vehicle of his employer, a presumption exists that he is using it in the course of employment. The presumption disappears, however, "when the surrounding circumstances are such that its recognition is unreasonable. We refuse to rest upon presumption, and put the plaintiff to his proof, when the departure from regularity is so obvious that charity can no longer infer an adherence to the course of duty."

The *Fiocco* court also articulates the re-entry test, which applies after an employee has abandoned his employment and the issue is whether he subsequently returned to his duties prior to the accident. Although location in time and space are important, it must also be proved that the "dominant purpose" of the employee is performance of the employer's business before re-entry will be found. As Judge Cardozo stated in *Fiocco*, "We are not dealing with a case where in the course of a continuing relation, business and private ends have been coincidentally served. Division [from the frolic] more substantial must be shown before a relation, once ignored and abandoned, will be renewed and re-established." Comment e to R3d § 7.07 captures these concepts: "De minimis departures from assigned routes are not 'frolics' ... and [f]rolics end when an employee reenters employment, that is, when the employee is once again performing assigned work and taking actions incidental to it."

In general, acts of a personal nature, such as smoking, are outside of the scope of employment on the reasoning that they are not the kind of thing the employee was hired to do and they are not done for the purpose of serving the employer. The employer will be liable, however, if engaging in the personal habit can fairly be characterized as a negligent way of doing one's job, such as causing an accident by taking one's hands off the wheel while driving in order to light a cigarette, or if the conduct can be characterized as "incidental to the employee's performance of assigned work." (R3d § 7.07, comment d).

Also, the "going and coming" rule prescribes that accidents of employees on their way to work or departing after work are outside the scope of employment on the reasoning that the employee is not working on behalf of nor under the control of the employer at that time. Nearly all courts come to the same result even if the employee is paid travel expenses or travel time, reasoning that the facts still do not fairly support an inference that the employee is on the job, working on behalf of and subject to the control of the employer, when traveling to or from work. If, on the other hand, an employee has been asked to do a special errand on the way to or from work, the focus shifts and one can start to construct a plausible case for conduct within the scope of employment.

B. Intentional Torts

(i) Intent to serve. Intentional torts pose a special problem for plaintiffs because it is difficult to characterize the employee's act as one "intended by the employee to serve any purpose of the employer" (R3d § 7.07(2)) when intentional misconduct is involved. Personal gratification, malice, or misappropriation (in cases of theft) are almost always written across the face of intentional misconduct, with no intent whatsoever to serve the employer. For this reason, the great majority of courts refuse to hold employers vicariously liable for intentional misconduct, especially when it also is criminal, unless the nature of the job is such that an employee's misconduct could be characterized as including at least a partial intent to serve the employer's purposes.

A frequent example of a partial intent to serve situation is the case of a bartender who overreacts to a situation involving control of a drunken patron and commits a serious assault on the patron. Because maintaining order is part of a bartender's job and the tort took place while the bartender was seemingly doing that, many courts hold that the tort falls within the scope of employment, unless the assault was too extreme. Cases involving security guards invoke the same response.

Several decisions have rejected the "intent to serve" test and have held employers liable for intentional torts even when it was clear that the employee had no intent to serve the employer. For example, the court in *Ira S. Bushey v. United States* (2d Cir.1968)(drunken sailor spun wheels controlling water intake valves and sunk ship being repaired in drydock) substituted a test of "characteristic risk," asking if the mishap may "fairly be said to be characteristic of its [the employer's] activities." The court also described this as a test of foreseeability, stating, "Put another way, [drunken sailor's] conduct was not so 'unforeseeable' as to make it unfair to charge [his employer] with responsibility." The Restatement (Third) rejects *Bushey*: "[F]ormulations based on assessments of 'foreseeability' are potentially confusing and may generate outcomes that are less predictable than intention-based formulations." (R3d § 7.07, comment b).

Two other illustrative cases are *Mary M. v. City of Los Angeles* (Cal.1991), holding Los Angeles liable in money damages for rape committed by a police officer, and *Doe v. Samaritan Counseling Center* (Alaska 1990), holding defendant counseling center could be found liable for the sexual abuse of a patient by a therapist. The court in *Mary M* upheld a trial court finding of liability by applying a test of "three policy objectives." Specifically, an employer would be liable if this would "prevent recurrence of the tortious conduct, give greater assurance of compensation to the victim, and ensure that the victim's losses will be equitably borne by those who benefit from the enterprise that gives rise to the injury." The *Doe* court reversed summary judgment for the center and remanded the case on the reasoning that the center could be held liable on an "enterprise liability" rationale if it was found below that the therapist's act was "incident to carrying on an enterprise."

There is a similarity to the characteristic risk, three policy objectives, and enterprise liability rationales of the above three cases. Each of them rejects the intent to serve test and instead substitutes broad questions about loss spreading and enterprise liability. It can be argued that these substitute standards are so open-ended that it is hard to focus analysis. In some circumstances arguments may consist of not much more than an exchange of conclusory assertions about whether the tortious act is or is not incident to the enterprise. With regard to tools of analysis, one virtue of the intent-based Restatement test is that it provides something more specific to consider when deciding these complex and emotional cases that deal with conduct everywhere viewed as offensive and repugnant.

In addition, it can be argued that the characteristic risk, three policy objectives, and enterprise liability rationales depart from the moral foundation of agency law. Conduct of an agent must be on behalf of the principal before it is fair to hold the principal to the strict liability of respondeat superior. If there is no "intent to serve," there is no action "on behalf of" the principal and therefore no moral justification for strict liability. Perhaps for this reason, the great majority of courts today continue to apply an intent-based test to scope of employment cases.

It is worth noting that in cases involving therapists, police officers, and others (like school teachers) who have particular control over people, the standard of due care in hiring and supervision is especially strict for employers. In some cases this may provide an appropriate alternative ground for recovery for a victim. If the employer has acted with due care, however, both the victim and the employer are innocent, making it difficult to find a principled basis of decision to place the loss on the employer whose employee has committed a self-serving intentional tort.

(ii) The implied contract argument. An alternative theory for intentional tort cases that avoids the awkwardness of arguing that rape is within the scope of employment has been advanced in several recent cases. The theory seeks to ground liability on an implied term of the contract between the victim and the employer that the employer will ensure the safety of the victim from misconduct by its employees. (This theory will cover only some intentional tort cases because of the necessity of a contractual relationship between victim and employer. It would not be useful in *Mary M*, for example.)

This argument was fully developed and analyzed in *G.L. v. Kaiser Foundation Hospitals* (Or.1988), a case involving a sexual assault on a patient by a respiratory therapist. It was conceded that the hospital was not negligent and that the employee was acting outside of his scope of employment, but plaintiff argued that the hospital impliedly undertook to be strictly liable to its patients for the intentional misconduct of its employees acting outside the scope of their employment. The court, after stating "the question before this court is a matter of first impression in Oregon, if not in the nation," rejected the argument on the reasoning that it "invents a legal fiction."

The assumption of the court in *Kaiser* appears to be that a court will imply terms into a contract only when it can fairly be inferred that both parties would have included the term in the contract had they thought about it. The court concluded that it cannot fairly be inferred that a hospital truly would have agreed to such a term and exposed itself to a risk of such magnitude and over which it had so little control. As the court of appeals said in the same case, "Plaintiff's theory [proposes to replace liability based on negligence or respondeat superior] with an absolute liability standard through the artifice of placing a contract label on what is inherently a matter of tort law." The Oregon supreme court concluded that the best forum for plaintiff's argument is the legislature, noting that the legislature had acted on similar matters before, including acts of theft by hotel employees, by providing a remedy under defined circumstances.

(iii) Torts "aided by the agency relation." The Restatement (Second) includes the concept that an employer would be vicariously liable for torts committed by an employee when the employee "was aided in accomplishing the tort by the existence of the agency relation." R2d § 219(2)(d). This concept can have far-reaching consequences for employers, as illustrated by the recent case of *Costos v. Coconut Island Corp.* (1st Cir. 1998). In *Costos*, the employee was the manager of a Maine inn. He used a key to which he had access, entered the locked room of the plaintiff, a guest at the inn, and raped her. The federal court, applying Maine law, applied the Restatement provision and reasoned that because, as manager, the employee was entrusted with the keys to the inn's rooms and knew where the victim was staying, he was aided in his tortious conduct by the agency relation. In a subsequent case, the Maine Supreme Court distanced itself somewhat from *Costos*, saying that it had not expressly adopted § 219(d)(2), and declined to apply the section to the case before, albeit one quite different from *Costos*. The Maine case, *Mahar v. Stonewood Transport* (Me. 2003), involved an instance of road rage by the employee and the Maine court concluded that the employee's conduct was not aided by the agency relation. In the course of its opinion, the Maine court noted that the ALI's deliberations preceding the adoption of § 219(2)(d) "demonstrate an intent to limit the section's application to cases involving apparent authority, reliance, or deceit." The Restatement (Third) also seems to reject *Costos*:

> This Restatement does not include "aided in accomplishing" as a distinct basis for an employer's (or principal's) vicarious liability. The purposes likely intended to be met by the "aided in accomplishing" basis are satisfied by a more fully elaborated treatment of apparent authority and by the duty of reasonable care that a principal owes to third parties with whom it interacts through employees and other agents.

Restatement (Third) of Agency, § 7.08 (T.D. No. 5, 2004).

§ 26. Punitive Damages

Courts divide on whether an innocent employer can be held liable for punitive damages in addition to compensatory damages for the misconduct of an employee. Some courts are willing to allow punitive damages in any case in which the employer is liable for compensatory damages under respondeat superior. The majority of courts disagree and follow the "complicity rule" which "results in employer liability for punitive damages only when a superior officer in the course of employment orders, participates in, or ratifies outrageous conduct." *Loughry v. Lincoln First Bank* (N.Y.1986).

The *Loughry* court uses the phrase "superior officer." It defines that to mean "more than an agent, or 'ordinary' officer, or employee vested with some supervisory or decision-making responsibility.

Indeed, since the purpose of the test is to determine whether an agent's acts can be equated with participation by the employer, the term must contemplate a high level of general managerial authority in relation to the nature and operation of the employer's business."

The reasoning underlying the complicity rule is well expressed in *Campen v. Stone* (Wyo.1981). The court stated that the purpose of punitive damages is "to punish the wrongdoer and deter him and others from duplicating his misconduct. Unless the employer is himself guilty of some tortious act (or omission) . . . an award punishing the employer and deterring him and others situated to act likewise (i.e., other employers) makes no sense at all."

§ 27. Liability to Invitee of Employee

Even if conduct is within the scope of employment, a defense may be available to the employer if the plaintiff was injured upon the employer's premises or in the employer's vehicle at the invitation of an employee who had no authority or apparent authority to extend the invitation. An adult hitchhiker is a good example of this. The Reporter's Notes to R2d § 242 state that, "by accepting the hospitality of the servant and causing him to commit a breach of duty, the intruder has so identified himself with the servant that it is just that his claim against the master should be forfeited. Further, although the servant drives in the scope of employment, he is also driving for the benefit of the intruder." Courts divide on this issue, however.

Some jurisdictions conclude their inquiry with scope of employment.

§ **28.** **Vicarious Liability for Nonphysical Torts**

The vicarious liability of a principal for an agent's intentional torts includes liability for fraud and other nonphysical torts. These materials will focus on the tort of fraud, which generates nearly all the litigation in the area of nonphysical torts.

The element of control over the physical conduct of the wrongdoer, essential to respondeat superior liability, is irrelevant here. Also, the motive element in respondeat superior plays no role in fraud cases. Instead, focus shifts to the expectations of the victim. It is useful to recall that the elements of fraud, broadly defined, include a knowing misrepresentation by the tortfeasor and justifiable reliance by the victim.

The Restatement (Third) seeks to capture many cases in this area with a single section, eschewing the approach of the Restatement (Second), which utilized several sections. R3d § 7.08 (Tentative Draft No. 5, 2004) provides:

A principal is subject to vicarious liability for a tort committed by an agent in dealing or communicating with a third party on or purportedly on behalf of the principal and actions taken by the agent with apparent authority constitute the tort or enable the agent to conceal its commission.

The concept of apparent authority, which focuses on the reasonable expectations of third parties created by the principal's manifestations, is covered in § 38 of these materials.

Billups Petroleum Co. v. Hardin's Bakeries (Miss. 1953) provides an example of liability under this concept. A salesman for Hardin's Bakeries overcharged Billups for bread over a period of several months and kept the excess for himself. The court held Hardin liable for its agent's fraud. In this case the agent's position facilitated commission of the fraud and the customer reasonably could assume under the circumstances of the case that the salesman was authorized to prepare bills and accept payments for the delivered bread, thus establishing apparent authority.

Another case reaching a similar result, although phrasing the test for liability in different terms, is *Rothman v. Fillette* (Pa.1983). In this case P, a person injured in a car accident, hired an attorney (A) to represent him in litigation against the other driver (T). A, the attorney, misrepresented to T and T's insurance company that P had approved a $7000 settlement that A previously had worked out with T and the insurance company. A delivered to them a settlement agreement and release purportedly signed by P but actually forged by A. The insurance company presented a check payable to both P and A. A forged P's signature and absconded with the funds. The court held P responsible for A's fraud on the reasoning that, "Where one of two innocent parties must suffer, the loss should be borne by him who put the wrongdoer in a position of trust and confidence [inviting others to deal with the wrongdoer] and thus enabled him to perpetrate the wrong."

§ 29. The Exculpatory Clause

One way a principal can protect itself from liability for money damages for the fraud of its agents is to include an exculpatory clause in its contract with the third party. A typical exculpatory clause reads as follows: "It is understood that the authority of seller's agents is limited and confined to securing purchasers for its property upon the terms and conditions set out in the agreement, and not otherwise; that sales representatives have no authority to make any change, modification, promise or any representation whatsoever other than those herein stated." (Based on language contained in *Eamoe v. Big Bear Land & Water Co.* (Cal.App. 1950)).

Such a clause protects the principal from liability for money damages for fraud unless the principal knows of and encourages the fraudulent behavior, ratifies it, or exercises an inadequate amount of supervision over its agent. It does not, however, preclude rescission of the contract and recovery in restitution by the defrauded party of funds paid to the principal on the reasoning that a principal cannot benefit from its agent's fraud. This limitation does not apply if the principal has in good faith changed position prior to receiving notice of the fraud.

§ **30.** Vicarious Liability by Estoppel

Under the concept of vicarious liability by estoppel one can be held vicariously liable for the tort of another in the absence of an agency relationship, which sounds extraordinary. Liability is based on appearance, not reality, however. *Crinkley v. Holiday Inns, Inc.* (4th Cir.1988), is a typical case. Plaintiffs, who were staying at a Holiday Inn and were criminally assaulted on the motel premises, filed a negligence claim against Holiday Inns. The defense was that the particular inn in question was owned and operated by a franchisee of Holiday. The franchisee was allowed to use the Holiday name in return for granting Holiday a percentage of gross income. Holiday argued that it was not actually in charge of the premises nor was there any agency relationship between it and the franchisee, which was running its own business, and thus any negligence was attributable to the franchisee, not Holiday.

The court nevertheless upheld a judgment for plaintiffs, holding that the evidence at trial was sufficient to show that Holiday had permitted the franchisee to create the appearance that the inn was owned and operated by Holiday and that plaintiffs had relied on Holiday's good reputation for safety of its guests. The only disclosure of the franchisee's ownership was by a sign in the restaurant in the building, which the court found insufficient. Thus Holiday was estopped from denying that it did not own the motel in question.

Reasonable reliance is part of a plaintiff's claim under this concept. A similar case, *Hayman v. Ramada Inn, Inc.* (N.C.App.1987), was lost on that ground when defendant Ramada Inn proved that plaintiff stayed at the inn in question because she was required to by her employer, rather than by her choice in reliance on the good reputation of the franchisor.

§ 31. The Joint Enterprise Relationship

Joint enterprise liability is a form of vicarious liability that exists independently of respondeat superior. It is an unusual feature of American law that seems to be rapidly fading, although it remains law in a number of states. It flourished during the time when automobile liability policies did not contain an omnibus clause, which provides insurance coverage for anyone who drives a car with the consent of the insured owner. Although not all joint enterprise cases involve automobile accidents, a large percentage of them do. It may be that courts created the joint enterprise doctrine in order to increase the chances of recovery for an injured plaintiff.

A succinct definition of a joint enterprise is contained in *Howard v. Zimmerman* (Kan.1926): "An enterprise is a project or undertaking, and a joint enterprise is simply one participated in by associates acting together." The court further stated, "The basis of liability of one associate in a joint enterprise for the tort of another is equal privilege to control the method and means of accomplishing the common design. It is sufficient that, at the beginning of the enterprise, or as it progressed, or at any time before the tortious event, he [the passive party who is being held vicariously liable for a co-enterpriser's negligence] possessed equal authority to prescribe conditions of use."

Note that control over physical conduct is not required, as it is in respondeat superior. The court is satisfied with a much broader, less focused standard of control. In *Howard* a passenger in the rear seat of a car was held liable for the negligent driving of a friend. The two teenagers had borrowed a car from the passenger's father and were aimlessly driving around the Kansas countryside. Although the doctrine was used to impose direct liability on the passenger in *Howard*, its most frequent use today is as a defendant's doctrine, imputing contributory or comparative negligence and blocking or limiting a cause of action by an injured co-enterpriser against a stranger whose negligence contributed to the loss.

The passive joint enterpriser who pays a judgment is entitled to indemnity from the active wrongdoer. If there were more than two joint enterprisers, the passive party would be entitled to contribution from his fellow joint enterprisers. (Although the words are not always used consistently, indemnity involves shifting the entire loss from one tortfeasor who has been required to pay it to another who should bear it. Contribution involves distributing a loss among tortfeasors by requiring each to pay a proportionate share to the one who has discharged their joint liability.) Also, an injured joint enterpriser can recover from the negligent co-enterpriser on the theory that the actual wrongdoer always is personally liable to the persons he injures. Despite this, the exposure of an innocent person to liability is substantial under this doctrine.

The joint enterprise doctrine strikes many people as unfair because it imposes vicarious liability on a person who does not have control over the physical conduct of the tortfeasor and thus realistically is not in a position to minimize the risk of loss. For this reason, as noted above, there is a trend away from the doctrine today, confining liability to commercial ventures. See *Holliday v. Bannister* (Wyo.1987), refusing to apply the doctrine to a hunting accident in which one hunter in a joint outing negligently shot and killed an outsider. The court stated, "[B]y limiting the doctrine of joint enterprise to those having a business or pecuniary purpose, it avoid[s] the imposition of a basically commercial concept, derived from the law of partnership and principles of agency, to non-commercial situations which are more often matters of friendly or family cooperation and accommodation."

With regard to commercial ventures, which usually are called joint ventures, it is nearly everywhere agreed that the law of partnership (see Part IV) applies to such relationships. Both control and sharing of profits are required for liability under the law of joint venture. For example, in *Connor v. Great Western Sav. and Loan Ass'n.* (Cal.1968), the court held that Great Western was not involved in a joint venture with a real estate developer of a large tract development despite the exercise by Great Western of considerable control over the project. The court stated: "Although the profits of each were dependent on the overall success of the development, neither was to share in the profits or losses that the other might realize or suffer. Although each received substantial payments ... , neither had an interest in the payments received by the other."

§ 32. The Unincorporated Association Relationship

Unincorporated associations are formed, typically, for some sort of nonprofit activity like clubs, fraternal societies, organizers of a soccer tournament or a race for charity, and so forth. A key concern is the liability of members of an association for the acts of other members or employees of the association. Unincorporated associations are not recognized as legal entities under the common law, which triggers the law of individual agency with respect to this issue. A number of states have passed statutes making associations capable of suing and being sued, however.

The usual rule is that membership alone does not render one vicariously liable for torts committed by fellow members, officers, or employees of an association. The individual member must have participated in the wrongful act or have authorized or ratified it in order to incur personal liability. The same rule applies to contractual liability. If a member authorizes or ratifies an act of another, however, the relationship is conceptualized as one of agency and liability follows. The member is viewed as a principal and the actor his agent.

Membership in an unincorporated association can be a trap, especially if the concepts of prior authorization or subsequent ratification are broadly applied to attendance and voting affirmatively on vaguely worded resolutions at meetings. Because of this uncertainty, a uniform act, called the Uniform Unincorporated Nonprofit Association Act, was promulgated in 1992. It has been adopted in eleven jurisdictions to date. The Act creates a limited liability entity upon formation of an association even without filing any document (an extraordinary step in American law), absolving a member of any liability for the acts of others in the association unless the member is personally guilty of wrongdoing.

§ 33. The Co-Principal Doctrine

The co-principal doctrine has been used to immunize a member of an unincorporated association, or the association itself, from vicarious liability for an injury caused to one member by another member or an employee of the association. This defense to vicarious liability is based on characterizing the wrongdoer as an agent of the plaintiff as well as the defendant. For example, assume that Pam, a member of a speedboat-racing club, is injured by the negligent driving of Ted, another member of the club, on the way to a race sponsored by the club. Pam sues the club for the loss caused by Ted in a state where a statute allows suit against an association. The co-principal doctrine will provide a defense to the club, as it would to any member (other than Ted) whom Pam sues. (The uniform act mentioned in § 32 also would provide a defense to a member of the club in the eleven jurisdictions that have adopted it.)

The reasoning underlying the co-principal doctrine is that each member acting with consent is an agent of every other member and employees are agents of all members. Thus the wrongdoer is an agent of the plaintiff as well as the other members. Since one cannot base a cause of action on a wrong attributable to her, the association has a defense to a claim of vicarious liability, as does any member of the club who is joined in the suit on agency grounds. With respect to the liability of the association itself, however, case authority exists that rejects application of the co-principal doctrine under circumstances where it cannot realistically be said that the injured member has any authority over the day-to-day operation of the association, such as a labor union or a condominium association.

It should be emphasized that the wrongdoer (Ted) is personally liable to Pam, the injured party, in all states. No doctrine of vicarious liability provides immunity for the negligent actor, nor does a statutory grant of limited liability (such as the uniform act noted in § 32) provide immunity for personal wrongdoing. With the exception of worker's compensation statutes in some states that provide immunity for a negligent worker who causes harm to another worker, it is everywhere acknowledged that personal liability results from personal wrongdoing.

§ 34. Procedural Consequences of Vicarious Liability

The liability of the employer and the employee is joint and several, with the employee directly liable for personal tortious conduct and the employer vicariously liable. This triggers the customary rules with regard to the procedural consequences of joint and several liability, including the rule that plaintiff can choose whom to sue (since each joint tortfeasor is liable for the whole), or can sue both. Also, in most jurisdictions a release of one joint tortfeasor releases all joint tortfeasors, unlike a covenant not to sue. A prior judgment against either a principal or an agent is not binding on the other, who has not had his day in court, unless the first action was controlled by the defendant in the second action. The damages awarded in a subsequent judgment against a principal can be no greater than those previously obtained against the agent in order not to compromise the principal's right of indemnity against the agent. Finally, a prior judgment in favor of either the principal or the agent is a bar in a subsequent action against the other unless the judgment is the result of a personal defense.

With regard to personal defenses, although wrongful behavior by an employee is a necessary precondition to respondeat superior liability, the derivative nature of this liability does not, in most states, mean that the employer is able to take advantage of an immunity enjoyed by the employee. As an example of this unusual situation, consider *Schubert v. August Schubert Wagon Co.* (N.Y.1928). An employee injured his wife while driving on his employer's business. The employee was not liable because of intra-family tort immunity. The wife sued the employer. The employer argued that the employee's immunity gave it a defense to the wife's suit because respondeat superior liability is derivative in nature. The court rejected the defense, stating "the [employer] is not exonerated when the [employee] has ... escaped liability upon grounds not inconsistent with the commission of a wrong unreleased and unrequited."

It was argued in response that the consequence of upholding an action against the employer may be to cast the burden on the husband anyway, despite his immunity, because of the employer's right of indemnity. The court rejected this argument on the reasoning that indemnity does not rest upon a theory of subrogation to the claim of the victim but instead rests upon breach of an independent duty owed to the employer. If, however, there is collision between the principles of immunity and of indemnity, the court stated that intrafamily immunity would give way, as an anomalous exception to the responsibility to act with due care.

CHAPTER 5

CONTRACTUAL POWERS
OF AGENTS

---

§ 35. The Authority of an Agent

The word "authority," standing alone, is ambiguous. It covers several distinct situations, ranging from the agent acting pursuant to the clearly articulated consent of the principal to the agent who acts without consent, knows it, and is able to commit the principal anyway. The usual breakdown of authority is into categories of actual (also known as genuine or privileged) authority, which in turn breaks down into express and implied authority, and apparent authority. These materials will follow this approach. The doctrines of estoppel and inherent agency power also are relevant to the subject matter of this chapter and will be discussed below.

The words and phrases "apparent authority," "implied authority," and "inherent agency power" are not always used consistently by courts. It sometimes will be necessary to ascertain the meaning of the words used from their context.

§ 36. Express Authority

Express authority is created when a principal manifests consent to its agent to act on its behalf in a particular matter. The term express authority "often means actual authority that the principal has stated in very specific or detailed language." R3d § 2.01, comment b (T.D. No. 2, 2001). A manifestation is an expression of will, as distinguished from undisclosed purpose or intention.

A bilateral contract is created by a manifestation of mutual assent. If an agent is expressly authorized, a contract is made when the third party and the agent exchange manifestations of assent. A court does not ask whether or not the expectations of the third party are reasonable, an issue which is central to the doctrine of apparent authority. Instead, if there has been an exchange of consent and the transaction is lawful, the legal relationship of contract between the principal and the third party exists as of that moment.

The existence of the principal's consent to the agent's actions is an issue of fact. Consent can be expressed in many forms, from an express verbal instruction to a nod of the head to an elaborate written set of instructions to a failure to object to actions that repeat previously authorized actions. A frequently used vehicle for the manifestation of the principal's consent is the power of attorney, to which we now turn.

A. The Power of Attorney

A power of attorney is a written instrument by which a principal appoints another as agent and sets forth the authority conferred upon the agent. Its primary purpose is to evidence the authority to third persons. If the act the agent seeks to perform falls within the language of the power, the agent is expressly authorized.

In general, courts tend to construe powers of attorney cautiously and narrowly, perhaps because a power of attorney grants authority to the power holder over the property and assets of another. Courts are especially reluctant to recognize the validity of gifts of the principal's property or attempts by the agent to borrow money or to issue guarantees in the name of the principal in the absence of express language authorizing such acts or proof of clear intent to authorize as evidenced by the surrounding facts and circumstances. Courts tend to disregard broad, all-encompassing expressions in powers of attorney, such as "[agent] is authorized to do any and all acts that I could do if personally present."

(i) Statutory short form power of attorney. A number of states have created an optional statutory short form power of attorney based on the Uniform Statutory Form Power of Attorney Act. The statutory form contains thirteen specific subdivisions describing particular kinds of transactions (e.g., real property transactions, stock and bond transactions, claims and litigation, banking transactions, and so forth) that can be activated by initialing the form in the proper place. The act describes in some detail for each subdivision the powers that have been granted through the act of initialing the subdivision, thus identifying the circumstances under which a power containing such terms would be effective as a matter of statutory law. The goal seems to be to offer a standard form of power of attorney that is convenient and reliable. It is useful to note that some institutions, such as brokerage houses and banks, insist on use of their own forms in nearly all circumstances.

(ii) Durable power of attorney. The durable power of attorney functions primarily to deal with incompetency and can be written to cover financial matters, hospitalization, and health care under circumstances where recovery of the maker of the power (the principal) is unlikely. The common law rule is that a power of attorney terminates automatically when the principal becomes incapacitated, on the theory that the consent of the principal can no longer be presumed (see § 59). Legislation exists in nearly all states creating an exception to this rule by allowing decisions to be made and bills to be paid under a durable power of attorney following incapacity of the principal and prior to death. Legislation allowing the durable power was promulgated on the theory that this is what most people would want under such circumstances and that their prior consent should be honored. Customarily there are two separate durable powers, one for financial matters and one for health care and medical decisions.

(iii) Springing power of attorney. The springing power of attorney is one that does not activate the agency powers until a certain event has happened, which almost always is the incapacity of the maker. This device allows the maker to stay in sole control of her own affairs while she is competent. The ability to postpone the activation of the power is regarded as particularly desirable when the power is a general one granting the agent broad financial discretion.

B. The Equal Dignity Rule

In general, the common law rule is that when a statute requires that a contract be in writing the authority of an agent to contract on behalf of the principal need not be authorized in writing. In some states, however, statutes requiring that contracts for particular transactions be in writing also mandate that the authority of the agent must be in writing. This rule is sometimes referred to as the "equal dignity" rule. It appears to reflect the same concerns about fraud and verifiability that underlie the statutes of frauds.

The written nature of a power of attorney is useful not only for its permanence and reliability but also because, properly drafted, it can satisfy the equal dignity rule. In some states the writing that is required for a particular transaction must also be notarized, which means the power of attorney also would have to be notarized in order to satisfy the rule.

§ **37.** Implied Authority

Express authority rarely covers every action an agent is supposed to take, either because a principal assumes that the granting of authority to take certain steps beyond those expressed in the instructions is obvious or because the principal did not think of all the acts that would be necessary to accomplish the transaction. See R2d § 7, comment c:

> [M]ost authority is created by implication. Thus, in the authorization to "sell my automobile," . . . there may be power to take or give possession of the automobile or to extend credit or to accept something in partial exchange. These powers are all implied or inferred from the words used, from customs and from the relations of the parties. They are described as "implied authority."

A. Conceptual Basis of Implied Authority

The Restatement (Third) conceptualizes implied authority as falling within the definition of actual authority (R3d § 2.01 (T.D. No. 2, 2001)) and provides these definitions of implied authority:

> The term "implied authority" has more than one meaning. "Implied authority" is often used to mean actual authority either (1) to do what is necessary, usual, and proper to accomplish or perform the agent's express responsibilities or (2) to act in manner in which the agent believes the principal wishes the agent to act based on the agent's reasonable interpretation of the principal's manifestation in light of the principal's ob-

jectives and other facts known to the agent. These meanings are not mutually exclusive. Both fall within the definition of actual authority.

B. Incidental Authority

Incidental authority is included within the agent's actual authority. The Restatement (Third) describes the basis for incidental authority:

> If a principal's manifestation to the agent expresses the principal's wish that something be done, it is natural to assume that the principal wishes, as an incidental matter, that the agent proceed in the usual and ordinary way, if such has been established, unless the principal directs otherwise. R3d § 2.02, comment d (T.D. No. 2, 2001).

The drafters then provide this simple example:

> 1. P employs A, an auctioneer, to sell goods owned by P. A has authority to accept bids on P's behalf. This result is consistent with the interest being protected by the concept of implied authority, which is the agent's reasonable expectation about what he is authorized to do. Of course, when the agent is in doubt about his authority, he should contact the principal and obtain express consent to do the contemplated act, unless an emergency or the unavailability of the principal makes that impossible.

C. Delegation of Authority

One situation that arises with some frequency is the delegation of authority by an agent. Ordinarily an agent is not authorized to delegate his authority, if the matter involves discretion or judgment, in the absence of express consent or an emergency. This limitation is reflected in the Latin phrase *delegatus non potest delegare* (a delegate cannot delegate). The underlying policy is that one cannot presume consent of the principal to have his business carried on by a stranger rather than the person he chose and trusted. Nevertheless, in certain situations it is natural to presume implied consent to delegation of authority, as developed below.

The issue of delegation of authority can generate substantial relational complexities. Courts and secondary authorities sometimes confuse the terminology set forth below, making it necessary to be alert to context when seeing these terms.

(i) Subagent. Subagency involves authorized delegation by agents, resulting in agents acting for other agents. R3d § 1.04 (T.D. No. 2, 2001). An understanding of the relationships can get tricky in this setting, in part because one person is acting both as agent and as principal. As noted in the Glossary, an agent (A) may be authorized expressly or implicitly to appoint another person (B) to perform all or part of the work she has agreed to do for her principal (P). If A remains responsible to the principal for the work done, the agent she appoints (B) is a subagent and A is both an agent (to P) and a principal (to B). It seems convenient to refer to A as the immediate principal of B and P as the remote principal. As far as the relations between the principal and third persons are concerned, a subagent has the same power as an agent.

B is an agent of P as well as A, which means that the actions of B within the scope of the agency can bind P as the remote principal and expose P to liability for wrongdoing. This underscores the importance of consent by P to the subagency relationship. The customs and usages of particular industries can play an important role in determining consent, especially implied consent.

If P is held liable for B's wrongdoing, P has a right of indemnity both against B (as the primary wrongdoer) and A (as the immediate principal of B). A (vicariously liable) in turn would have a right of indemnity against B (primary wrongdoer), which also is true if A instead of P is held directly liable for B's wrongdoing. If, on the other hand, B incurs a reasonable and ordinary expense or suffers a loss flowing from authorized conduct, the right of indemnity flows in the opposite direction (see § 8).

An example of subagency is when a person (P) engages a large law firm (A) to represent her in a complex commercial transaction and the law firm uses its regular employees (B) to carry out some of the tasks of the agency. Subagency is necessarily involved whenever a corporation is an agent because a corporation can only act through others. This result also applies to other business entities.

(ii) Agent's agent. If P did not authorize A to appoint another to perform work for P, and A engages B to do some of the work A had agreed to do, B is an "agent's agent," which means that B does not have the power to bind P. A, as principal, is solely responsible for B's misconduct. The phrase "agent's agent" is ambiguous because a subagent also is an agent's agent. This imprecision makes it necessary to ascertain its meaning from the context in which it is used. Once a situation is analyzed, however, it serves the useful purpose of sharply delineating the relationship of the parties in just a few words, as noted in the Glossary.

(iii) Co-agent. If A's authority is simply to engage an agent for P, B is a co-agent of A and an agent of P, not a subagent. Under that circumstance, A is not a principal and incurs no liability for B's actions. Instead, both A and B are agents of P. An example of this is the hiring officer for a corporation whose job involves placing ads, interviewing people, and making hiring decisions. The people hired are co-agents of A, the hiring officer, not subagents. If instead A is a manager or other officer who hires B as her assistant, and thereafter issues orders to B, this still does not make B her agent, although this relationship looks confusingly like subagency. Instead, both A and B are employed by and acting on behalf of P and are working in a hierarchical relationship. The restatement (Third) refers to the relationship of A and B and "superior and subordinate co-agents." R3d § 1.04, comment j. (T.D. No. 2, 2001).

§ 38. Apparent Authority

An agent has the capacity to bind his principal under two circumstances: when he has the *right* to commit the principal, and when he has the *power* to do so. An agent has the right to bind the principal when he acts with the actual authority (express or implied) of the principal (see §§ 35–37). An agent has the power to bind the principal when circumstances of apparent authority, estoppel, or inherent agency power enable him to bind the principal to a transaction without the consent of the principal. Under these circumstances the agent is acting in an unprivileged manner and incurs liability to the principal for whatever damages may be occasioned by this departure from instructions. Apparent authority is discussed in this section. Estoppel and inherent agency power are covered in §§ 39 and 40.

Apparent authority addresses the situation in which a person acting professedly as agent for another is unauthorized to so act but the third party reasonably believes the actor is authorized and contracts accordingly. The law protects these expectations if the purported principal is responsible for them. Apparent authority thus is a subset of the objective theory of contracts. The objective theory validates the reasonable expectations of parties to a contract, rejecting the notion that there must be a subjective meeting of the minds (of the principal and the third party in this context) before a contract is made.

Both actual and apparent authority depend on manifestations of the principal. The difference is that the manifestations are to the agent in actual authority situations and are to the third party in apparent authority. R3d § 2.03, comment c (T.D.

No. 2, 2001) expresses this idea clearly: "Apparent authority holds a principal accountable for the results of third-party beliefs about an actor's authority to act as an agent when the belief is reasonable and is traceable to a manifestation of the principal."

For examples of manifestations in this context, consider the following language from R3d § 2.03, comment c:

> Manifestations. . . may take many forms. These include explicit statements that the principal makes directly to the third party, as well as statements made by others concerning the actor's authority that reach the third party and are traceable to the principal. For example, the principal makes a manifestation about an agent's authority by directing that the agent's name and affiliation with the principal be included in a listing of representatives that is provided to the third party. The principal may make a manifestation directing an agent to make statements to third parties or by directing or designating an agent to perform acts or conduct negotiations, by placing an agent in a position within an organization, or by placing the agent in charge of a transaction or situation. See § 3.03, Comments *b*, *c*, *d*, and *e*.

The comment goes on to state that an agent "may have actual authority to make statements concerning the agent's own authority." It is important in this regard to emphasize the word "authority" in that phrase. An agent cannot create apparent authority by his own statements or there would be no limit to the liability imposed on the principal by this doctrine. Although it seems odd that apparent authority can be created by statements of the agent, the fact that the statements are authorized is deemed sufficient to constitute a manifestation by the principal. Implied authority plays a major role in this context because usually an agent would be reasonable in assuming that he can state his authority to third persons.

The language in R3d § 2.03 states that apparent authority can be created "by placing an agent in a position within an organization." This well-accepted and frequently invoked source of apparent authority is explained more fully in R3d § 3.03 (T.D. No. 2, 2001):

> Apparent authority in an organizational setting may also arise from the fact that a person occupies a type of position that customarily carries specific authority but in which the organization has withheld such authority from that agent.

As one example of apparent authority by "power of position," see *Bucher & Willis v. Smith* (Kan.App. 1982), involving the apparent authority of an attorney to order a survey of the property owned by an estate. After noting that general managers, presidents, and partners are illustrative cases of apparent authority by position, the court stated: "In our view, the mere appointment of Johnson as attorney for the estate clothed him with sufficient apparent authority to obligate the estate for services, such as the survey, which were routinely and directly connected with the administration of the estate."

A principal is responsible for authority that he knowingly or negligently permits the agent to assume. For example, suppose that P writes to A directing A to act as her agent to contract for the sale of a valuable oriental rug, with full power to negotiate and close the deal. P sends a copy of this letter to T, a prospective purchaser. The following day P tells A in a private conversation that she does not want A to strike a final deal until she has approved the price. Two days later A sells the rug to T without first communicating with P. P is dissatisfied with the price and wants to avoid the sale on the ground that A was unauthorized to make the contract. T can ignore this and enforce the bargain because A had apparent authority to bind P to the contract. The "secret instructions" of P did not come to T's attention and thus his expectations, based on the letter he received from P, that he had a contract with P were reasonable. This would be true even if P had terminated A's agency relationship before the contract was made. T's expectations would be the same, created by P's manifestation. This variation underscores the point that nonagents can possess apparent authority.

Assume, alternatively, that P had not sent a copy of the letter to T, but A displayed to T his copy of the letter and concluded a contract on the same terms. Is P bound? Courts would answer yes because P was *responsible for* the manifestation to T on the assumption that reasonable people in her position would understand that agents will display whatever indicia of authority they have in order to enhance the prospects of making a sale.

Assume further that P had not sent a copy of the letter to T and had expressly instructed A not to display his letter of authority and the facts are otherwise the same. Would P be liable? Again, nearly all courts would find liability on the reasoning that P should realize that her conduct is likely to result in a manifestation to T because of the considerable risk that an agent will succumb to the temptation to display indicia of authority in order to enhance his bargaining posture.

This result demonstrates that placing documents of authority in an agent's hands, even with instructions to the agent that limit their display, can be a hazardous business from the principal's perspective. Among other things, one consequence of this liability is that the principal bears the risk of obtaining the return of indicia of authority after terminating an agent's authority. This may make it advisable under some circumstances to consider dating indicia of authority and providing on the face of it a limitation on the period of time it will be effective, subject to renewal or reissue at the principal's choice.

Finally, suppose P anticipated the above difficulties and inserted a paragraph in the letter stating that A was not authorized to sell without confirming the price with P. A convincingly covers over that paragraph and sells the rug without talking to P. Is P bound? This is a troubling issue. Judicial authority on the matter of alteration of documents does not point in a clear direction. On the one hand, it can be argued that to find the principal liable because, by placing indicia in the hands of the agent, the principal is "responsible for" the information that comes to T, runs the risk of making the liability of a principal for altered documents limitless. The agent could forge the document to say almost anything and to grant himself very substantial apparent authority. On the other hand, it can be argued that the principal did invite people to rely upon indicia of authority she placed in her agent's hands, and good faith reliance should be protected. The responsibility should lie with the principal to choose her agents carefully and to bond her agents if the exposure to liability can be substantial.

Apparent authority can be "stacked" within an organization in the sense that it is possible, depending on the circumstances, for one agent to provide apparent authority to another agent within the same organization. For example, the Secretary to a board of directors of a corporation customarily prepares and certifies the minutes of the board. If a Secretary falsely prepares and certifies a board resolution that purports to grant authority to B, another officer of the corporation, to borrow money in the name of the corporation, B will have apparent authority to borrow upon display of the resolution based on the Secretary's apparent authority by power of position to certify the minutes of the board.

Duty of inquiry. The other person has to act reasonably in addition to having a subjective belief that the agent is authorized. See *Link v. Kroenke* (Mo. App. 1995), stating, "A person dealing with a supposed agent ... must display that degree of common sense which distinguishes good faith from blind faith." Thus, knowledge that an agent has a power of attorney can make a difference in a third person's case. See *Bayless v. Christie, Manson & Woods Intern, Inc.* (10th Cir.1993), quoting language to the effect that, "[I]f a person has means of knowledge reasonably open to him as to the limit of the agent's authority, he cannot hold the principal unless he uses ordinary diligence to ascertain them.... He has means of knowledge if he knows or has reason to know that the authority is evidenced by a document open to and intended for his inspection."

With regard to the duty of inquiry under corporate law when an argument is based on power of position, the case of *Jennings v. Pittsburgh Mercantile Co.* (Pa. 1964) is instructive. *Jennings* involved the apparent authority of Elmore, the vice-president and treasurer-comptroller of a corporation, to accept the offer of a sale and leaseback of all the real property of the corporation for a period of 30 years. The court saw the issue as involving "the apparent authority possessed *virtute officii* to consummate an extraordinary transaction." It denied apparent authority, stating that "any other conclusion would improperly extend the usual scope of authority which attaches to the holding of corporate offices, and would greatly undercut the proper role of the board of directors in corporate decision-making."

See also, *Chase v. Consolidated Foods Corp.*, (7th Cir. 1984), stating: "Even . . . the title of 'president' [does not invest the holder] with apparent authority to 'make a contract which is unusual and extraordinary,' that is, beyond the usual authority of a president, as a contract to sell a major corporate division would be."

Suppose Elmore had falsely stated to plaintiff that the board of directors had met, had approved the offer, and had authorized him to inform plaintiff of this. Would that statement bind the corporation to the deal? The *Jennings* case came close to this situation. The court denied apparent authority, stating: "An agent cannot, simply by his own words, invest himself with apparent authority."

Liability of agent. An agent is under a duty to obey the principal's instructions (see § 11), which provides the principal with a cause of action against the disobedient agent. The practical difficulty is that often the agent is not in a fiscal position to compensate the principal for the damages caused by disobedience of instructions.

Government agents. The rules of apparent authority and estoppel (§ 39) do not ordinarily apply to government agents. See R3d § 2.03, comment g (T.D. No. 2, 2001). Court decisions have placed the burden of ascertaining the actual authority of government employees squarely on the third person for the reason that "no agent of the government can hold out to have an authority not sanctioned by the law." *Blake Constr. Co. v. United States* (D.C.Cir. 1961). For an exception to this, see *Giglio v. United*

States (S.Ct.1972), dealing with the unauthorized representations of an assistant United States attorney in a criminal case.

§ 39. Estoppel

Estoppel is fundamentally a principle of torts developed to prevent loss to an innocent person that is caused by relying upon a representation or promise of the estopped person. It is distinguished from apparent authority because a person can be estopped from denying liability based on inaction, whereas apparent authority requires a manifestation by the principal. Also, apparent authority is based on the objective theory of contracts, making the principal a party to the contract the third person makes with the apparently authorized agent. In contrast, estoppel "protects third parties who reasonably believe an actor to be authorized as an agent when the belief cannot be shown to follow directly or indirectly from the principal's own manifestations." R3d § 2.05, comment d (T.D. No. 2, 2001).

The distinction between apparent authority and estoppel is clearly drawn in *Hoddeson v. Koos Bros.* (N.J.1957). An imposter posing as a salesman in a furniture store took cash from a customer, promising later delivery of the furniture, and absconded with the money. The disappointed customer sued the store on apparent authority grounds and lost. The court held that no manifestation was made by the store that the person purporting to be a salesman was authorized to act for the store. That court stated that for an apparent authority case to succeed the plaintiff must prove that the manifestation that a particular person was authorized to act on behalf of the principal came from the principal. "Assuredly the law cannot permit apparent authority to be established by the mere proof that a mountebank in fact exercised it."

The court remanded for a new trial on the ground of estoppel, however, noting that plaintiff should be allowed to prove that the event would not have happened had the store exercised reasonable surveillance over its place of business. As stated in R2d § 8 B, "A person who is not otherwise liable to a party to a transaction purported to be done on his account, is nevertheless subject to liability to persons who have changed their positions because of their belief that the transaction was entered into by or for him, if (a) he intentionally or carelessly caused such belief, or (b) knowing of such belief and that others might change their positions because of it, he did not take reasonable steps to notify them of the facts."

Although this language imposes an affirmative duty to act, which seems inconsistent with the no duty to rescue rule of torts, the law has long required an owner of property to act affirmatively and assert his interest in it when another is purporting to sell it as owner. Perhaps an explanation for the affirmative duty to act in *Hoddeson* is that one's name and reputation are like property and thus a principal should take affirmative steps when someone is purporting to act in his name. (There is a distinction, however, between losing a piece of property and being subject to the open-ended liability created by holding one to the acts of an imposter.)

§ 40. Inherent Agency Power

This controversial doctrine extends the liability of a principal beyond apparent authority and estoppel. It was created in the second Restatement of Agency and rests upon a vague kind of enterprise liability, by analogy to the law of respondeat superior. The term has been expressly abandoned in the Restatement (Third). Comment b to § 2.01 (T.D. No. 2, 2001) provides:

> The term 'inherent agency power,' used in the Restatement Second of Agency and defined therein by § 8 A, is not used in this Restatement. Inherent agency power is defined as 'a term used. . .to indicate the power of an agent which is derived not from authority, apparent authority or estoppel, but solely from the agency relation and exists for the protection of persons named by or dealing with a servant or agent.' Other doctrines stated in this Restatement encompass the justifications underpinning § 8 A, including the importance of interpretation by the agent in the agent's relationship with the principal, as well as the doctrines of apparent authority, estoppel, and restitution.

However, because the term inherent agency power does appear in some cases and in the literature on agency law, a few words on the concept are in order. As an initial matter, the concept applies only in the context of actions by a general agent. Although not defining the term, the Restatement (Third) has this to say about general agents: "The prototypical general agent is a manager of a business, who has authority to conduct a series of transactions and who serves the principal on an ongoing as opposed to an episodic basis." R3d § 2.01, comment d (T.D. No. 2, 2001). The comment goes on to describe the principal's relationship with a special agent: "The transaction-by-transaction nature of the principal's relationship with a special agent limits the principal's potential benefit from associating with the agent but also limits the principal's risk." Id.

The inherent agency power ramifications of general agency are set forth in R2d § 161, which states that a general agent can bind his principal to contracts where there is neither authority nor apparent authority so long as the acts done "usually accompany or are incidental to" transactions that the agent is authorized to conduct. At first glance this limitation is puzzling because there seems to be almost a complete overlap of inherent agency power with apparent authority, in particular the "power of position" type of apparent authority (see § 38), which ordinarily would accompany general agency. That is, acts that "usually accompany" or "are incidental to" authorized acts of an agent in a certain position would almost certainly fall within the ambit of conventional apparent authority. One of the difficulties in understanding the inherent agency power doctrine is that almost all of its well-known cases can be classified as apparent authority cases.

The Second Restatement attempts to avoid this difficulty with the following illustration to § 161: A general manager of a foundry violates instructions to purchase an alloy from a certain firm and instead purchases the alloy from T, a different firm, writing to T on personal stationery and signing the letter only "A, agent of P." The Restatement concludes that "P is bound upon this transaction." An alternative apparent authority analysis is avoided in this illustration by having A write on personal stationery, thus destroying a power of position argument.

It is difficult to muster much enthusiasm for this illustration. T's expectancy interest seems weak, A's conduct bizarre, and the interest of the law in enforcing this unauthorized transaction obscure. The explanation in R2d § 161, comment a, is that the principal's liability exists solely because of his relation to the agent. It is based primarily upon the theory that, if one appoints an agent to conduct a series of transactions over a period of time, it is fair that he should bear losses which are incurred when such an agent, although without authority to do so, does something which is usually done in connection with the transactions he is employed to conduct. Such agents can properly be regarded as part of the employer's organization in much the same way as an employee is normally part of the employer's business enterprise.

The case that involves the inherent agency doctrine in its purest form is an undisclosed principal case from England, *Watteau v. Fenwick*, discussed below in § 44. In that case a manager of a beer house ran it in his own name. The owner wanted to remain undisclosed. Against instructions, the manager purchased cigars and other items from plaintiff. The court held the owner liable to plaintiff, noting that the purchases were incidental to the manager's authorized transactions. An apparent authority argument, which requires a manifestation from the principal to the third party, is impossible in this case because the principal is undisclosed. A plausible estoppel argument could be made in this situation due to the misleading appearance of apparent ownership of the assets of a business. But the inherent agency power doctrine applies well beyond that. *Watteau* has been subject to criticism, but has been embraced by the Restatement (Third). (See § 44).

Some recent cases and, of course, the Restatement (Third) of Agency, have expressed doubts about the inherent agency power doctrine, perhaps because it is unclear what interest of the third person is being protected and perhaps also because it introduces uncertainty into an area of law that already has gone far in protecting the third person's interests. Apparent authority protects the third person's expectancy interest and estoppel protects a change of position in reliance on a misimpression that can be traced to a lack of care and attention by the principal. One can conclude that the liability of a principal should go no further when dealing with a claim based on contract.

CHAPTER 6

THE UNDISCLOSED PRINCIPAL

§ 41. Definition of Undisclosed Principal

A principal is undisclosed when the other party to a contract (T) has no idea that the party she is contracting with (A) is in reality an agent. As far as T is concerned, she thinks she is making a contract solely with A. The legal consequences of this hidden arrangement are described below.

§ 42. The Rights of an Undisclosed Principal

The law of agency declares that the principal (P) is a party to the contract between T and A, if A intended to be acting on behalf of P when making the contract and the contract is within A's power to bind P. Once P reveals his identity and interest in the contract, T is not thereafter free, for example, to pay A (or otherwise perform) without running the risk of having to pay again to P. The parol evidence rule does not prevent assertion of undisclosed principal rights even when the contract is an integrated, written agreement, perhaps on the functional reasoning that T's rights against A remain fully intact and thus the evidence is not contradicting the obligations involved; instead, it is adding a party.

The undisclosed principal doctrine is unusual because the principal is a party to the contract without a manifestation of mutual assent between T and P. This formally contravenes the basic principle of contract law that a contract results from such manifestation. The law allowing assignment of rights under contracts makes a substantial inroad into the notion that a contractual relationship is inherently personal, however. Also, the status of the agent as a party to the contract does not change when the undisclosed principal discloses his interest and asserts his rights under the contract. In that sense T's expectation rights remain protected.

The undisclosed principal doctrine also is unusual because it appears to endorse prearranged misleading behavior. The doctrine exists in all states, however, perhaps in part because it serves a useful role by, for example, addressing the problem of the holdout in a private land assemblage. The problem of the holdout would exist if the identity of the buyer had to be disclosed. Under such circumstances the last few owners in an area targeted for assemblage would hold out for a price vastly in excess of the market value of the land independent of the assemblage. Disneyworld, Rockefeller Center, and large portions of Grand Teton National Park (subsequently given to the federal government) are all illustrations of private land assemblages that took advantage of the undisclosed principal doctrine.

§ 43. Limitations on the Rights of the Undisclosed Principal

The limitations described in this section are designed to ensure that the expectations of parties contracting with the agent are not materially disadvantaged by the assertion of the rights of the undisclosed principal. As one illustration of this, the undisclosed principal cannot claim status as a party to the contract if the terms of the contract exclude other parties. For example, in *Arnold's of Mississippi v. Clancy* (Miss. 1965), the court held that a clause in a lease prohibiting subletting without the landlord's consent excluded an undisclosed principal, stating, "Lessor has a right to elect the person with whom he will deal. There are elements of confidence other than credit involved in leasing property." A clause in a contract prohibiting assignment may operate as evidence of intent to exclude an undisclosed principal, but does not in itself prevent suit by an undisclosed principal on the contract.

Another example of the principle that the expectations of the other party are not to be materially disadvantaged is that P cannot tender his own performance if T has a substantial interest in receiving the performance of A. Also, P must disclose his existence prior to a disadvantageous change of position by T.

In addition, T is not bound if P's existence was fraudulently concealed and if T would not have dealt with P as a party to the contract. This limitation applies even if no express misrepresentation was made if P knew that T would not deal with him and A, whether knowing or innocent, failed to disclose P's interest. This defense does not arise, however, if P merely suspected that T will not deal with him (if P and T are competitors, for example).

In most jurisdictions a misrepresentation by A of her status as an agent will not in itself avoid the underlying transaction on the reasoning that the misrepresentation is not material if it affects only the price of the property. Thus T's complaint that she was disadvantaged because she would have charged a lot more money if she had been aware of P's existence is not alone regarded as sufficient to avoid the contract.

§ 44. Liabilities of the Undisclosed Principal

A. Authorized Transactions

The undisclosed principal is liable on the contract despite the fact that T was satisfied solely with the credit of A. The policy underlying P's liability is that P "is the one who initiated the activities of the agent and has a right to control them. [Thus, P is liable] in accordance with the ordinary principles of agency." R2d § 186, comment a. As stated in W. Seavey, Law of Agency 7 (1964), "It is not unfair to the principal to make him liable on an authorized contract since it was his business which was being done, and there is no reason why the ordinary rules that the principal is responsible for authorized acts should not be followed." The rationale provided by the Restatement (Third) is somewhat less persuasive:

> If an agent acts with actual authority in making a contract on an undisclosed principal's behalf, the basis for treating the principal as a party to the contract is that the agent acted reasonably on the basis of the principal's manifestation of assent to the contract.

R3d § 6.03, comment b (T.D. No. 4, 2003). This is more descriptive of the situation than analytical.

The election rule. As noted above, P is liable on the contract. A also is liable, of course, because A is the party with whom T contracted. In some states T, if she discovers the existence of P prior to obtaining judgment from A, has to elect from whom she will recover. This is known as the election rule. It does not apply if T obtains judgment against A prior to discovering the existence of P. It apparently rests on the reasoning that if T was satisfied with only one credit at the time of contracting, she should be satisfied with only one credit now.

The election rule has been under successful attack recently in a number of states on the theory that T should have a right to two judgments (but only one satisfaction), one on the contract and the other based on the agency principle underlying the liability of P. The right against the principal thus is

viewed as additional, not alternative, in those jurisdictions that have recently overturned the election
rule. See *Grinder v. Bryans Road Building & Supply Co.* (Md. 1981), quoting the following language:
"They [the cases supporting the election rule] are
unjust, since as a result the principal who ordinarily
profits from the transaction and who has not met
his obligations is relieved by the mistake of the
other party in believing that the agent has sufficient assets to pay the debt, since in all cases where
the matter is of importance, the agent is insolvent."

In § 6.09 (T.D. 4, 2003), the Restatement (Third)
rejects the election rule, stating that:

(1) the liability of the principal or the agent is
not discharged if the third party obtains a judgment against the other;

(2) the liability of the principal or the agent is
discharged to the extent a judgment against the
other is satisfied .

B. Unauthorized Transactions

Case authority is divided with regard to the liability of an undisclosed principal when the agent is
unauthorized to do what she did. To some authorities liability for unauthorized transactions is inap-
propriate because T is not even aware that an
agency relationship exists and thus has no expectation that anyone is standing behind A nor, absent
special facts, does any estoppel claim exist. T can
assert contract rights against A, which is all T
bargained for.

The Restatement (Second) takes the contrary view, favoring liability for certain unauthorized transactions by invoking the inherent agency power doctrine (see § 40). If A is an unauthorized general agent doing something she usually does, liability for the undisclosed principal follows, in the Restatement view. The primary case authority for this view is *Watteau v. Fenwick* [Q.B.1893]. In that case Humble, the owner of a tavern, sold it to Fenwick. Fenwick retained Humble as manager of the tavern and left Humble's name over the door. The license for the tavern was taken out in Humble's name. Humble agreed to purchase his supplies from Fenwick but departed from these instructions and bought cigars and other tavern accessories on credit from plaintiff, who sued Fenwick for payment upon discovering his interest. The court held Fenwick liable, stating that an undisclosed principal is liable for all acts of the agent that are within the authority usually confided to an agent of that character and noting without explanation that "very mischievous consequences would often result if that principle were not upheld."

The result in *Watteau* is appealing but the basis of liability is troubling because it seems too broad. The arrangement established by Fenwick sent a misleading signal to persons who dealt with Humble, a signal of apparent ownership of the tavern and all of its assets. Fenwick should be responsible for that and thus should be estopped from denying Humble's ownership under these circumstances, allowing Watteau to execute against the tavern and its assets after obtaining a judgment against Humble. But to base liability on an inherent agency power that would hold an undisclosed principal liable for all transactions that usually accompany an agency of that character, whether or not there is a misleading appearance of ownership, seems to go too far when the other party has no idea an agency of any character is involved in the transaction.

The Restatement (Third) of Agency § 2.06 (T.D. No. 2, 2001) adopts *Watteau v. Fenwick* in these terms:

> An undisclosed principal may not rely on instructions given an agent that qualify or reduce the agent's authority to less than the authority a third party would reasonably believe the agent to have under the same circumstances if the principal had been disclosed.

Comment c following this black-letter rule explains that the focus of the rule is on the reasonable expectations of the third party. Not knowing that it is dealing with an agent, the third party has no reason to inquire into the extent of the agent's authority. To allow the principal to escape liability under these circumstances "might otherwise permit the principal opportunistically to speculate at the expense of third parties."

§ 45. Payment and Setoff Issues

A. Payment by the Other Party

The other party's act of paying A prior to learning about P is binding against P in recognition of the policy of limiting the doctrine of undisclosed principal so that it does not disadvantage T's expectation interest.

B. Payment to the Other Party

Courts split on an undisclosed principal's liability when the agent fails to make payment to the other party after receiving payment from the principal. The majority rule is that a principal who settles in good faith with his agent while still undisclosed, expecting that the agent will pay T, is protected from liability to T if A neglects to discharge her duty to pay T. The minority rule is that an undisclosed principal is not discharged by payment to the agent unless he does so in reasonable reliance upon the conduct of T that indicates that A has settled the account.

Policy arguments can be made on both sides of this issue. In favor of the majority rule is the argument that P's good faith payment to A does not harm T, who had no expectation that A was anything other than a sole contracting party and who thus took a credit risk with A. To the extent that T's rights against P can be viewed as subrogation (in effect) to A's indemnification rights against P (see § 8), P's payment to A discharges those rights and so should discharge T's rights as well. In favor of the minority rule, embraced by R2d § 208 and R3d § 6.07 (T.D. No. 4, 2003), is the argument made in the Reporter's Notes to § 208 that, "An agent receiving support from the principal is a different kind of person from an independent trader who by hypothesis the third person believes to be the owner of the business. Further, the principal has ample means to protect himself.... The other party should not lose because the principal has chosen to rely upon his agent's honesty rather than upon his own investigation." The Restatement (Third) also notes that the undisclosed principal is a party to the contract between the agent and the third party, thereby entitled to the performance of the third party, and, in exchange, has a duty of performance to the third party. "That duty is not discharged by rendering performance to someone else, including the agent." R3d § 6.07, comment d.

C. Setoff

Restatement Second and Third differ in their treatment of the ability of a third party, when making payment to the principal, to setoff claims that she has against the agent. Under R2d § 306, if the agent is authorized to conceal the existence of the principal and T does not know or have reason to know of the principal, T can setoff claims she had against the agent at the time of making the contract and until she becomes aware of the existence of the principal. Again, this is consistent with protecting the expectations of T, who may have entered into the contract only because she could setoff a pre-existing claim she had against A. If A is not authorized to conceal P's identity, T's setoff right exists only if A has been entrusted with possession of goods or if P has otherwise misled T into extending credit to A (R2d § 306(2)).

Under R3d § 6.06 (T.D. No. 4, 2003), if the third party had no notice that it was dealing with an agent, its setoff rights are not affected if the agent acted without actual authority in not revealing the principal's existence or identity. The drafters of the Restatement note that "[w]hether an agent acted with actual authority depends on interactions between the principal and agent that the third party is not in a position to observe. Regardless of instructions the principal has given the agent, a principal may be tempted to claim that the agent acted without actual authority in not revealing the principal's identity if by so doing the principal may defeat the third party's right to set off amounts that the agent owes the third party." R3d § 6.06, comment c. For this reason, the drafters reject the rule of the Second Restatement.

CHAPTER 7

LIABILITY OF THE AGENT TO THIRD PERSONS

---

§ 46. Contractual Liability

Under what circumstances does an agent incur contractual liability as a consequence of acting as agent for another? Unless there is a personal guaranty or other commitment by the agent, the answer to this question depends on the status of the principal at the time a contract with another party is made. Whether a principal is disclosed, undisclosed, or unidentified plays a major role in the exposure of an agent to contractual liability to other parties, as explained below.

Disclosed principal. A principal is disclosed when the other party has notice of the principal's existence and identity at the time of a transaction. Under these circumstances the agent acting in the transaction incurs no contractual liability (absent special facts, such as expressly agreeing to be a party or guarantying the contract).

Unidentified principal (sometimes described as partially disclosed principal). A principal is unidentified when the other party has notice that the agent is acting on behalf of someone but does not know the identity of the principal. Under these circumstances it is inferred, subject to contrary agreement, that the agent is a party to the contract on the reasoning that the other party ordinarily would not contract solely on the liability of an unknown party. The Restatement (Second) uses the term "partially disclosed principal," while the Restatement (Third) has opted for the term "unidentified principal."

Undisclosed principal. A principal is undisclosed when the other party is unaware that the agent is acting for a principal. The assumption that the other party is making is that the agent is a person contracting on his or her own behalf. Under that circumstance the agent is a party to the contract, as noted in Chapter 6.

A. The Principle of Direct Representation

In contrast to Roman law and primitive legal systems, the common law of agency has always embraced the principle of direct representation, which allows a person to make contracts through others rather than requiring that contracts be made personally. Under this principle a legal transaction by A acting manifestly on behalf of P and with P's authority binds P without creating liability for A. Thus, if an agent is expressly authorized to make a contract for a principal, does so and the principal is disclosed, the agent is not liable in the absence of special facts.

It is important that the agent make it clear that he is acting in a representative capacity. If the contract is in writing, it would be advisable for the agent to sign the contract as "P, by A, agent" or "A as agent for P" or "P corp. by A, Vice-president." The parol evidence rule can create a problem for the agent who signs an apparently complete and final written agreement in just his own name or in both the principal's and his names without any indication of agency status. At a minimum, the agent who does not make his representative status clear runs a risk of litigation and the expense of introducing extrinsic evidence of the actual understanding of the parties (assuming the language of the writing is ambiguous, allowing the introduction of extrinsic evidence).

B. Liability When the Principal is Disclosed: Special Circumstances

Sometimes even when a principal is disclosed the other party will insist on a guaranty by an agent or an agent will by custom be liable for its client's account, as can happen in the advertising industry under some circumstances. Also, many states hold litigating attorneys liable for services, including the fees of expert witnesses, that the attorney orders for a client unless the attorney expressly and clearly disclaims such liability. This liability exists even if the identity of the client is fully disclosed, on the reasoning that this reflects the expectations of most service providers in the litigation context.

C. Liability When the Principal is Unidentified (Partially Disclosed)

Issues involving the partially disclosed principal generate the most litigation, involving in large part an agent's sometimes unwitting exposure to contractual liability. An unidentified principal exists when the other party has notice that the agent is acting in a representative capacity but has no notice of the principal's identity. R3d § 1.04 (c) (T.D. No. 2, 2001). This can happen deliberately, when an agent refuses to disclose the principal's identity on the principal's request. For example, assume an accountant bids for an expensive fur coat at a prestigious private charity auction, explaining that she is acting on behalf of someone who is "very well-known but does not wish to be identified." (Her principal does not want to run the risk of angering animal rights groups and thus prefers to remain unidentified.) It also can happen accidentally, when the agent thinks he is identifying his principal and fails adequately to do so, as developed below.

Unless otherwise agreed, an agent for a unidentified principal is a party to the contract, based, as noted earlier, on the reasoning that ordinarily one would not expect to contract solely with an unknown party. Thus, the accountant is liable on the contract in the above example.

An agent must disclose the identity of his principal with such complete information that the principal can be readily distinguished from all others. This rule is adopted and applied in the overwhelming majority of jurisdictions. It can catch an agent by surprise, especially an agent contracting on behalf of an organization that operates with a trade name. For example, in *Van D. Costas, Inc. v. Rosenberg* (Fla.App.1983), Rosenberg, the president of Seascape Restaurants, Inc., a corporation that owned a restaurant called "The Magic Moment," contracted for the creation of a "magical entrance" to the restaurant. Rosenberg signed the contract "Jeff Rosenberg, The Magic Moment." Seascape did not pay for the work done.

Rosenberg was sued for breach of contract and was held liable. The court rejected his defense that he was a mere agent, holding that "the use of a trade name is not a sufficient disclosure of the identity of the principal so as to eliminate the liability of the agent." Although this exposes an innocent, naive agent to unexpected liability, the underlying theory apparently is that the agent is usually the one who initiates the transaction and who knows or should know the identity of his principal. Thus, between the agent and the other party, the agent is the cheapest cost avoider. See also, *Benjamin Plumbing, Inc. v. Barnes* (Wis. 1991)(agent held liable on a $10,000 contract for plumbing work because he left off the word "Inc." when signing a contract on behalf of his corporate principal, thus failing to signal plaintiff that his principal was a limited liability entity).

Courts split when the identity of the principal can be located in a public registry. Some courts hold that a public filing satisfies the disclosure of identity while other courts hold that the burden is on the agent, not the other party, to search the records and identify the principal to the other party. The Restatement (Third) § 6.02, comment d (T.D. No.4, 2003) notes that whether the third party has notice is a question of fact and "[i]t is a presumption that notice of facts that form a basis for further sleuthing by a third party, such as searches in public records, do not constitute reasonably sufficient notice of a principal's identity."

The unidentified principal also is a party to the contract, based on the inference that normally the person dealing with an agent desires the liability of the person on whose account the contract is made. As noted above, these liabilities can be altered or extinguished by agreement of the agent and the other party. For example, they may agree that the agent alone is a party or that the principal alone is a party (by, for example, signing the contract "A, as agent only"), or that both the agent and the principal are parties.

There is no election doctrine in the unidentified principal context. The other party has cumulative (up to one satisfaction) and not alternative rights against agent and principal.

D. Liability When the Principal is Unintentionally Undisclosed

As noted above, an agent who seeks to avoid contractual liability has the burden of proving that the other party was aware of the agency relationship and the identity of the principal. The problem of unintentional nondisclosure of agency often arises when a person incorporates her business but fails to notify persons with whom she has been dealing. She thinks she is no longer personally liable for the debts of the business but from the perspective of the persons with whom she is contracting nothing has changed. Although she does not know it, she is an agent for an unidentified principal and thus is fully liable on the contracts.

Sometimes people try to establish notification by showing they paid with corporate checks or billed on corporate invoices. It is a question of fact whether notice was reasonably given through those means.

§ 47. The Agent's Warranty of Authority

An agent who purports to contract on behalf of another makes an implied warranty of authority to the other party. The warranty is that he has the power to bind his principal. The warranty operates against even an innocent agent who in good faith thinks he is authorized but who subsequently discovers that he did not have the power to bind his principal.

This strict liability is based on the reasoning that the agent is the one who by his actions created expectations of the other party by expressly or impliedly representing that he was authorized. See *Collen v. Wright* (Ex. 1857), stating, "[The agent's] moral innocence, so far as the person whom he has induced to contract is concerned, in no way aids such person or alleviates the inconvenience and damage which he sustains." The Restatement (Third) § 6.10, comment b (T.D. No. 4, 2003) adds that the agent "is better able than the third party to ascertain the truth at the time of making the representation." An agent does not, in the absence of express agreement, warrant his principal's honesty or solvency, however.

The warranty does not exist if the other party knows the agent is unauthorized, although he can recover against the agent even if he should have known or had reason to know the agent was unauthorized. For example, in *Husky Industries v. Craig Industries* (Mo. App. 1981), plaintiff Husky sued defendant Craig Industries, a corporation, for specific performance of a promise to sell to Husky one of the two charcoal plants owned by Craig Industries. The unauthorized promise was made by D.C. Craig, the president of Craig Industries. Plaintiff lost its suit against the corporation on the reasoning that D.C. Craig did not have apparent authority (see § 38) to sell half the assets of the corporation without board of director approval. Plaintiff's expectation that D.C. Craig was authorized was unreasonable.

Plaintiff won, however, in its suit against D.C. Craig for breach of his warranty of authority. Plaintiff did not know Craig was not authorized and the fact that its expectation that he was authorized was unreasonable did not defeat its suit. Perhaps the reasoning underlying this outcome is that of the two parties, the agent is more at fault. (If, on the other hand, Craig had been apparently authorized, he would not have breached his warranty of authority because under that circumstance he would have had the power to bind his principal, which is what he purported to have.)

Damages for breach of a warranty of authority are described in R3d § 6.10, comment b, as including "the benefit of the bargain," although recognizing that some courts "limit the third party's recovery to the damage or loss the third party suffered and exclude the third party's expected gain from the contract." If the contract with the principal would not have been beneficial due to insolvency or some defense to the contract, however, "the contract would not be of benefit to the third party had the principal been bound" and there are no damages.

The warranty of authority can be disclaimed by the agent. For example, an agent would be in effect disclaiming any warranty of authority if he said to the other party, "If I am authorized to do this." Also, if the agent fully discloses to the other party the sources of his authority the risk is then put upon the other party, assuming the agent is careful not to warrant impliedly the genuineness of whatever documents he displays.

§ 48. Harm to the Economic Interests of others

The issue of harm to the economic interests of others arises when an agent fails to perform his duties to his principal and a third party is injured. See, for example, *Coker v. Dollar* (11th Cir.1988), in which Coker was instructed by his principal to open an escrow account for the plaintiff third party and place funds in the account. Coker failed to open the account and was sued for the resulting substantial loss to plaintiff. The court found no liability, stating, "The general rule is that an agent is not liable for pecuniary harm to a person other than his principal that results from his failure to perform his duties to his principal." See, also, Restatement (Third) of Agency § 7.02 (T.D. No. 5, 2004).

It may be that under some circumstances the other person could make a plausible claim to be a third party beneficiary of the principal-agent contract and hold the nonperforming agent liable on that ground. This liability is difficult to establish, however, because ordinarily the plaintiff must prove intent to benefit him on the part of both the principal and the agent. That would be highly unlikely in most situations.

On a somewhat related issue, dealing with an agent's liability to the other party for money had and received, in general an agent is required to return funds received (or their equivalent) that were paid by the other party by mistake or as a result of the fraud of the principal. The agent has a defense of good faith transfer to the principal, but not if the principal was undisclosed.

§ 49. Liability of the Agent in Tort

An agent is fully liable for personal tortious behavior. Acting as the agent of another does not somehow confer immunity upon the actor. An exception to this exists by statute under the worker's compensation laws in many states. These statutes absolve from liability a negligent worker who injures a fellow worker, assuming the injured worker is successful in claiming worker's compensation.

It is unclear whether liability of an agent in tort follows from nonfeasance as well as misfeasance. In most jurisdictions the agent is not liable for mere nonfeasance. Recall the language quoted in § 21 to the effect that, "No man increases or diminishes his obligations to strangers by becoming an agent." But see R3d § 7.01, comment a (T.D. No. 5, 2004) which states, without explanation or illustration, that an "agent's tort liability extends to negligent acts *and omissions* as well as intentional conduct." (emphasis added)

CHAPTER 8

THE DOCTRINE OF RATIFICATION

This unusual doctrine, which operates retroactively, is recognized in all jurisdictions. It can serve a useful function by curing defects in an agent's authority. It also can be a trap for the unwary.

§ 50. The Concept of Ratification

In the words of R3d § 4.01, comment b (T.D. No. 2, 2001): "The art of ratification consists of an externally observable assent to be bound by the prior act of another person." For example, Ann, acting wholly without authority, contracts on Tuesday to sell Pam's oriental rug to Tom. Pam hears about this on Friday, likes the price, and says to Ann, "I'm not happy that you did this without even talking to me but I like the price, so I'll go along with it." By that statement the sale immediately becomes binding on Pam and the effective date of the contract is Tuesday.

Ratification applies to situations in which the actor, who may or may not be an agent, did not have the power to bind the principal to the purported contract. It thus is a source of liability independent of actual authority, apparent authority, or estoppel. It sometimes is joined in cases as an alternative ground of liability to one or more of those doctrines, however, if the facts support its use.

One of the consequences of ratification is that it releases the person purporting to bind the principal from warranty of authority liability to the other person. Warranty of authority liability would otherwise apply because by hypothesis the actor did not have the power to bind the purported principal.

Also, under some circumstances the actor might be entitled to claim compensation from the principal following ratification, subject to any conditions imposed by the principal at the time of ratification and agreed to by the actor, who may be willing to agree because he will be relieved of warranty of authority liability. A claim to compensation would rest on the rationale that the affirmance operates retroactively, granting the actor the same rights against the principal as if the act originally had been authorized, including compensation and indemnity (see §§ 7 and 8). Also, if the actor was not an agent when he acted, ratification has the effect of making him a fiduciary of the principal with respect to the transaction.

The actor would not be entitled to compensation if the principal is obliged to ratify in order to avoid losses, such as ratifying by filing a claim in a bankruptcy proceeding of the other party in order to validate a security interest the actor had obtained in the course of making an unauthorized loan to the bankrupt. Also, the actor would not be entitled to compensation if the principal was induced to affirm by the fraud or duress of the actor.

§ 51. The Act Constituting Ratification

The ways in which a person may ratify the act of another are described in R3d § 4.01 (T.D. No. 2, 2001):

(2) A person ratifies an act by

(a) manifesting assent that the act shall affect the person's legal relations, or

(b) conduct that is justifiable only on the assumption that the person so consents.

Thus defendant's statement "I will pay you" in response to plaintiff's request for payment following work done by plaintiff at the request of an unauthorized independent contractor who purported to represent the defendant is an effective ratification. *Evans v. Ruth* (Pa.Super.1937).

Also, in *Dempsey v. Chambers* (Mass.1891), an unauthorized person delivered some of defendant's coal to plaintiff, accidentally breaking a large window at plaintiff's building while depositing the coal. Defendant was informed about the broken window. He thereafter sent plaintiff a bill for the coal. Plaintiff sued defendant for the damage to the window. The court held that the act of billing with knowledge of the tort constituted a ratification of the negligent act.

The manifestation need not be communicated to the other person, although that happened in both *Evans* and *Dempsey*, and in that sense ratification is different from accepting an offer of a contract. The manifestation need not even be communicated to the unauthorized actor in order to be effective, although of course it will have to be proven in some way.

Ratification can create liability either in contract or in tort, as the *Evans* and *Dempsey* cases demonstrate. In most jurisdictions, and under the formulation set forth in R2d § 82, an undisclosed principal cannot ratify (although an unidentified principal can ratify because the other party does intend to deal with a principal). A number of relatively recent cases and R3d § 4.03 (T.D. No. 2, 2001), however, take the contrary view, allowing the undisclosed principal to ratify the acts of its agent.

R3d § 4.30 (T.D. No. 2, 2001) provides that "[a] person may ratify an act if the actor acted or purported to act as an agent on the person's behalf." This limits, in certain circumstances, the liability of one who appears to have ratified a tort. For instance, in *Matulis v. Gans* (Conn.1928), the statement of a car owner that he would pay for damages caused by a prospective purchaser of the car who was aimlessly driving the car around town with two friends was not binding on the reasoning that the owner "could not ratify an act which was not done in his behalf." The statement instead was a mere voluntary assumption of liability, which requires consideration or a substitute for consideration (such as reliance on the statement) in order to be binding on the car owner.

Ratification of an employee's tortious conduct can expose an employer to punitive damages. For example, in *Novick v. Gouldsberry* (9th Cir. 1949), a bartender savagely attacked a customer for purely personal reasons (the bartender was married to the customer's ex-wife; the customer made a comment the bartender did not like). Clearly the assault by the bartender was not done on the principal's account. A few days later the owner of the bar saw the customer on the street and said, "What's the matter with you, Gouldsberry? If I had been there I would have broken your [expletive deleted] neck." The court characterized this statement as ratification of the tort and upheld an award of punitive damages against the owner.

One recurring question in ratification relates to forgery. Under the formulation set forth in R2d § 82, only those "acts done or professedly done" for a person could be ratified by that person. Thus, a forgery could not be ratified because it neither was done nor was it purportedly done on the victim's behalf. Although at one time forgeries could not be ratified in many jurisdictions, the law on this issue has changed, in part due to the influence of the Uniform Commercial Code § 3–403, which states that a forgery can be ratified (noting that this does not affect civil or criminal liability of the forger).

R3d § 4.03, comment c (T.D. No. 2, 2001) recognizes this U.C.C. section and rationalizes the principle that it reflects: "It may be in the principal's interest to ratify a forgery to obtain the benefit of a transaction not otherwise available."

§ 52. Uniqueness of the Concept and its Justification

The following language from Comments c and d to R2d § 82 expresses clearly both the uniqueness of ratification and its justification. Nothing in Restatement (Third) of Agency would call into question this succinct observation of the law:

c. *A unique concept.* The concept of ratification ... is unique. It does not conform to the rules of contracts, since it can be accomplished without consideration or manifestation by the purported principal [to the other party] and without fresh consent by the other party. Further, it operates as if the transaction were complete at the time and place of the first event, rather than the last, as in the normal case of offer and acceptance. It does not conform to the rules of torts, since the ratifier may become liable for a harm that was not caused by him, his property, or his agent. It cannot be justified on a theory of restitution, since the ratifier may not have received a benefit, nor the third party a deprivation. Nor is ratification dependent upon estoppel, since there may be ratification although neither the agent nor the other party suffer a loss resulting from a statement of affirmance or a failure to disavow. ...

d. Justification. . . . In many cases, the third person is a distinct gainer as where the purported principal ratifies a tort or a loan for which he was not liable and for which he receives nothing. This result is not, however, unjust, since, although the creation of liability against the ratifier may run counter to established tort or contract principles, the liability is self-imposed. Even one who ratifies to protect his business reputation or who retains unwanted goods rather than defend a law suit, chooses ratification as preferable to the alternative. Further, the sometimes-derided doctrine of relation back not only is used in other parts of the law, but it tends to give the parties what they wanted or said they wanted. If it sometimes happens that a mistaken or over-zealous agent is relieved from liability to the third person, the net result causes no harm to anyone. However, perhaps the best defense of ratification is pragmatic; that it is needed in the prosecution of business. It operates normally to cure minor defects in an agent's authority, minimizing technical defenses and preventing unnecessary law suits. In this aspect, it is a beneficial doctrine, which has been adopted in most systems of law.

§ 53. Implied Ratification

Ratification can be implied by conduct. In that sense, it can be a trap for the unwary. *Dempsey* (§ 51) may constitute an example of that. The defendant may have billed plaintiff for the coal without even considering the possibility of ratification.

It is possible that all he was thinking about was getting paid for the coal that was in the plaintiff's possession. Yet the court in effect construed the billing as "conduct . . . justifiable only if there was an election to treat the act as originally authorized by him."

Silence can constitute ratification under certain circumstances. See R3d § 4.01 (2)(b) (T.D. No. 2, 2001), requiring only "conduct that is justifiable only on the assumption that the person so consents [to the act of another]." Two common examples are the silent retention of benefits after being informed that the benefits were obtained by actions purported to be on one's account and silence after being informed that an admitted agent has exceeded his powers in a moment of zeal.

In both of the above circumstances a number of cases exist that characterize such behavior as implied ratification. For a case recognizing but distinguishing those circumstances, see *Myers v. Cook* (W. Va. 1920). In this case, Cook signed his wife's name to a promissory note without her consent. The wife discovered this and said nothing. The holder of the note claimed implied ratification. The court rejected this claim, holding that the wife's silence was not sufficient evidence of ratification in the absence of a pre-existing agency relationship or of receipt and retention of benefits.

The concept of indirect or implied ratification through conduct or lack of conduct is soft-edged and can be difficult to apply. It may be that sometimes the equities of a case will lead a court to draw an inference of ratification under ambiguous circumstances. This sometimes happens to employers in sexual harassment cases when the employer failed to stop the misconduct after notice and ratification is an alternative ground of recovery for the plaintiff. Also, it may be that many implied ratification cases can be argued in the alternative as estoppel or restitution cases. There is not a complete overlap with these doctrines, however, as noted in § 52.

It is sometimes argued that retaining an employee in employment after the employee committed a tort constitutes ratification of the tort. Nearly all courts have rejected this claim on the reasoning that one cannot fairly infer approval from retention and that to hold the contrary would be damaging to employees as a class.

§ 54. Limitations on Ratification

A. Principal Must Have Been Able Initially to Authorize the Act

R3d § 4.04 (T.D. No. 3, 2002) makes clear that a person may ratify an act only if the person existed at the time of the act and had the necessary legal capacity. Among other things, this rule means that a promoter who is organizing a corporation and who signs contracts on behalf of the contemplated corporation cannot count on ratification to protect her from warranty of authority liability. Because the corporation was not in existence at the time of the contract, it cannot later ratify it. The corporation can adopt the contract, but adoption does not relate back to the time of original signing. Thus a promoter is not released from liability except by novation, when all three parties agree to substitute a new contract for the original contract, rescinding the original contract.

On a separate point, when formalities are requisite for the authorization of an act, its affirmance must be by the same formalities in order to constitute a ratification. For a recent case involving this concept, see *Estate of Huston v. Greene* (Cal. App. 1997). In this case an agent operating under a power of attorney granted by Ms. Huston purchased an annuity for a person who had devotedly cared for the elderly Ms. Huston long after others had abandoned her. The power of attorney did not authorize gifts. Ms. Huston, mentally alert up to the time of her death, orally approved the gift in a conversation with her banker, among others. After her death her relatives challenged the gift as not properly authorized. The court agreed with this, stating: "Because a power of attorney must be in writing, any act performed by the agent acting under the power must therefore be ratified in writing. Even though it is apparent decedent in fact wished to make [the] gift, nonetheless she failed to comply with the formalities necessary to do so."

B. The Knowledge Requirement

One of the conventional rules of ratification is that the purported principal must have knowledge of all the material facts before being held to an affirmance, unless he assumes the risk of lack of knowledge. See R3d § 4.06 (T.D. No. 2, 2001): "A person is not bound by a ratification made without knowledge of material facts involved in the original act when the person was unaware of such lack of knowledge." See *Page v. Suraci* (Vt.1984)(retention by plaintiff buyers of second deed for eight months before objection was not ratification of attorney's unauthorized act of recording the deed because plaintiffs were unaware of the material fact that the second deed differed substantially from the first).

With regard to assuming the risk of lack of knowledge, R3d § 4.06, comment d (T.D. No. 2, 2001) states in part as follows: "A factfinder may conclude that the principal has made...a choice [to ratify] when the principal is shown to have had knowledge of facts that would have led a reasonable person to investigate further, but the principal ratified without further investigation." Also, estoppel can play a role in this context. That is, even if one does not have knowledge of material facts and does not assume the risk, nevertheless if the other party relies on the ratification, the principal will be bound.

C. The No Partial Ratification Rule

The principal cannot pick and choose the best parts of a contract, refusing to ratify the rest. The no partial ratification rule decrees that ratification of part of a transaction is deemed to be ratification of the whole transaction. Thus ordinarily a principal cannot affirm a sale and disavow unauthorized representations or warranties that the purported agent made to induce the sale. Realizing this, a sophisticated principal may, instead of ratifying, condition affirmance upon a modification of the original contract. If the other party accepts this, a new contract is created.

D.   Withdrawal by the Other Party

The other party has the option to withdraw prior to ratification. This rule is a limitation on the fiction of relation back. The other party can withdraw even if he does not realize that the contract is unauthorized and thus his withdrawal appears to him to be a breach of contract. The withdrawal must be manifested either to the agent or the principal. The manifestation can be implied as well as express, such as the act of suing the agent for breach of warranty of authority.

E.   Changed Circumstances

One cannot ratify after circumstances have changed in a way that would make it inequitable to the other party. An example of this is when A, purporting to act on behalf of but without the power to bind P, contracts on Monday to sell to T land with a house on it owned by P. On Tuesday the house, uninsured, burns to the ground. On Wednesday P discovers the facts and hastily ratifies. The ratification is ineffective.

The factor of changed circumstances has relevance beyond disputes between the immediate parties. The doctrine of relation back cannot deprive others of rights that have accrued prior to ratification. R3d § 4.02, Illustration 5 (T.D. No. 2, 2001), provides an example of this:

> P owns Backacre. A forges P's name on a lease of Blackacre to T that contains an option to purchase. P then enters into a contract to sell Blackacre to S. Thereafter, P ratifies A's forgery of P's name on the lease, and T wishes to exercise the purchase option. S's contract to buy Blackacre is specifically enforceable. P may be liable to T for money damages for breach of contract.

F. Time Limitations

If an act to be effective must be performed before a certain time, ratification is not effective unless made before such time. For example, assume that an option to purchase property expires on July 1. A, acting without authority, accepts on P's behalf on June 30. P seeks to ratify on July 2. The ratification is ineffective.

CHAPTER 9

NOTICE AND NOTIFICATION;
IMPUTED KNOWLEDGE

A notification is an act that is intended to convey information to another. Knowledge is cognitive awareness of a fact. When a person has received a notification or has knowledge of a fact, he or she is deemed to have "notice" of the fact and must act accordingly. The law of notice has significance in the law of agency when notification or knowledge is claimed to have taken place through an agent, binding the principal whether or not the information actually is received by the principal.

Not all courts and commentators use the words "notice, notification, and imputed knowledge" consistently. Sometimes it will prove necessary to ascertain the meaning of the words used from the context of the language.

§ 55. Notification

Notification involves a deliberate effort to bring some fact to the attention of a person. The key agency issue is, under what circumstances will notification to an agent bind the principal? The law of apparent authority plays a major role in resolving notification issues unless the agent is actually authorized to receive the particular notification.

A. Reasonable Expectations

A notification will be effective if the expectation of the party making it is reasonable in assuming that the agent is authorized to receive it. If the agent appears to be on duty at the time and the notice seems to fall within the scope of his duty, so that he could reasonably be expected to communicate the information to his principal, the notification will be effective. This is true even if the agent has an adverse interest and has no intention whatsoever to communicate the information, so long as the other party is unaware of that.

For example, consider the following two illustrations from R3d § 5.02 (T.D. No. 3, 2002):

1. P, who owns a garden center, employs A to manage it. P enters into a contract with T providing that T shall supply the garden center's requirements for mulch for five years. The contract provides that either party may cancel by giving the other 60 days written notice and further provides that any notice to P shall be given to A. T mails a written notice canceling the contract to A. A opens and reads T's notification but does not tell P. T's notification is effective against P.

2. Same facts as Illustration 1, except that P tells A that A may not accept any notices from T. T's notification is effective against P. A had apparent authority to receive the notification from T.

Illustration 5 makes clear that if P fires A, A may still have the apparent authority to affect P's legal relations (e.g., accept notice of renewal), if T is unaware of the firing. Obviously, if T gives notice to one who does not appear to have authority to accept notice, the notice is ineffective. See, for instance, *Thompson v. Sun Oil Co.* (Fla. 1939), holding ineffective an attempted notification of the assignment of a lease of a gasoline station that was given to an attendant at the gas station.

It is useful to note that one must be especially careful when attempting to notify government agencies. Statutes or administrative regulations often specify in detail the steps required to make an effective notification to a particular agency and specifically reject notification by any other means.

B. When a Notification is Effective

A notification can in some cases be effective at the moment it is given. For example, ordinarily a notice of acceptance of an offer given to an authorized or apparently authorized agent of the offeror is effective at the time it is given. But under other circumstances, in particular when action is required on the part of the one being notified, reasonable time must be given for the transmission of the information to the one who is to act.

If there is a contract between the parties, the requirements for notification and when it is effective often are established by agreement. Also, the issue of effective notice is sometimes defined by statute. A significant example of this is Uniform Commercial Code § 1–201(27), dealing with notice to an organization: "[N]otification received by an organization is effective for a particular transaction from the time it is brought to the attention of the individual conducting that transaction, and in any event from the time it would have been brought to his attention if the organization had exercised due diligence."

C. Duration

In general, a notification is effective whether or not the person authorized or apparently authorized to receive the notification forgets it and does nothing with it. As stated in Seavey, Law of Agency 173 (1964), "Since a notification, as such, operates to determine the rights of the parties to it, the effect continues indefinitely." A notification "crystalizes the rights of the parties." Id.

§ 56. Imputed Knowledge

The doctrine of imputed knowledge involves holding a principal to the knowledge of, and sometimes the wrongs (broadly defined) committed by, his agent. It does this through the fiction of imputing the agent's knowledge to the principal. It is most frequently applied in the context of acquisition of assets for the principal, although it is not limited to that situation. The doctrine has several rationales. First, like respondeat superior, it creates an incentive on the part of principals to select and monitor their agents with care. Second, it discourages the use of agents to "insulate" principals from information of which principals consciously wish to remain ignorant. Finally, the doctrine recognizes it is more efficient for third parties to communicate with agents rather than directly with principals and if the doctrine did not exist, third parties would be discouraged from communicating with agents. Closely related to this rationale, R3d § 5.03, comment b (T.D. No. 3, 2003) points out that "[b]y treating the principal as knowing relevant facts known to the agent, imputation encourages dealings that more fully reflect material facts."

Some of these rationales are captured in illustration 1 to R3d § 5.03:

> P wants to sell good to the government of country X but is concerned that pay-offs may be necessary to effect such a sale. P employs A in country X and advises A that P does not wish to know of any commissions or other payments A may need to pay to effect the sale of P's goods. P may nonetheless be charged with violations of anti-bribery laws. Notice may be imputed to P of A's knowledge of payments made by A.

Comment b following this illustration demonstrates that P may not avoid imputation by instructing A "to disclose to P any risk that payoffs might be made or by showing that A knew or suspected their occurrence but did not tell P."

Because the doctrine of imputed knowledge is not expectation based, perhaps it makes sense to return to the core issues of responsibility stemming from the agency relationship.

A. Forgotten Knowledge

All authorities agree that in order for knowledge to be imputed it must be "present in the mind" of the agent at the time he conducts the transaction for the principal. This rule raises the issue of forgotten knowledge. As noted earlier, knowledge is subjective and consists of cognitive awareness of a fact. All authorities agree that relevant information acquired by an agent *during* a transaction should be imputed to the principal. A defense that it was forgotten by the agent is not viewed as plausible. But what about knowledge acquired *prior* to the transaction at issue? The standard applied by courts to resolve this issue is set forth in *Pee Dee State Bank v. Prosser* (S.C.App.1988): "As a general rule, a principal is charged with the knowledge of an agent acquired before the relationship only when the knowledge can reasonably be said to have been in the mind of the agent while acting for the principal or where he acquired it so recently as to raise the presumption that he still retained it in his mind."

Pee Dee Bank involved a priority dispute between two mortgagees. The mortgagee first in time, Pee Dee Bank, argued that the second mortgagee (Universal) was on notice of Pee Dee's unrecorded prior interest because the attorney who had performed a title search for Pee Dee in conjunction with its mortgage subsequently represented Universal in its closing with regard to the same property. The time span between the mortgages was one year. Pee Dee argued that the attorney's knowledge of Pee Dee's prior interest should be imputed to Universal. The court rejected the argument, concluding, because so much time had passed, that it was not proven that the information about Pee Dee's outstanding interest was "in the mind of the agent" at the time he acted on behalf of Universal.

B. The Duty Requirement

A principal is bound by his agent's knowledge when the agent has a duty to convey it to him. See, for example, *Sexton v. United States* (E.D.N.C. 1991), in which the knowledge of a welder's assistant (Rosser) that a door had fallen into a pit on a construction site, posing a safety hazard, was not imputed to his employer, a subcontractor on the job. The court stated: "[T]he general rule is that a principal is chargeable with, and bound by, the knowledge of defects [known by] his agent which [is] received while the agent is acting as such within the scope of his authority. Rosser was not a supervisory employee or one engaged in safety concerns [for his employer. Thus the matter] was not one over which his authority extended."

Composite knowledge. At times, an argument is made that an organization should be held to the composite knowledge of several of its employees. Assume, for example, that a power company ("Power") enters into a contract with a bridge company ("Bridge") to string high tension wires above the bridge. Power promises to provide safety personnel whenever Bridge paints the bridge upon receiving notice of that fact. Bridge decides to paint the bridge and does not give notice to Power. One employee of Power sees painters working on the bridge. Another employee knows that Power is supposed to supply safety personnel under that circumstance. Is Power subject to the composite knowledge of the two employees? The answer would be no unless this "affair was entrusted" to the agent who observed the painters. In other circumstances, however, the courts will hold a corporation to the composite knowledge of its employees. See, for instance, *Gutter v. E.I. DuPont De Nemours* (S.D. Fla. 2000)(cumulative knowledge of several corporate agents, including outside counsel to the corporation, imputed to the corporation and resulted in a finding that the corporation committed fraud on the court).

C. The Adverse Interest Exception

The adverse interest exception is similar to the scope of employment defense in respondeat superior (see § 25). If an agent is acting adversely to the principal and entirely for his own or another's purposes, his knowledge is not imputed. (In one sense, the agent is "on a frolic" of his own.) The fact, however, that an agent has conflicting goals (like the desire to earn a commission and thus keep silent about an outstanding equity) will not rise to the level of an adverse interest. For instance, assume P retains A to negotiate on P's behalf to acquire Blackacre from T, provided A finds no defects in T's title. P promises A a commission on the purchase price if the deal closes. In investigating T's title to Blackacre, A discovers an unrecorded equitable interest in favor of S. A withholds this information from P so as not to jeopardize A's commission on the purchase, thus clearly acting adversely to P. P, unaware of S's interest, agrees to buy Blackacre from T. If T did not know or have reason to know that A did not disclose S's interest, T may enforce the contract against P. See R3d § 5.04, illustration 2 (T.D. No. 4, 2003). The risk that A may act adversely to P, given the incentive structure that P created, is one that P should bear. This provides a justification for protecting the rights of T, who acted in good faith in the transaction. It is only when the agent totally abandons the principal's business, such as taking a bribe to keep quiet, that the knowledge will not be imputed.

D. The Sole Actor Rule

The sole actor rule is an exception to the adverse interest exception. It is difficult to get a clear sense of the sole actor rule but it seems to apply when the agent, even though clearly acting as an adverse party to the principal by, for example, selling some of his own property to the principal, also receives that property in the capacity of agent for the principal and is the only agent acting in that capacity.

Under this circumstance the agent is in effect wearing two hats, one as adverse party and the other as sole recipient of the property for the principal. It is in the latter capacity that the sole actor rule applies, imputing the agent's knowledge (of an outstanding equity, say) to the principal. As stated in *First Nat. Bank of Cicero v. United States* (N.D.Ill. 1987): "The law will charge the principal with whatever the agent knew, as the fair price of claiming the benefit through the agent."

As an example of the sole actor rule in operation, consider *Munroe v. Harriman* (2d Cir.1936), a classic sole actor case. In that case Harriman borrowed securities from Munroe on a personal basis, committing fraud in the process. He then pledged the securities as collateral for a loan from a bank of which he was the president and used the loan proceeds for his own purposes. Harriman dominated the bank's other officers and employees, including the loan committee that approved the loan. The court held that his knowledge of the fraud was imputed to the bank, allowing Munroe to rescind the transaction and obtain the securities from the bank.

Harriman's knowledge was imputed even though he obviously was an adverse party borrowing money for his own benefit and even though the bank gave value for the securities and thus was not unjustly enriched. Also, estoppel did not play any role in these facts. The bank was held to Harriman's knowledge because he dominated the loan committee. In the words of the court, "Harriman's domination was exerted to affect the action of the bank with respect to the particular transaction. His will alone caused the making of the loan and the acceptance of the collateral. Therefore he should be treated as the sole actor on behalf of the bank as fully as though he had physically placed the note and securities in the bank's vault.''

CHAPTER 10

TERMINATION OF THE AGENCY
RELATIONSHIP

---

§ 57. Termination by Will

A principal has the *power* to terminate the agency relationship and thus the agent's authority at any time. This rule holds true even if the principal had contracted not to terminate the agency and thus did not have the *right* to do so. The underlying theory is that it should always be in the power of the principal to manage its own business and to determine who shall act on its behalf, subject to paying damages for breach of contract when appropriate. An agent also has the power to quit the agency at any time, again subject to paying damages for breach of contract if, for example, a term contract is involved.

If a principal does not have the power to end a relationship, it is not an agency relationship even though it may look like one. For example, a power of attorney authorizing a lender to sell an asset of the borrower in the event of nonpayment of the loan does not create an agency relationship. Although the instrument looks like a conventional power of attorney, in reality it is a security power. Exercise of it by the holder of the power has nothing to do with acting on behalf of the best interests of the borrower. Instead, it is designed and intended to help the lender secure payment of the loan. The power thus is given to the lender to do something for itself, not for the borrower; it is not a true agency power. It would be held irrevocable during the maker's lifetime by nearly all courts. (As an aside, it is not wise for a lender to cast a security interest in this form, in part for reasons explained in § 59. Instead, the lender should receive an assignment of the security interest.)

With regard to true agency, unless termination results from the completion of the purpose of the agency or the expiration of an agreed term, it is necessary for the principal to notify the agent of termination of the relationship. Until the agent receives notice, he or she continues to be actually authorized to commit the principal to transactions within the scope of the agency.

Notification can be express or implied. As with the creation of authority, the objective theory controls, imposing a standard of reasonableness on expectations. For example, P authorizes A to sell Blackacre for $10,000. Subsequently A observes that P has built an expensive home on Blackacre. A's authority is terminated.

Even if there is not an express breach of contract, a principal's right to end an agency relationship is subject to equitable considerations. For example, even with a rightful termination, as stated in *Beebe v. Columbia Axle Co.* (Mo. App. 1938):

> The limitation is that, in any case of indefinite agency where it is revoked by the principal, if it appears that the agent, induced by his appointment has in good faith incurred expense and devoted time and labor in the matter of the agency without having had a sufficient opportunity to recoup such from the undertaking, the principal will be required to compensate him in that behalf; for the law will not permit one thus to deprive another of value without awarding just compensation.

This limitation includes the revocation by a principal of an offer of compensation in order to avoid paying a commission or bonus or with the intent to give the benefit to another.

§ 58. Notice of Termination to Third Parties

In order to avoid the problem of "lingering apparent authority," in addition to recovering indicia of authority, a principal must send individual notice to all persons who extended credit to or received credit from the principal through the agent (their names presumably are on the principal's books and records) and to persons "with whom the agent has begun to deal, as the principal should know" (R2d § 136). Reasonable public notice ordinarily suffices for all others.

§ 59. Termination by Operation of Law

Death or incapacity automatically terminates an agency relationship at common law. Legislation has been enacted in nearly all states addressing specifically the issue of incapacity, making the durable power of attorney (see § 36 A) possible by declaring that incapacity does not revoke a durable power.

It is the majority rule at common law that death terminates not only authority but also apparent authority of an agent, which means notice by operation of law of termination is automatic at common law. Among other things, this rule exposes an agent to warranty of authority liability to third persons. Legislation exists in a number of states that have adopted the Model Probate Code that tempers the common law rule by stating that an agent's authority under a power of attorney continues until he receives notice of the principal's death. R3d § 3.11, comment b (T.D. No. 2, 2001) rejects earlier Restatements and the common law rule: "A principal's death or loss of capacity does not by itself or automatically end the agent's apparent authority."

The power coupled with an interest problem. Death was found to revoke a nonagency power in the famous case of *Hunt v. Rousmanier's Administrators* (S.Ct.1823), on the formalistic ground that,"A conveyance in the name of a person who was dead at the time would be a manifest absurdity." The power was a power of attorney given for security for a loan on some ships. It gave the power holder a power of sale in the event of nonpayment.

Chief Justice Marshall acknowledged in his opinion that the power would be irrevocable during the lifetime of the parties but he could not overcome the formalistic impact of death.

Only if a power is coupled with an interest, Justice Marshall noted, could it become irrevocable at death. A power is coupled with an interest when the interest is conveyed at the time the power is created, thus allowing sale without the necessity of selling in the name of the deceased. A power of sale in a mortgage in a title theory state, where the lender is conveyed title to the property subject to defeasance if the loan is paid, is the purest example of a true power coupled with an interest because the power holder can convey in his own name.

Courts have found the power coupled with an interest concept difficult to apply. A number of decisions depart substantially from the test advanced by Justice Marshall and have found nonagency powers irrevocable even when no interest was conveyed to the power holder at the time of creation of the power. The underlying equities of a case often seem to play a major role in a court's willingness to find powers coupled with an interest.

The Restatement (Second) (§§ 138–139) attempts to avoid this problem by rejecting the power coupled with an interest terminology, substituting the phrase "power given as security" and characterizing all nonagency powers as irrevocable by death. Although this seems sensible and straight-forward, the "power coupled with an interest" language has proven remarkable durable in many states.

PART IV

THE LAW OF UNINCORPORATED BUSINESS ENTERPRISES

INTRODUCTION

Contained below is an overview of the various ways of doing business in unincorporated form. Most of the forms of doing business discussed in this overview are covered in detail in Chapters 11–15.

There are several matters of common concern for persons who contemplate becoming co-owners of a business with others. These include (1) the right to manage or at least share in the management of the business, (2) avoidance of personal liability for the debts of the business, (3) enjoyment of favorable tax treatment, and (4) the right to exit the business and cash out one's holdings in a reasonably prompt way. These are not the only issues of importance to co-owners. For example, owners may be concerned about what statutory limitations, if any, exist on distributions from the business to them and what fiduciary obligations they might be subject to, among other things. But the four matters listed above are of such common concern and vary sufficiently among the different business forms that it is useful to look at the different ways of doing business from this perspective.

A. The Corporation

The topic of the corporation appears to fit poorly into material covering the law of unincorporated business organizations. It provides a useful contrast to the different forms of unincorporated business associations, however, and will be discussed in that context.

A full development of the concepts mentioned below, as well as the application in detail of the law of agency specifically to corporations, will have to await the course on corporations. It is important to note that some (but not all) states have adopted legislation that allows the closely held business (one with a relatively limited number of owners) to be operated in corporate form with less formality than that described below.

As noted in § 5E, a corporation is a legal entity formed under a state statute by filing articles of incorporation with the proper state office. The articles designate, among other things, the number and kinds of shares of stock that the corporation may issue. Such shares may differ by classes in such rights as voting, share of profits, and property rights on liquidation. A corporation is owned by persons who hold shares of its stock. As a legal entity a corporation can sue and be sued, own property, and is required to pay taxes on its income. General policy is set by a board of directors, which is elected by the shareholders. The board of directors in turn appoints officers, who are employees and who run the day-to-day business of the corporation.

A corporation can act only through its employees-agents. The board of directors may act only as a group. Individual directors have no authority to establish policy or run the business unless they also are officers.

Debts of a corporation ordinarily are satisfied only out of the assets of the corporation. Thus, the shareholders, members of the board, and officers all enjoy limited liability in the sense that they are not personally liable for the debts of the business. Corporations are required in most states to file annual reports with the state and to operate with a certain degree of formality. A corporation may be established with a perpetual life.

With regard to the four main concerns of co-ownership expressed above: (1) Management is not in the hands of the owners. Instead, the board of directors manages the corporation, assisted by officers appointed by the board. Thus, ownership and control are separated in a corporation, although individual owners can become officers and members of the board. (2) Liability of owners is limited, as explained above. (3) Taxation is a problem, due to the double taxation created by the corporate form. Income generated by a corporation is taxed first to the corporation. Then, when income is distributed to the shareholders, usually in the form of dividends, it is taxed again as income to the shareholders. (Double taxation can be avoided by electing to be treated as an S corporation, but that form is subject to a number of technical restrictions.) (4) Exiting from the business and cashing out are extremely easy when the shares of a corporation are publicly traded. Exit is more of a problem for the closely held corporation because there is no established market in the shares and thus exit usually depends on contractual buyout arrangements.

The corporate form is most widely used for large businesses, which need to accumulate substantial amounts of capital and have available a public market (like the New York Stock Exchange) for trading in the shares of the corporation. Historically the corporate form also has been used by closely held businesses when limited liability for owners of the business was so important that it outweighed the income tax and operational irritations and drawbacks posed by operating in corporate form.

1.   The Historical Price Paid for Limited Liability

Although, as noted above, some states have legislated ways in which the closely held corporation can be operated informally, it is nevertheless true that in most instances the corporate form entails some inconvenience structurally and managerially, in addition to the problems created by double taxation. This was the price paid for limited liability for all the owners of a business. That price existed for many years. It no longer need be paid by closely held businesses because of two recent extraordinary changes in the law, which make operating in unincorporated form much more attractive: (i) the availability of limited liability in unincorporated form and (ii) a change in the income tax laws allowing favorable taxation for unincorporated limited liability entities, as explained below.

2. Recent Changes in Limited Liability and Pass–Through Taxation for Unincorporated Businesses

It seems a safe assumption that today many lawyers think first about recommending that clients do business in LLC (limited liability company) or LLP (limited liability partnership) form when dealing with a closely held business. In large part this is because operating as an LLC or LLP can be informal and flexible, carries no disadvantage in terms of limited liability, and provides the benefits of partnership taxation. Under partnership taxation the income of the partnership flows directly through to the partners and is not first taxed separately to the partnership (this is commonly referred to as taxation on a "flow-through" or "pass-through" basis).

Limited liability recently was made available to unincorporated businesses by the enactment of legislation that provides for acquiring limited liability by the act of filing papers under the appropriate statute. The change in taxation came about as a result of the adoption of "check-the-box" regulations by the Internal Revenue Service (see Chapter 15), abandoning the rigid four-factor test used for years by the IRS for distinguishing between corporations and partnerships. It is now possible for an unincorporated business with more than one owner to be taxed as a partnership even if its owners have limited liability and the business has other corporate characteristics, like centralized management, free transferability of interests, and continuity of life.

B.   The Different Forms of Unincorporated Businesses

The sole proprietorship and the business trust will receive most of their coverage at this point. A more detailed treatment of the partnership, the LLP, the limited partnership, the LLLP (limited liability limited partnership), and the LLC will take place in Chapters 11–15.

1.   The Sole Proprietorship

In one sense, the sole proprietorship is not a "form" of doing business at all. A sole proprietorship is simply one person going into business without making any plans for an entity to carry on the business. No papers are filed in order to create the business. The sole proprietorship is one of the two "default" ways of doing business, in the sense that it applies if no other form is chosen. (The other default form, covering the situation in which there is more than one owner, is the general partnership.)

The business may be carried on in the owner's (proprietor's) name or it may be given a trade name. The net income from the business is taxable income to the proprietor. All losses are indistinguishable from losses related to the proprietor's personal life and thus are paid from personal assets. Although it is wise to separate business and personal assets and have a separate accounting for the business, there is no significance in doing so with regard to taxation or liability.

The sole proprietorship is widely used in this country. Some 18 million nonfarm sole proprietorships were active in 2001, the most recent year for which statistics are available, with the number constantly rising (there were 5 million in 1970 and 9 million in 1980). This is over two times the combined number of partnerships and LLCs (2 million) and corporations (5 million) in 1997. Internal Revenue Service, Statistics of Income Bulletin 52 (fall 1999).

This surprisingly large number may reflect the informality and small size of most sole proprietorships. Also, the incentive to spend time and money adopting a limited liability form is minimal for a business owned and operated by one person because of the reality that individuals always are liable for their personal wrongdoing and by hypothesis wrongs committed by a sole proprietor would be personal wrongs, even though committed in the course of the business. In addition, with regard to contractual liability, although it is true that the entity and not the individual is the contracting party on contracts relating to a business organized as an entity, in reality if the contract involves substantial sums the personal guaranty of the owner is almost always required by the other party to the contract in the small business context. Finally, many people tend not to revisit arrangements when a business starts to grow and hire employees and thus do not get around to consulting an attorney and obtaining protection from vicarious liability for the torts of their employees by, for example, becoming a single member LLC or a sole shareholder corporation.

It is important to emphasize that liability protection does not exist for the personal wrongdoing of an owner in *any* form of doing business. Thus realistically, with the exception of minor contracts, the issue of limited liability becomes important in many sole proprietor businesses only when the owner starts to engage the services of others in an agency capacity or brings in other owners for the business.

2.   The Business Trust

The business trust originated at common law. The concept of a trust was utilized to create an unincorporated business association, usually known as the Massachusetts trust. The business trust was used early in the 20th century primarily as a device designed to provide limited liability for owners of a business while avoiding certain restrictions in some states (in particular, Massachusetts) on operating in corporate form. The business trust is used today primarily for asset securitization ventures in which income-generating assets, such as mortgages, are pooled in a trust, with participation (ownership) interests in the trust sold to investors. The common law business trust has certain drawbacks, as explained below. In 1990, Delaware passed a statute that avoids the common law defects and provides considerable freedom of contract among the owners and managers. Several other states have followed suit.

A business trust is created by placing the assets of a business in trust with trustees. The trustees hold title to the assets for the benefit of holders of shares in the trust and thus are technically the legal owners of the business. The holders contribute capital, receiving shares reflecting the extent of each individual's contribution, and are the beneficial owners of the trust. The shares can be made freely transferable without disrupting the continuity of the organization. The trustees manage the business. In the absence of a statute to the contrary, the trustees sue and are sued in their individual names and as legal owners of the business are personally liable for obligations incurred in the business. They have a right to reimbursement from the trust assets, however, if the obligation paid does not stem from their own wrongdoing.

One concern at common law is the risk of liability of the beneficial owners if they exercise control over the trustees. Liability is based on the reasoning that the trustees become the agents of the beneficial owners under such circumstance or the trust may be classified as a partnership. The Delaware statute resolves this by expressly stating that beneficiaries of a Delaware business trust cannot be held responsible for the debts of the trust beyond their original investment. Also, the Delaware statute specifies that the trustees are not personally responsible for the obligations of the business and that a business trust has a perpetual existence unless the governing instrument provides otherwise.

With regard to the four common concerns: (1) Management is in the hands of the trustees. With respect to common law trusts, the owners cannot control the trustees in any substantial way without running the risk of personal liability; this risk does not exist by statute in some jurisdictions. (2) Liability for owners is limited at common law because they are not the legal owners of the business and it is limited by statute in Delaware and some other states. (3) Taxation may be on a flow-through basis for the business trust that takes advantage of the check-the-box change in the tax laws. Like public limited partnerships, however, business trusts that are traded on national exchanges are subject to taxation as corporations pursuant to a special provision of the Internal Revenue Code. (4) Exit is accomplished by a routine sale of shares and does not cause a dissolution of the trust.

3.   The Partnership

As explained in the Glossary, a general partnership is created when two or more persons carry on as co-owners a business for profit. No documents need be filed to create a partnership. It exists as soon as two or more people start doing business together without choosing another form of business. In that respect the partnership is a "default" form of doing business. People can become partners without realizing they have done so and with no understanding of the consequences of being in this relationship. Chapters 11–13 cover the partnership.

The law has for centuries provided the two default forms of business operation, the sole proprietorship and the partnership, as a "back-up" for people who enter into business without planning. It is important to note that people sometimes choose these forms deliberately. It is only the default status that is being emphasized at this stage due to its importance to an overall understanding of the legal consequences of certain decisions relating to business. The other alternatives of doing business in unincorporated form require filing a document with a designated office in the state of origin before the particular entity can come into existence.

With regard to the four matters of common concern: (1) Partners have equal rights to manage the business, unless they agree otherwise. (2) Partners are personally liable for the debts of the firm. (3) Partnership taxation is on a flow-through basis, which as noted above means that income is taxed only once, a desirable feature in small businesses that distribute most of their income to the owners. (4) Partners can exit a business whenever they desire, although contractual liability to fellow partners may result from this under some circumstances. Cashing out one's partnership interest can be difficult due to the absence of a ready market for the interest in most cases. Contractual buyout arrangements with fellow partners are common. Subject to agreement, a departing partner has a liquidation right against the partnership, allowing a forced sale of the business, as explained in Chapter 13. Unless otherwise agreed, partners share income and losses equally and must unanimously agree on new partners, thus reducing exit options as a practical matter. Each partner is a general agent of the partnership.

4.   The Limited Liability Partnership (LLP)

The limited liability partnership ("LLP") is a relatively new creation of the law. It makes available limited liability for all partners of a general partnership if a proper filing is made with the state. An LLP is a general partnership in all other respects. All fifty states have amended their partnership acts to make filing for LLP status possible.

5.   The Limited Partnership

The limited partnership is a creature of statute. It is quite distinct from the LLP, although the names are confusingly similar. It is formed by filing a document with a designated office in the state. All states recognize the limited partnership, which is covered in Chapter 14.

A limited partnership has at least one general and one limited partner. General partners in a limited partnership are like general partners in a general partnership, which includes personal liability for the debts of the business. (Sometimes a limited partnership will have only a corporate general partner as an "end around" the liability issue.) Limited and general partners are owners and enjoy the tax benefits of being partners in a partnership. By statute the limited partners are not liable for the debts of the business, although care must be exercised in some states about their participation in control. They do not have management rights in their status as limited partners, although they can contract otherwise.

With regard to the four common concerns of co-ownership: (1) As noted above, limited partners do not have management rights as a matter of status. Management of a limited partnership is in the hands of its general partners. Because of this clear-cut separation of managerial rights and responsibilities, limited partnerships are regarded as "hard-wired," a desirable feature for business and estate planning. (2) Limited partners are exempt from liability for the debts of the firm, unlike the general partners of the firm. (3) The taxation benefits of operating in partnership form are fully available to general and limited partners in a limited partnership. (4) Exit privileges are more confined for limited partners. Under the uniform act (see Chapter 14) they must give six months' notice before they can exit, unless the partnership agreement specifies otherwise, as almost all agreements do. Also, some state statutes recently have been amended to take away the limited partners' default exit privilege in order to take advantage of discount valuations for federal transfer tax purposes. In some firms limited partnership interests are by agreement freely transferable and may even be evidenced by certificates and traded on national securities exchanges (most public limited partnerships are by special provision taxed as corporations).

6. The Limited Liability Limited Partnership (LLLP)

The limited liability limited partnership ("LLLP") is an entity authorized by statute and has only very recently arrived on the scene. A filing with the state is required to create an LLLP. If a filing is properly made, limited liability is extended to the general partners of a limited partnership in the same manner as it is to partners in an LLP. In all other respects the LLLP is like a regular limited partnership. As of the date of this writing at least sixteen states provide for LLLPs.

7. The Limited Liability Company (LLC)

The limited liability company ("LLC") is a relatively new form of doing business as an unincorporated entity. It offers owners the benefits of limited liability, taxation as a partnership, and management flexibility. Liability is limited in the sense that owners (called "members") are not liable for the debts of the business and in that respect are in a similar position to shareholders of a corporation. The LLC is covered in Chapter 15.

It is necessary to file a document with the state in order to create an LLC. All states have adopted enabling legislation for LLCs, with considerable variation from state to state. The National Conference of Commissioners on Uniform State Laws ("NCCUSL") has promulgated a Uniform Limited Liability Company Act (1995)("ULLCA"), which has been adopted in whole or in substantial part in eight states to date.

With regard to the four major concerns: (1) Management is shared among the owners, just as it is among partners in a partnership, in a "member-managed" LLC. Owners are free to form a "manager-managed" LLC, placing management in the hands of one or more managers. (2) Liability of owners is limited, as explained above. (3) Taxation, as in a partnership, is on a flow-through basis, unless an election is made under the check-the-box regulations to be taxed as a corporation. (4) Exit from the entity need not cause dissolution of the LLC under statutes that have been amended following adoption of the check-the-box regulations.

The organizing document of an LLC is referred to nearly everywhere as an "operating agreement." The LLC is desirable for small businesses due to the enactment of enabling legislation in all 50 states and the flexible management and operational structure of the LLC, as contrasted with the corporation.

CHAPTER 11

THE CREATION OF A PARTNERSHIP

§ 60. Creating the Partnership Relationship

A general partnership is easy to form. If two or more persons associate as co-owners of a business and take no steps to formalize their relationship, they have created a partnership. No documents need be written or filed. This lack of formality is the fundamental characteristic that distinguishes the partnership from all other co-owner business organizations, which are statutory in origin and require that a document be filed before an organization can come into existence.

The partnership thus is a residual (or "default") form of doing business in a co-ownership relationship, applying to people who have done no planning and may not even know they are in a partnership relationship. Its use is not limited to that function, however. The partnership also is a widely and deliberately chosen form of doing business for many kinds of enterprise, including many professional businesses, like lawyers, doctors, and accountants.

The Uniform Partnership Act (1914) ("UPA"). UPA was promulgated in 1914 by the National Conference of Commissioners on Uniform State Laws ("NCCUSL"), an organization that prepares and recommends uniform laws to state legislatures. At one time UPA was adopted in all states except Louisiana. It still is governing law over a third of the states. (The other states have adopted RUPA, which is described below.) UPA is set forth in Appendix A to this book. A partnership is defined in § 6(1) of UPA as "an association of two or more persons to carry on as co-owners a business for profit."

UPA serves a dual function. It establishes certain basic principles of law that operate regardless of agreement among the partners ("mandatory rules"), such as §§ 11–15, which state when a partnership is bound by notice to and admission of a partner and which define the nature of a partner's liability to third parties. It also establishes certain principles that are subject to change by agreement among the partners ("default rules"), such as UPA § 18, which sets forth rules determining rights and duties among partners.

The Uniform Partnership Act (1997) ("RUPA"). In 1997 NCCUSL promulgated the latest version of RUPA. The "R" in "RUPA" stands for revised and RUPA indeed is a substantial revision of UPA. Although the word "revised" is not in its official title, the act is referred to as RUPA in its official Comments and in nearly all of the literature on it. RUPA has replaced UPA in 32 states and is currently under consideration in several other states. There are 1992, 1993, 1994, and 1996 versions of RUPA, all of which were superseded by the 1997 Act.

RUPA's definition of a partnership in § 202 is identical to that in UPA in all material respects. RUPA also contains mandatory and default rules. The delineation between the two is more clearly determined than in UPA because all rules of RUPA are declared default in nature in RUPA § 103(a) except a list of ten set forth in § 103(b). For example, RUPA § 103(b)(3)-(5) states that the fiduciary duties (and several other duties, including the duty of care and the obligation of good faith and fair dealing) may not be eliminated, thus classifying them as "mandatory" duties. As noted, nearly all other duties under RUPA are classified as "default" duties, which means that they are subject to the bargain of the partners.

RUPA is set forth in Appendix C to this book. A conversion table for UPA and RUPA is set forth between the two acts in Appendix B.

Elements of the Partnership Relationship. The elements of the definition of a partnership can be broken down as follows:

(i) "association"—An association is an organized body of persons who have some purpose in common. A partnership is created by agreement, express or implied, including *delectus personae* (choice of the person). The personal liability of a partner for the debts and obligations of the business (see § 72) doubtless provides much of the rationale underlying delectus personae, since one partner can create liabilities for the others. (It may be that the creation and widespread adoption of the LLP—see § 61—will have an impact on the practical importance of the delectus personae principle to some partners. Under "broad shield" LLP statutes a partner is not liable for the obligations of the partnership and thus need not fear personal liability for the obligations incurred by fellow partners. Nevertheless, each partner is a general agent of the firm (see Chapter 12) and has dissolution powers (Chapter 13), creating additional incentive to exercise care when choosing one's partners.)

This right of personal choice is expressed in UPA § 18(g) ("No person can become a member of a partnership without the consent of all the partners"). *Id.* RUPA § 401(d). All rights under §§ 18 and 401 are subject to agreement, however, which means that the right of choice over one's partners can be waived. Thus, a partner can leave the choice of future partners up to a majority vote of the other partners, or of an executive committee, or whatever other arrangement is desired or casually fallen into.

(ii) "persons"—This word includes not only individuals but also corporations and other partnerships. Capacity to contract is required because the partnership agreement is a contract.

(iii) "to carry on as co-owners a business"—
Ownership is defined in the Comment to UPA § 6
and RUPA § 202 as including "the power of ultimate control." The comment is referring to ownership of the business, not of the capital contributed
to the partnership (capital can consist of cash, property, or intangible assets; capital contributions can
vary among the partners). "Business" is defined in
UPA § 2 as "every trade, occupation, or profession"
and consists of "a series of acts directed toward an
end." *Id*. RUPA § 202, Comment 1.

(iv) "for profit"—Partnership law is a branch
of commercial law. Thus, "the operation of the act
should be confined to associations organized for
profit." UPA § 6, Comment and RUPA § 202, Comment 2.

§ 61. The LLP

A limited liability partnership (LLP) is created
when a partnership files a statement of qualification invoking limited liability for its partners under
a statute making that option available to partners
(see, e.g., RUPA § 1001). All 50 states have adopted
LLP statutes.

The creation of the LLP makes a major change in
Anglo–American partnership law as it has existed
for over a thousand years. Historically all partners
were jointly and severally liable for the obligations
of the partnership (this remains true for partnerships that have not filed a statement). That was the
common law rule and it was adopted in UPA and
the first three versions of RUPA. The LLP change

may be in part a response to the LLC (see Chapter 15), which established the principle that a person can do business in noncorporate form and yet enjoy both limited liability and the benefits of partnership taxation (see Introduction to Unincorporated Businesses, immediately preceding this Chapter, or see Chapter 15). A partner in an LLP enjoys a liability status similar to that of a shareholder in a corporation. RUPA § 306(c). Of course, a partner's capital interest is subject to the debts and obligations of the business, but that is distinct from the personal liability being discussed in this section.

Nevertheless, a partner is not shielded from the consequences of personal wrongdoing or from negligent supervision of others. The Delaware statute, for example, states that its liability limitation "shall not affect the liability of a partner in a registered limited liability partnership for his own negligence, wrongful acts, or misconduct or that of any person under his direct supervision and control." Del. Code, title 6, § 1515. (As an aside, the language extending liability to a partner for misconduct of persons "under his direct supervision and control" carries probably unintended overtones of respondeat superior liability. That is, it is possible that a court could read that language broadly to include vicarious liability based on control, rather than narrowly to cover only the negligent exercise of control. Not all LLP statutes contain such language.)

All statutes require that an LLP identify itself as such by including the initials "LLP" or some close approximation thereof in its partnership name. This serves to warn persons that they are dealing with a limited liability entity. Some states require a minimum amount of liability insurance for LLPs and many states require that LLPs file an annual report.

§ 62. The Business Role of the Partnership

The partnership form of doing business is widely used. The most recent figures available (U.S. Census Bureau, Statistical Abstract of the U.S. 2004–2005) show that in 2001 there were 2 million partnership returns filed, with net income of over 276 billion dollars.* (This compares to 5 million corporations with net income of $604 billion and 18 million nonfarm sole proprietorships with net income of $217 billion.)

The informality involved in the creation and operation of a partnership, together with its widespread and centuries-old use, making precedent available on many issues, may in part account for its significant role in today's business economy. Also, as noted briefly in the Introduction preceding this chapter, there are tax advantages to the partnership form. Unlike corporations, partnerships do not pay federal income tax on their business income. Instead, each partner is taxed directly on his or her share of the partnership's taxable income and also

* The Internal Revenue Service, the source of data, does not differentiate between partnerships and LLCs, so the figures represent all unincorporated business entities. However, other IRS data indicates that of those 2.0 million returns, 800,000 were for LLCs.

takes losses, including losses generated only on paper (like depreciation) directly into his or her personal return. As noted previously, this kind of taxation is often referred to as "flow through" or "pass through" in nature. In addition, the function of partnership law as a residual category for the joint ownership of business means that it will always play the important role of governing the relations of those who do not wish to engage in the planning and expense involved in choosing another form of doing business, or who are unaware of other choices.

With regard to liability protection, many professional businesses, including lawyers and accountants, use the partnership in LLP form today, instead of using the LLC or the professional corporation. If the professional business is formed as an LLC or professional corporation, there is a danger that co-owners will refer to each other as "partners," a natural form of reference and far more comfortable to use than "member" or "shareholder." It is dangerous for a co-owner in a nonpartnership to consent expressly or impliedly to being held out as a partner because it runs a risk of partner liability by estoppel (see § 65), resulting in a loss of liability protection. This danger does not exist in a true partnership that is an LLP.

§ 63. History

The partnership form of doing business has existed for over one thousand years. It originated in the

Societas, a form of general partnership well known in the law merchant of Europe in the middle ages. The Societas was recognized by the English courts from the earliest days of the common law. After a complicated interplay between law and equity, the English law of partnership became statutory in nature with the passage of an act in 1890. American partnership law also was based on the common law until UPA was promulgated by NCCUSL in 1914 and soon thereafter enjoyed widespread enactment by the states.

§ 64. Litigation over Partnership Status

The law of partnership contains ample evidence of frequent battles over partnership status, with a large share of the litigation brought by creditors seeking additional pockets for payment of outstanding debts of a firm. Section 7 of UPA sets forth rules for addressing this issue, including language that the "receipt by a person of a share in the profits of a business is prima facie evidence that he is a partner in the business." It then lists five situations in which "no such inference shall be drawn." These include the receipt of profits as wages for an employee, as rent to a landlord, or as interest on a loan. RUPA restates essentially the same test in its § 202, adding language declaring that shared appreciation mortgages and other equity participation arrangements do not convert lending arrangements into partnerships.

Martin v. Peyton (N.Y.1927), is a famous and respected case in the law of partnership involving

litigation over partnership status in a setting where
lawyers drafted agreements that went to the edge of
liability. In *Martin* an investment banking partnership had gotten itself into serious economic trouble
through a series of bad investments. Hall, one of
the partners of the firm, had three wealthy friends
who were persuaded to make substantial sums of
money available to the partnership but who wanted
more than a mere loan with interest.

An elaborate agreement was entered into between
the partnership and the three individuals. The
agreement provided that the three individuals
would make a substantial loan to the firm, receiving
40% of the profits of the firm as interest on their
loan, and that the management of the firm would
be placed in Hall's hands. Also, the three individuals were entitled to inspect the firm books, to be
kept advised on the conduct of the business, and
consulted on important matters. They had veto
power over any business they considered injurious
or highly speculative. In addition, they were given
an option to join the firm as partners. Finally, each
partner of the firm placed his resignation in the
hands of Hall. If at any time Hall and the three
agreed, the resignation would be accepted and the
partner forced to retire.

Creditors of the firm sued the three individuals,
claiming that this combination of profits and extensive control created a partnership, not a creditor
relationship. A unanimous court decided that there
was not enough evidence to support a fair inference
that a partnership was created at the time the

agreement was entered into and there was nothing in the subsequent conduct of the parties that added to the agreement. The three were merely creditors with a very strong presence in the business. Although they had the right to veto business, they did not have the right "to initiate transactions as a partner may do." Their receipt of profits was as interest on their loan and thus did not constitute presumptive evidence of partnership status under UPA § 7(4).

Martin is significant in part because of its express distinction between affirmative and negative control by creditors. It appears to sanction creditor control by veto power and to characterize a right to initiate transactions as inherently inconsistent with creditor status, at least in ordinary situations.

§ 65. Partner Liability by Estoppel

Under what circumstances is a person who is not a partner estopped to deny nonpartner status? Of course, if a person carelessly or intentionally creates a misimpression that he is a partner, he is estopped to deny partner status with people who have changed position in reliance on it. But suppose someone else holds him out, he hears about it, and does nothing. Does he have a duty to act to dispel the belief?

The existence of an affirmative duty to take action when one is being held out as a partner without consent is doubtful under the statutory law of partnership. The language of § 16 of UPA reads in part as follows: "When a person, by words spoken or written or by conduct, represents himself, or consents to another representing him to anyone, as a partner. . . ." The word "consents" in § 16 seems to require actual consent to the holding out before partner liability by estoppel exists. This reading is reinforced by the Comment to § 16, which states, "[T]he weight of authority is to the effect that to be held as a partner he must consent to the holding and that consent is a matter of fact. The act as drafted follows this weight of authority and better reasoning." The Comment does not further explain its reasoning.

RUPA in its § 308, the counterpart to UPA § 16, also uses the word "consents" and in its Comment states that, "As under UPA, there is no duty of denial, and thus a person held out by another as a partner is not liable unless he actually consents to the representation." This language is strong and clear, but conflicting case authority exists on this issue under UPA. Some courts have ignored the statutory language and required a nonconsenting person to prevent such holding out by some action on his part even if he has played no role in the holding out. Other case authority exists that applies the language exactly as it reads.

On a separate issue, RUPA has resolved any doubts about the necessity of a creditor to prove reliance in a public holding out case. The confusion about whether creditor reliance was necessary was created by some abstruse language in UPA § 16 that, carelessly read, seemed to obviate the requirement of reliance in a public holding out. Section 308 clearly states that reliance is a necessary element for all claims under the section, a resolution that was adopted in the better opinions under UPA § 16.

§ 66. The Underlying Theory of Partnership

The law of partnership has long struggled with the underlying theory of the nature of a partnership. Two competing theories have dominated analysis for many years.

The aggregate theory. UPA is based largely on the aggregate theory, known sometimes as the common law theory. That theory views a partnership as an aggregate of persons acting with a common purpose, sharing profits and losses, and holding partnership assets in joint ownership. It follows from this approach that a partnership is in existence only as long as its exact aggregate of partners exists. If a new partner joins, or a partner dies or resigns, the partnership is dissolved. Although this makes doing business in partnership form seem tenuous, the appearance is more frightening than the reality. Dissolution of the *partnership* does not mean termination of the *business*. Termination of the business does not necessarily (or even usually) follow from dissolution of the partnership, as developed below.

If, following dissolution, the remaining partners continue the business in partnership form, they do so in a different partnership than the former partnership because the cast of persons is different. The remaining partners may continue to operate under the prior agreement to the extent applicable. This will often happen by implication if nothing express is said. Nevertheless, as a formal matter they are a new and distinct firm.

The case of *Mazzuchelli v. Silberberg* (N.J.1959), provides a practical example of the aggregate theory playing a determinative role in a lawsuit. In *Mazzuchelli* an employee (Mazzuchelli) of a partnership was injured by the negligent driving of a partner of the firm while on firm business. Mazzuchelli recovered in worker's compensation for his injuries, then sued the negligent partner for personal tort liability. Mazzuchelli invoked the rule in worker's compensation that allows an injured employee to sue a third party tortfeasor for damages even though the employee has recovered worker's compensation from his employer. The partner invoked the aggregate theory, arguing that he was plaintiff's employer and thus in effect had already paid plaintiff for his injuries. The court upheld this defense, noting that § 15 of UPA, which mandates personal liability of each partner for the debts of the partnership, adopts the aggregate theory.

The entity theory. RUPA is based on the entity theory, reversing the approach of UPA. RUPA § 201 states: "A partnership is an entity distinct from its partners." The comments to § 201 make it clear that at least part of the reason for shifting expressly to the entity theory is to promote contract stability.

A well-known case under UPA, *Fairway Development Co. v. Title Ins. Co.* (N.D. Ohio 1985), involved a claim under a title insurance policy that was purchased by a partnership consisting of three persons. Subsequently two of the original partners left the firm, selling their interests to the third partner and a new person. The new partnership continued the real estate business of the former partnership. An easement was discovered on a piece of partnership real estate, precipitating a claim for damages under the title insurance policy. The title company defended by saying that it wrote a policy for the first partnership, not the second, and the first partnership had dissolved. The court agreed, stating, "[T]he court holds that the terms of the title guaranty extended only to the named party guaranteed, and that [the new partnership] had no standing to sue the defendant for breach of the contract in question."

Fairway caused consternation in legal circles. Some saw *Fairway* as taking the aggregate theory too far, creating doubts about the enforceability of executory contracts whenever a partnership dissolves. In general, this fear is exaggerated. Dissolution does not in itself destroy executory contracts. Destruction of an executory contract is very rare and depends on the terms and subject matter of the contract. Even guaranty contracts, which courts tend to construe strictly, are enforced despite dissolution "if the business risks remain substantially unchanged and this was the parties' apparent intent." Bromberg & Ribstein on Partnership 7:150.

Nevertheless, because of this fear *Fairway* apparently added substantially to the impetus to adopt

RUPA with its entity theory, reducing the occasions when dissolution will occur (see Chapter 13). As the Comment to RUPA § 201 states, "Under RUPA, there is no 'new' partnership just because of membership changes. This will avoid the result in cases such as *Fairway Development*." (RUPA still recognizes automatic dissolution for a partnership at will when a partner leaves if the partners have not agreed otherwise, however (see Chapter 13), which should qualify this statement.)

§ 67. The Aggregate Theory and the Property Rights of a Partner

UPA. There is a substantial conceptual difference between UPA and RUPA with regard to the property rights of partners. The treatment in UPA of the property rights of partners is subtle and complex, in large part due to conflicting goals. One goal of those drafting UPA was to stay as consistent as possible with the aggregate theory. Another goal was to resolve the confusion at common law (stemming largely from the aggregate theory) concerning the rights of partners in partnership property.

Partners at common law were treated as joint owners of partnership property—tenants in common of real property and joint tenants with right of survivorship (for purposes of winding up) of personal property. One consequence of this was that creditors of individual partners were able to execute against partnership property in satisfaction of personal judgments, disrupting the partnership business. Courts of equity intervened and established a right of the other partners to apply partnership property to partnership obligations, but property rights were not clearly defined and varied in theory and application from state to state. The desire to clear up confusion regarding property rights was a major impetus for uniform legislation, contributing to the promulgation of UPA.

In its § 24, UPA defines the property rights of a partner as follows: "The property rights of a partner are (1) his rights in specific partnership property, (2) his interest in the partnership, and (3) his right to participate in the management." (It might seem odd to classify a partner's right to participate in management as a property right. Apparently those drafting UPA used this as a shorthand way to gather in one spot a description of the complete rights of a partner, making convenient the act of identifying and separating the economic interest of a partner for purposes of transfer and assignment (see § 84 of this book)).

With regard to the nature of a partner's right in specific partnership property, UPA in its §§ 24(1) and 25 gives a nod to the aggregate theory by *formally* maintaining the ownership of a partner in specific partnership property but then strips away almost all of the customary rights of ownership. This is accomplished by creating a "tenancy in partnership" in § 25(1) ("A partner is co-owner with his partners of specific partnership property holding as a tenant in partnership"), but defining the incidents of this tenancy in § 25(2) to include only a right to possess partnership property for partnership purposes. Section 25(2)(a) states that a partner "has an equal right with his partners to possess specific partnership property for partnership purposes; but he has no right to possess such property for any other purpose without the consent of his partners."

UPA § 25(2)(b) states: "A partner's right in specific partnership property is not assignable except in connection with the assignment of rights of all the partners in the same property," and in § 25(2)(c): "A partner's right in specific partnership property is not subject to attachment or execution, except on a claim against the partnership." Only partnership creditors can attach partnership property. On dissolution partnership creditors have priority over partnership property. UPA § 40(h).

This statutory scheme, while complex, has served its function of preventing disruption of the partnership business. It also facilitates loans and other credit to the partnership.

RUPA. RUPA has a far less elaborate scheme. It jettisons the tenancy in partnership concept by its adoption of the entity theory. It states simply in § 203, "Property acquired by a partnership is property of the partnership and not of the partners individually." This makes unnecessary the elaboration of property rights found in UPA § 25.

§ 68. When is Property Partnership Property?

It is not always an easy matter to separate partnership property from the individual property of partners, especially in the small, informally run firm. UPA § 8(2) creates a presumption to address one aspect of the confused ownership cases, stating, "Unless the contrary intention appears, property acquired with partnership funds is partnership property." This helps, but it is not always easy to identify the source of funds in some small firms. See *Quinn v. Leidinger* (N.J.Ch.1930)("The section [8(2)] is perhaps not controlling since it is undisputed that these partners were in the habit of indiscriminately paying individual obligations with partnership funds.").

A frequent subject of confusion arises when it is unclear whether a partner has contributed ownership of certain property to the partnership or merely the use of the property. Ultimately, the intention of the parties controls but sometimes the intent is not clearly expressed. For example, suppose Pam, a partner, transfers 1000 shares of stock of a growth company to her partnership. The terms of her transfer allow the firm to pledge the stock as collateral for loans to the firm. The shares are put in the partnership name in order to facilitate their use as collateral. Pam later decides to leave the firm with the consent of her fellow partners. The stock has sharply increased in value since her transfer of it to the firm. Who is entitled to that increase, Pam or the firm? If the transfer was a contribution of ownership of the stock to the firm, then the firm enjoys the increase in value. If it was merely of the use of the stock, Pam gets the shares back and she enjoys the increased value.

The following language may prove helpful in dealing with confused ownership cases when the statutes do not provide specific guidance: "When the intention of the partners to convert [individually owned property] into firm property is inferred from circumstances, the circumstances must be such as do not admit of any other equally reasonable and satisfactory explanation." *Robinson Bank v. Miller* (Ill.1894). Also, other guidelines, all rebuttable, include the inferences that ownership follows title, that the use or possession of property is a sign of ownership, that the way an item is carried on the partnership books is an important indication of ownership, whether the item is depreciated on the partnership's tax return, and so forth.

With regard to Pam and the stock, probably a court would characterize the transaction as a mere loan despite the fact that the stock was transferred to the firm name. The terms of Pam's transfer were quite limited, providing only for the use of the stock as collateral for loans. Thus, the circumstances do admit of another "equally reasonable and satisfactory explanation," to the one that the firm had the mere use of the stock. The inference would be different if the firm had the right to sell the stock and use the proceeds for business purposes. Of course, the expectations of third persons arising from title being in the firm name would be protected.

RUPA takes fundamentally the same approach as UPA but provides more detail. Among other things, in its § 204 it establishes two presumptions. One presumption restates the UPA presumption that property purchased with partnership funds is partnership property, even if not acquired in the partnership name. The other presumption states that property acquired in the name of one or more of the partners without an indication of the person's status as partner and without use of partnership funds is presumed to be separate property, even if used for partnership purposes.

§ 69. Real Property

The common law had considerable difficulty with title to real estate owned by a partnership. Because of the aggregate status of a partnership, it was not itself a legal "person" and thus could not hold title to real property. Instead, title had to be in the name of a partner or partners. If title was not so held, only equitable title would pass to the firm. If, for example, a partnership was named "Laundry Supply Co." and real estate was conveyed to it in that name, only equitable title would pass, rendering the partnership vulnerable to the claims of a bona fide purchaser.

As a result, conveyances usually were made to all the partners as individuals. This raised problems not only with conflicting claims of individual versus firm creditors, but also when the membership of the firm changed during the period of ownership of the property.

This problem was addressed in UPA in §§ 8 and 10, providing that a partnership could acquire title to real property and prescribing detailed standards for conveyances from the partnership, depending on how title was taken by the firm. For example, if title was taken in the partnership name, it must be transferred out in the partnership name in order to pass legal title. If title was taken in the name of all of the partners, it must be conveyed out in the same way in order to pass legal title. In this respect UPA treats a partnership as an entity, a sensible solution to a difficult problem.

RUPA § 302 is the counterpart to UPA § 10. It provides detailed rules for the transfer and recovery of property, expanding upon the rules in UPA. As part of its effort to simplify the transfer of real property from a partnership, RUPA created in its § 303 an option for a partnership of filing and recording a statement of authority limiting or specifying the authority of partners to transfer real property held in the name of the firm.

CHAPTER 12

THE OPERATION OF
A PARTNERSHIP

This chapter will focus on the ongoing operation of a partnership. In some instances there will be an overlap with Chapter 11 because formation and operation issues sometimes are intertwined. This is also true with regard to issues of dissolution and termination discussed in Chapter 13. Nevertheless, many of the issues involved in the ongoing operation of a partnership are distinctive and make up a large part of partnership law.

§ 70. Contractual Powers of Partners

Partners are general agents of their partnership. See UPA § 9(1)("Every partner is an agent of the partnership for the purpose of its business"). Also, § 18(e) of UPA states that, unless otherwise agreed, "All partners have equal rights in the management and conduct of the partnership business." These provisions relate to the actual and apparent authority of partners to transact partnership business. RUPA adopts the same concepts in virtually identical language in its §§ 301 and 401(f). Thus the discussion of authority, apparent authority, inherent agency power, and estoppel set forth in §§ 35–40 of this book is fully applicable to the actions of partners as well as to employees of the partnership.

Actual authority. A partner is actually authorized to act with the express or implied consent of his or her fellow partners. The test for determining the existence and scope of actual authority is similar to that in ordinary agency law (see §§ 36–37 of this book): was the acting partner reasonable in assuming that he was authorized to act? This expectation must be based on the manifestations of one's fellow partners. As in agency, much of authority is implied, based on a reasonable interpretation of the language of the partnership agreement, if any, on the customary way the business is run, on prior authorizations, ratification of similar acts, acquiescence in the assumption of authority, and other manifestations raising reasonable expectations in the mind of the acting partner.

An example of implied actual authority is provided by *Elle v. Babbitt* (Or. 1971). In this case a partnership of 19 partners owned two tube mills for making welded steel pipe. It leased the mills to a corporation in the steel business. One partner (John Beall) conducted the business of the partnership. No meetings were called nor were the other partners consulted on decisions made in the ordinary course of business. One day Beall agreed with the lessee to a sharp cut in the income the partnership would receive from a particular job in order that the lessee could make a low bid for the job. When the other partners heard of Beall's action they complained and eventually filed a law suit on this and other issues. The complaint of the other partners was that they were deprived of their right to participate equally in the management of the partnership business (UPA § 18(e)) and thus that Beall's act was unauthorized. The court quoted the following testimony from the trial below:

Q: In other words, all the partners did, the nineteen partners during this period of time [7 years] were to put up the money initially for their original investment and receive the profits each year, is that right?

A: It sounds a little ridiculous but [those are] the facts.

In rejecting plaintiff's claim, the court noted that, "None of the partners ever objected to this manner of conducting the partnership business; John Beall became, by tacit agreement among all the partners, the managing partner with authority to conduct the ordinary business of the partnership. . . . The decision was clearly part of the ongoing management of the partnership's business [and thus was actually authorized]."

When partners disagree. One issue relating to authority and the management of a partnership concerns disagreement among the partners on a particular course of action. UPA § 18(h) is a default provision addressing this issue. It states: "Any difference arising as to ordinary matters connected with the partnership business may be decided by a majority of the partners; but no act in contravention of any agreement between the partners may be done rightfully without the consent of all the partners."

Section § 18(h) could be read to require a partner who receives an objection from *any* other partner to a planned course of action, even action that has been routinely authorized for years, to obtain a majority vote of all partners before proceeding with the routine action. On the other hand, the language could be interpreted to require the objecting partner to carry the burden of calling a meeting and obtaining a majority vote before the routine action becomes unauthorized. This latter reading seems more sensible, but a cautious lawyer would worry about the literal language of § 18(h) and probably advise the acting partner to make some phone calls to other partners before proceeding. As noted, § 18(h) is a default rule and can be altered by agreement among the partners. RUPA § 401(j) is the counterpart to 18(h) and contains identical wording to the clause being addressed except that it substitutes "*A* difference" for "*Any* difference."

The language of § 18(h) leaves open the issue of what vote is required for extraordinary matters that have not been addressed in the partnership agreement. For example, assume that a majority of partners in the business of farming want to develop part of the farm as a residential subdivision, but one or more partners object. Nothing is said in the partnership agreement about this issue (or there is no partnership agreement). Common sense suggests that unanimity should be required because of the change in the nature of the business. Courts have read a gloss onto § 18(h) requiring unanimity in this circumstance. RUPA § 401(j) expressly fills the gap by adding the words "an act outside the ordinary course of business of the partnership" to the clause requiring unanimity among partners.

Deadlock. Deadlock occurs when a partnership contains an even number of partners and they split evenly on a matter. Courts tend to address this by inquiring whether the matter at issue involves a change in the business or a mere continuation of an already established way of doing business. See *Summers v. Dooley* (Idaho 1971), holding that the decision of one of two partners to hire an employee, something the firm had never done before, was not authorized. The court quoted language from a treatise stating, "if the partners are equally divided, those who forbid a change must have their way."

In *National Biscuit Co. v. Stroud* (N.C.1959), on the other hand, one partner of a two person partnership in the grocery business could not stop routine deliveries by a major supplier of bread to the firm when his fellow partner objected. The court quoted the following language:

In cases of an even division of the partners as to whether or not an act within the scope of the business should be done ... it seems that logically no restriction can be placed upon the power to act. The partnership being a going concern, activities within the scope of the business should not be limited, save by the expressed will of the majority deciding a disputed question; half of the members are not a majority.

The only option available to the dissenting partner in this situation is dissolution (see Chapter 13). While drastic, dissolution seems appropriate because the dissenting partner impliedly agreed upon joining the business to be bound by decisions made in the ordinary course of the business.

Unless agreed otherwise, all partners, including dormant or silent partners, have equal rights in the management and conduct of the business under UPA § 18(e) and RUPA § 401(f). Thus the fact that partners in a general partnership are sometimes spoken of as "general partners" has little practical utility in that context. The phrase "general partner" has considerable utility in limited partnerships, however, as developed in §§ 97–98 of this book.

Apparent authority. Section 9(1) of UPA states, "Every partner is an agent of the partnership for the purpose of its business, and the act of any partner ... for apparently carrying on in the usual way the business of the partnership of which he is a member binds the partnership ... unless [he is unauthorized and] the person with whom he is dealing has knowledge of the fact that he has no such authority." Courts have construed this language as adopting the traditional law of apparent authority (see § 38 of this book), which includes the requirement of a manifestation from the partnership to the other party.

The creation of apparent authority by power of position plays a significant role in partnership law. Partners are by force of statute general agents of the partnership and thus are in a power of position simply by their status as partners. Of course, exactly what powers of apparent authority a particular partner has depends on the nature of the business and the way it customarily is conducted. At one time the distinction between trading and nontrading partnerships played a major role when courts were faced with the issue whether a partner could bind the partnership to a negotiable note or other borrowing of funds. A trading partnership was one that, by the nature of its business, continually borrowed funds. Examples are the construction and retail businesses, whose inventory constantly needs replenishing. Nontrading partnerships included professional businesses, like doctors and lawyers. Today courts tend to use those terms less frequently and instead refer to the general standard of apparent authority set forth in the acts.

One issue that has arisen under UPA § 9(1) is whether the phrase "apparently carrying on" refers just to the business of the particular partnership or does it include the way other firms in the same business and locality carry on their trade. Courts have split on this, with the leading authority adopting the broader view. The broader view seems to reflect more fairly the expectations of persons dealing with a partnership. One would expect warning if the particular business one was dealing with operated in a manner different from other similar businesses. RUPA § 301 expressly adopts the broader view of apparent authority. (As an aside, it is useful to note that if an act is actually authorized by the other partners, a partner can bind the firm whether or not the act involves carrying on the business in the usual way. See UPA § 9(2) and RUPA § 301(2).)

RUPA in its § 301(1) takes an unusual and controversial step away from one feature of the traditional law of apparent authority, the requirement of a duty of inquiry by the other party under suspicious circumstances. Unlike UPA § 9(1), which states that persons who have "knowledge" that a partner is unauthorized cannot base a claim on apparent authority, the language of § 301(1) states if the person "knew or received a notification" in place of "knowledge." The word "knowledge" is defined in UPA to include not only actual knowledge of a fact but also "knowledge of such other facts as in the circumstances shows bad faith." Courts have interpreted this language to mean that a person whose expectation is not reasonable cannot base a claim on apparent authority, which rests on the objective theory of contracts and thus protects only reasonable expectations. See § 38 of this book. Another way of expressing this is that a person has a duty to inquire when circumstances appear suspicious.

RUPA § 301(1) rejects the duty of inquiry by confining "knew" to mean actual knowledge of a fact and "notification" to mean when one takes steps reasonably required to inform another of a fact. The language of § 301(1) thus does not take the reasonableness of the other person's expectation into account. This is made clear in the Comments to the section, which state: "Thus, RUPA does not expose persons dealing with a partner to the greater risk of being bound by a restriction based on their purported reason to know of the partner's lack of authority from all the facts they did know."

This is an odd result. It departs from the objective theory underlying apparent authority for no particular reason. Also, a person who has reason to know that a partner is acting in an unauthorized manner is almost certainly the cheapest cost avoider in that circumstance. That is, it is cheaper for the person to inquire into suspicious circumstances surrounding a particular transaction than it is for partners to engage in widespread surveillance of each other's activities in order to reduce the "agency costs" of misbehavior by fellow partners. Usually the other partners would not even know the transaction at issue was being undertaken by the unauthorized partner.

Statements of authority. RUPA has added a significant feature to the law of authority of partners by providing in § 303 for the centralized filing by a partnership of a statement of authority. The comment to § 303 states that, "Since § 301 confers authority on all partners to act for the partnership in ordinary matters, the real import [of a statement of authority] is to grant extraordinary authority, or to limit the ordinary authority, of some or all of the partners."

A filed *grant* of authority under RUPA § 303 is conclusive in favor of a person who gives value without knowledge to the contrary, unless it is limited by another filed statement (§ 303(d)(1)). A filed *limitation* of authority does not operate as notice to third persons, however (§ 303(f)), unless it relates to real property and a certified copy of the filed statement is *recorded* in the office for recording transfers of that real property (§ 303(e)). In this instance, under § 303(e), a third party is held to constructive notice of a limitation on authority. (RUPA provides for constructive notice in two other situations: 90 days after a statement of dissociation is filed (§ 704) and 90 days after the filing of a statement of dissolution (§ 805), cutting off lingering apparent authority in both instances, as noted in Chapter 13).

Apparent authority to receive notification. The above text dealt briefly with notice, knowledge, and notification, but not in the context of attribution of notice to a partnership. In general, the partnership rules of attribution follow closely the common law agency rules relating to imputed knowledge of and notification to an agent (see §§ 55–56 of this book), which is appropriate because partners are general agents of the partnership. Thus, partners have broad apparent authority to receive a notification. See UPA § 12 (dealing with notice and notification) and RUPA § 102 (defining in detail the concepts of knowledge and notice and stating as follows in its subsection (f): "A partner's knowledge, notice, or receipt of a notification of a fact relating to the partnership is effective immediately as knowledge by, notice to, or receipt of a notification by the partnership, except in the case of a fraud on the partnership committed by or with the consent of that partner").

§ 71. Tort Liability for the Wrongs of Partners

UPA § 13 (partnership bound by "any wrongful act or omission of any partner acting in the ordinary course of the business of the partnership"), § 14 (partnership bound by partner's breach of trust) and § 15 (partners are jointly and severally liable for everything charged to the partnership under §§ 13 and 14) make it clear that the partnership and individual partners are vicariously liable for the wrongs committed by partners acting within the scope of the business. RUPA establishes the same standards in its §§ 305 and 306. (As noted in § 61 of this book, these rules change if a partnership files a statement of qualification to be an LLP.)

There is no control over the physical conduct of partners in the typical partnership, but the commercial nature of a partnership historically has substituted a broader standard for vicarious liability in this context. Vicarious liability for the torts of employees of a partnership is like that of any other employer, of course.

The "ordinary course of the business" language in UPA § 13 is interpreted in a manner similar to the interpretation of "scope of employment" (see § 25 of this book). See, e.g., *Wheeler v. Green* (Or. 1979), in which a partner was held not liable for defamatory statements made by his fellow partner at a dinner party. The statements were made about Green, a trainer who worked for the partnership. The court held that there "was no basis for finding that this kind of dinner conversation was within the ordinary course" of the partnership business.

The Co-principal Doctrine. UPA § 13 states that a partnership is liable for the wrongful acts of partners to any person "not being a partner in the partnership." That language invokes the co-principal doctrine (see § 33 of this book). Although the wrongdoer remains personally liable to the injured party, under this doctrine there is no organizational vicarious liability under UPA when the injured party is a partner.

Under some circumstances an injured partner can establish a case for liability against his firm on other grounds, including the separate transaction concept. *Farney v. Hauser* (Kan.1921) is a classic case invoking this limitation on the co-principal doctrine. In *Farnay* a partner in a five person partnership that owned a grain elevator placed 10,-000 bushels of his own wheat in the elevator to be stored, cleaned, and loaded on railway cars. The wheat was misappropriated by Hagenmaster, the employee-manager of the elevator.

Plaintiff sued the partnership for his loss and was confronted with the co-principal doctrine as a defense. His fellow partners argued that Hagenmaster was the agent of plaintiff as well the other partners and the partnership. The court rejected this, stating: "Such a view fails to take note of plaintiff's additional relationship to the partnership, that of customer as well as partner. For the torts of Hagenmaster, as for all the losses of the firm, the plaintiff, like all the other partners, must bear his proportionate share; but as a customer of the partnership he is entitled to his due just as any outsider patronizing the firm would be."

RUPA deletes the language "not being a partner in the partnership" in its § 305(a), which is the counterpart to § 13 of UPA. Although the Comments to § 305 do not clearly explain that decision, perhaps it is because RUPA adopts the entity theory. Under the entity theory the partnership is the principal and partners are mere agents of the firm, at least for these purposes, which would make the co-principal doctrine inapplicable to injury done to partners.

Fraud. A particularly vexing and recurring problem of fraud involves misconduct outside of the practice of law by a lawyer in a partnership. For example, assume that a lawyer encourages a client of the firm to transfer funds to her as a partner of the firm, ostensibly for investments that will purportedly be safe and produce a high income. Acting as an investment adviser and handling funds for investment is outside of the practice of law, but the naïve client, impressed by the trappings of office and the sophistication of the lawyer, transfers funds to her, which are then misappropriated. The client sues the partners of the lawyer. Are they liable?

Courts split on this issue. Finding for the plaintiff, the court in *Cook v. Brundidge, Fountain, Elliott & Churchill* (Tex.1976), stated, "There is no claim ... that the law firm gave notice to [plaintiff client] that ... any act of Lyon [defrauding partner, who took plaintiff's money ostensibly for investment] for his individual profit, or in which he had a personal interest, would be outside his authority as a member of the partnership." Most authorities would describe this as an unusual application of apparent authority because it requires giving notice to clients that personal acts for individual profit are outside of a partner's authority. Apparent authority usually consists of a manifestation by the firm of the acts that a partner *is* authorized to do, created in this instance by placing the lawyer in the position of being a partner in a law firm, not notice of the acts that a partner is *not* authorized to do.

A contrary approach is contained in *Sheinkopf v. Stone* (1st Cir.1991). The court stated:

At bottom, [plaintiff's] argument rests on Saltiel's [defrauding partner] use of his office, secretary, and stationery in dealing with [plaintiff] to make out a jury question on apparent authority. But those few items cannot carry so much freight. ('Trappings of office, e.g., office and furnishings, private secretary, do not without other evidence provide a basis for finding apparent authority.') There is no evidence that these amenities were provided to Saltiel for anything other than the practice of law. On this record, [plaintiff] could not reasonably have believed, based on the words and deeds of [the law firm], that Saltiel was acting as its agent in respect to the investment.

§ 72. The Nature of a Partner's Liability

UPA § 15 in effect distinguishes between contract and tort liability when describing the nature of a partner's liability for partnership obligations. It prescribes joint liability for contractual obligations and joint and several liability for torts.

The distinction between joint and joint and several obligations is only procedural in nature. In both situations each person is liable for the whole amount, but in joint obligations the obligors are entitled to have all obligors joined in the suit by the creditor unless jurisdiction cannot be obtained over some joint obligors. In joint and several obligations no such privilege to demand joinder exists. Although the difference between the two kinds of liability does not appear to amount to much, it can cause inconvenience and expense. As a result, some states have amended UPA to declare all partnership obligations to be joint and several.

RUPA § 306(a) characterizes all obligations of a partnership as joint and several. This rule simplifies the process of enforcing the liability of individual partners, although as a practical matter the availability of the LLP in all 50 states makes the issue of personal liability less significant today for partners who have taken steps to protect themselves.

§ 73. Rights and Duties Among Partners

The nature and extent of fiduciary duties among partners will be developed at this juncture, where it fits naturally into a discussion of the partnership relationship at the operational stage. In some circumstances fiduciary duties apply to the formation and termination stages as well. These materials will specifically note when the issue of fiduciary duties applies to those stages.

§ 74. The Fiduciary Duties of Partners

Partners are agents. As noted earlier, § 9(1) of UPA states that, "Every partner is an agent of the partnership for the purpose of its business...." RUPA § 301(1) contains virtually the same language. Among other things, this statutory declaration of agency status establishes a fiduciary relationship among partners. The partnership relationship is a special kind of agency relationship, however, as developed below.

A frequently quoted statement setting forth in general terms the limitations set by fiduciary duties on a partner's conduct is contained in the following excerpt from a United States Supreme Court case, *Latta v. Kilbourn* (S.Ct.1893) (a few extraneous words have been deleted):

[A] partner cannot, directly or indirectly, use partnership assets for his own benefit; he cannot, in conducting the business of a partnership, take any profit clandestinely for himself; he cannot carry on another business in competition with that of the firm, thereby depriving it of the benefit of his time, skill, and fidelity, without being accountable to his copartners for any profit that may accrue to him therefrom; he cannot be permitted to secure for himself that which it is his duty to obtain, if at all, for the firm of which he is a member; nor may he avail himself of knowledge or information which may be properly regarded as the property of the partnership, in the sense that it is available or useful to the firm for any purpose within the scope of the partnership business.

UPA. UPA treats fiduciary duties briefly, leaving the full development of fiduciary duties up to the judiciary. UPA § 21 states that a partner is accountable to the partnership for "any profits derived by him without the consent of the other partners from any transaction connected with the formation, conduct, or liquidation of the partnership or from any use by him of its property." The only time the word "fiduciary" is used in UPA is in the title to § 21.

RUPA. RUPA takes a different approach from UPA with regard to the statutory treatment of fiduciary duties. All partnership fiduciary duties are defined in RUPA § 404, entitled "General Standards of Partner's Conduct." Comment 1 to § 404 states: "Section 404 is both comprehensive and exclusive." Section 404(a) declares that, "The only fiduciary duties a partner owes to the partnership and the other partners are the duty of loyalty and the duty of care." RUPA also specifies a duty to provide information in § 403, but does not characterize it as a fiduciary duty. Overall, the approach of RUPA appears to be to fully define and to limit the scope of fiduciary duties in an effort to increase the reliability of partnership agreements and to limit judicial tinkering at the margins of fiduciary concepts. In addition, as noted below (§ 75A), under RUPA § 103 the partnership agreement may significantly reduce (or, in some states, eliminate) fiduciary duties.

§ 75. The Duty of Loyalty

As noted above, in its § 21 UPA states that a partner is accountable to the partnership for "any profits derived by him without the consent of the other partners from any transaction connected with the formation, conduct, or liquidation of the partnership or from any use by him of its property." Courts have interpreted this language as prescribing a duty of loyalty. The duty of loyalty in RUPA is defined in § 404(b) as the duty to account for profits received (in language very similar to the language of § 21 of UPA), to refrain from dealing with the partnership as or on behalf of a party having an adverse interest to the partnership, and to refrain from competing with the partnership.

As noted in § 15 of this book, a fiduciary is required to be loyal to and act in the best interest of the principal, eschewing self-interest (except in so far as self-interest is advanced, as it obviously is, by doing a competent job in an honest way and receiving compensation therefor). This duty applies to partners, incorporated by statute as noted above.

As the quotation in § 74 from the *Latta* case indicates, it is a breach of loyalty to use for personal advantage information that belongs to the partnership. The *Meinhard* case (see § 15 C), involving a partner (co-venturer) who pre-empted a business opportunity by not calling a lease renewal to the attention of a fellow partner, is an example of that situation.

In one sense the fiduciary relationship of a partner is different from ordinary agency because a partner not only acts on behalf of others in an agency capacity but also has a strong personal stake in profits. As a result, a partner has the perspective of maximizing personal gain while operating in a partnership capacity. In that respect a partner is different, for example, from a trustee, who acts solely on behalf of another and has no personal gain in transactions engaged in by the trust.

This duality of function is expressly recognized in RUPA § 404(e), stating that, "A partner does not violate a duty or obligation under this [Act] or under the partnership agreement merely because the partner's conduct furthers the partner's own interest." Of course, this language, while realistic, does not supply answers to the many vague and conflicting situations that can arise in the course of personal and business dealings.

A.   Can Fiduciary Duties be Disclaimed?

To what extent can the scope or even existence of the duty of loyalty be resolved by agreement among the partners? In answering this question it is important to distinguish between agreements made in general terms in advance of any particular situation that may raise an issue of loyalty and agreements addressing a particular situation involving self-dealing or a conflict of interest. The latter circumstance often involves prior specific consent or subsequent ratification by fellow partners and usually raises no problems in the absence of duress or fraud.

With regard to the former situation involving an agreement made in general terms, usually at the onset of the partnership relationship, the issue raises complex questions about the nature of the partnership relationship. Because the partnership relationship is contractually based, one would assume that the parties can frame their contract and define their relationship in whatever terms they wish, as long as there is no fraud, duress, or unconscionability.

This is true to a certain extent, but it does not state the whole picture. For one thing, courts tend to construe narrowly language making inroads into the duty of loyalty. See *Jerman v. O'Leary* (Ariz. App.1985), construing language in a limited partnership agreement that allowed the general partner to purchase partnership property for itself "upon terms which the General Partner shall determine in its sole discretion." The court did not construe the language "in its sole discretion" literally. Instead, it approved a finding by the trial court that the general partner had not acted in good faith in paying a price below the fair market value of the property, granting damages to the limited partners, including punitive damages.

Also, courts respond differently to language dispensing with customary fiduciary duties. Some courts are quite willing to recognize the agreement made by the partners. The partnership agreement at issue in *Singer v. Singer* (Okl.App.1981) specified that "any partner will be free to deal on his or her own account to the same extent and with the same force and effect as if he or she were not and never had been members of this partnership." In *Singer* two partners purchased for themselves some property that they knew the partnership was considering buying, a flagrant breach of the duty of loyalty. The court refused to find the two partners liable to the partnership, holding in effect that the agreement had contracted away the duty of loyalty. The court stated that, "Absent fraud, illegality or overreaching in the *procurement* of written contract, parties rights are fixed by the contract."

Other courts refuse to recognize full freedom of contract with regard to fiduciary duties. See *Appletree Square I Limited Partnership v. Investmark, Inc.* (Minn.App.1993)(quoting language stating that, "While partners are free to vary many aspects of their relationship, . . . they are not free to destroy its fiduciary character.").

In a sense, the dispute on this issue defines the essence of the partnership relationship: is it simply a contractual relationship, admittedly a fluid and complex one, or is it something more than that, involving inherent duties that cannot be contracted away no matter how fair and open the contracting process is? This issue is not addressed in UPA. RUPA expressly addresses it in § 103, which lists ten matters that are not waivable by partnership agreement. These matters include the fiduciary duties of loyalty and care prescribed in § 404(b) and (c) and the duty of good faith and fair dealing prescribed in § 404(d). Section 103 provides that these duties may be modified by agreement if the modifications are not manifestly unreasonable, but they cannot be waived entirely. Those provisions of § 103 have generated a considerable amount of scholarly controversy.

As controversial as § 103 has proven to be, however, recent legislation in Delaware and elsewhere on the issue of fiduciary duties is likely to generate even more discussion. Delaware recently amended its partnership and LLC laws to liberalize further the ability of the owners of unincorporated business entities to contract out of fiduciary duties. For instance, § 15–103(f) of Delaware's general partnership law provides:

A partnership agreement may provide for the limitation or elimination of any and all liabilities for breach of contract and breach of duties (including fiduciary duties) of a partner or other person to a partnership or to another partner or to another person that is a party to or is otherwise bound by a partnership agreement; provided, that a partnership agreement may not limit or eliminate liability for any act or omission that constitutes a bad faith violation of the implied contractual covenant of good faith and fair dealing.

One obvious question raised by this provision is the extent to which courts will rely on the covenant of good faith and fair dealing to police what might otherwise be violations of fiduciary duties that have been disclaimed by contract. One might look for some guidance to the recent Delaware litigation challenging the actions of the board of directors of the Walt Disney Company in connection with the retention and termination of Michael Ovitz, who was hired to be the president of the company. The articles of incorporation of the company exempted the directors from personal liability for breaches of the duty of care, which seemed to be the essence of the complaint against the directors. Nevertheless, the Delaware court allowed a damages action against the directors to proceed on the basis that the complaint stated a claim that the directors breached their obligation to act in good faith. *In re Walt Disney Co. Derivative Litigation* (Del. Ch. 2003).

A second question raised by these statutory provisions is whether the courts will construe contractual provisions that disclaim fiduciary duties narrowly. This seems to be the case from recently reported cases. See, for instance, *Gelfman v. Weeden Investors, L.P.* (Del. Ch. 2004), where the good faith standard and a narrow construction of a partnership provision combined to thwart the general partner's actions.

B. Leaving the Business

A frequent source of friction among partners arises when a partner decides to leave the business. Two issues immediately arise: what steps can the partner take prior to severing the relationship in order to prepare ahead of time for setting up his own business? And what limits are there on competition with former partners once one has left a partnership? This latter issue deals with post-dissociation or dissolution matters and will be covered in detail in the next chapter. In general, subject to agreement, former partners are free to compete for business, including business with clients of the firm, after leaving the firm if the competition is fair, meaning in large part that it does not involve use of confidential information and trade secrets.

The former issue relates directly to the ongoing operation of a partnership. There are common law restrictions on behavior prior to leaving the firm, traced to the duty of loyalty. For example, while a partner can plan ahead by arranging for a lease, printing letterhead, preparing incorporation or LLC or LLP registration forms and agreements, and so forth, he cannot while still a partner solicit customers of the firm for his business. Nor can he conspire with other partners or employees to depart en masse in a way that will materially damage the partnership business.

§ **76.** The Duty of Care

All authorities hold that partners owe each other a duty of care in the conduct of the partnership business. This duty is often described as part of the fiduciary duties of partners. For example, as noted above, RUPA states in § 404(a) that, "The only fiduciary duties a partner owes to the partnership and the other partners are the duty of loyalty and the duty of care set forth in subsections (b) and (c)."

What is the scope of the duty of care? Is a partner required to act with reasonable care or is he subject to a lesser standard of care, such as gross negligence? UPA does not contain language addressing the duty of care, leaving that up to the common law. Apparently most courts apply a standard similar to that of the business judgment rule in corporate law, which shields officers and directors from liability for mere negligence while conducting the business of the corporation. The underlying policy apparently is to encourage robust decision-making. This approach is expressly adopted by RUPA, which states in § 404(c) that, "A partner's duty of care to the partnership and the other partners in the conduct and winding up of the partnership business is limited to refraining from engaging in grossly negligent or reckless conduct, intentional misconduct, or a knowing violation of law."

Perhaps another explanation for the RUPA gross negligence standard is that most partners, if they considered the matter, would agree to share losses equally, even losses caused by the negligence of a fellow partner, because each partner is exposed to the risk of personal negligence in an actively run business. Partners can always agree to hold themselves to a higher standard of care. The mandatory rule of RUPA § 103(b)(4) prohibits only unreasonable reduction of the duty of care. As noted above, in Delaware and some other jurisdictions, the duty of care could, by agreement, be eliminated. However, a partner who acts intentionally opposed to, or in reckless disregard of, the best interest of the partnership, would likely be found to be acting in bad faith.

§ 77. The Duty of Full Disclosure

The duty of full disclosure usually is regarded as part of the duties of care and loyalty, although sometimes courts will treat full disclosure as an independent duty owed among partners. UPA § 20 mandates a duty of partners to "render on demand true and full information of all things affecting the partnership to any partner." RUPA § 403 contains similar language, except that it also expressly requires each partner and the partnership to furnish information concerning the partnership's business reasonably required for the proper exercise of a partner's rights and duties *without* demand, a result courts reached by judicial decision under UPA.

Full disclosure of all material facts is required under circumstances where a partner reasonably knows or should know that the other partners would want the information. For example, full disclosure is required whenever a partner deals with the partnership as an adverse party (such as selling a personal asset to the partnership) or is seeking ratification for action he took that involved him in a conflict of interest or that created partnership liability for something outside the normal scope of business.

The theory underlying the duty of full disclosure is that the partnership relationship is one of trust and because of this partners expect to be fully informed of matters relating to the partnership business. They do not expect to have to investigate all facts and search for flaws, keeping up one's guard, as one would expect to do with a stranger.

One area of frequent litigation involves the extent of the duty of disclosure in buyouts, when one partner is buying out the partnership interest of another or the partnership is buying out a partner. The claim of a disappointed party is that facts were not disclosed which would have affected the price. Some courts are quite tough-minded on the issue of materiality when deciding such disputes, reasoning that each partner ordinarily has full access to information that would determine the value of the interest being sold and that the parties to the buyout agreement often are sophisticated. See *Burke v. Farrell* (Utah 1982) (although selling partner did not disclose value of partnership interest, no breach of fiduciary duty where buying partner had "ample access to information about the value of his partnership interest" and had "ready access to the records of the partnership").

Perhaps the fact that the relationship between buyer and seller ordinarily is by its nature adversarial plays an unexpressed role in these decisions.

It should be emphasized, however, that many courts state that fiduciary principles apply with full force to partnership buyout transactions.

§ 78. The Duty of Good Faith and Fair Dealing

The duty of good faith and fair dealing is well implanted in the law. It applies to all contractual relationships (see § 205 of the Restatement of Contracts), most of which clearly are not fiduciary in character. Nevertheless, it is closely related to the basic fiduciary duties in partnership law. See Bromberg & Ribstein on Partnership § 6:68, stating, "The main elements of the partners' fiduciary duties are well recognized: utmost good faith, fairness, and loyalty."

Good faith is mandated in UPA only in § 31(1)(d), which deals with the expulsion of a partner pursuant to a provision in the agreement. There has been some litigation under that section that has been useful in providing some context to the vague phrase "good faith." In general, courts have held that so long as the expelled partner's interest was fairly evaluated and paid, the courts will not look into the process of the expulsion nor will they require reasons be given, unless the partnership agreement so specifies. The rationale for this is well explained in *Holman v. Coie* (Wash. App. 1974):

> We conclude that these parties contractually agreed to the very method of expulsion exercised by the defendants, i.e., a clean, quick, and expedi-

tious severance, with a clear method of accounting. It is not difficult to understand why parties to such a professional relationship would find this method desirable. . . . The foundation of a professional relationship is personal confidence and trust. Once a schism develops, its magnitude may be exaggerated rightfully or wrongfully to the point of destroying a harmonious accord. When such occurs, an expeditious severance is desirable. To imply terms [of notice, hearing, and good cause] not expressed in this partnership agreement frustrates the unambiguous language of the agreement and the result contemplated.

Most courts agree with the *Holman* approach. A limitation on the interpretation of good faith as requiring only that the expulsion "not cause a wrongful withholding of money or property legally due the expelled partner at the time he is expelled" (*Lawlis v. Kightlinger* (Ind. App. 1990)) is contained in *Winston & Strawn v. Nosal* (Ill. App. 1996). In *Winston* a partner (Nosal) in a large law firm was denied the right to inspect the firm's books and records, which he contends would have revealed self-dealing on the part of the executive committee of the partnership. The executive committee determined the share of income for each partner. Nosal claimed that it gave unjustified increases to its own members. He was expelled soon thereafter. He sued, claiming his expulsion was in bad faith. The court held that Nosal raised a triable issue of bad faith. In its opinion the court relied heavily on the denial of the right to information Nosal was entitled to under both UPA and the partnership agreement, raising an inference that Nosal was expelled solely because he persisted in invoking those rights.

RUPA in § 404(d) includes the duty of good faith and fair dealing in its list of the obligations of a partner and declares it a mandatory duty under § 103. Yet RUPA expressly refuses to characterize it as fiduciary in nature on the reasoning that it is "a contract concept, imposed on the partners because of the consensual nature of a partnership.... It is an ancillary obligation that applies whenever a partner discharges a duty or exercises a right under the partnership agreement or the Act." (Comment to § 404). It may be that it will prove difficult to draw this line in practice, and that courts and other authorities will treat all duties described in § 404 as fiduciary in nature.

§ 79. The Managing Partner

To a certain extent, a partner who manages the business bears an even greater duty of full disclosure and denial of self-interest, doubtless because his fellow partners are more dependent on him for information and place greater trust in him than in a partnership in which control over the business is shared equally. See *Meinhard v. Salmon*, described in § 15 C, stating, "The very fact that Salmon was in control with exclusive powers of direction charged him the more obviously with the duty of disclosure ... He was much more than a coadventurer. He was a managing co-adventurer. For him and for those like him, the rule of undivided loyalty is relentless and supreme."

This generalization relating to managing partners is vague and impossible to quantify. Yet it has some appeal, perhaps because it encompasses the sense that the greater the trust, the greater the duty. Perhaps in practical terms it eases somewhat the burden of proof for an aggrieved party. Also, it may broaden somewhat the duty of disclosure, as it did in *Meinhard*, where the court held in a 4–3 decision that Salmon violated a duty of disclosure (although that conclusion was not obvious in light of the limited nature of the venture between the parties).

It can be argued that this same intensification of the duty of disclosure and loyalty should apply to general partners in a limited partnership because they manage the business. As developed below (see § 98), in most limited partnerships the limited partners are passive investors and thus place considerable trust in the general partners.

§ 80. The Right to an Accounting

An accounting is a statement of receipts and disbursements that covers the period of time from the last accounting (or waiver of one) or, if there never has been one, from the beginning of the partnership to the time of the accounting. It shows all of the detailed financial transactions of the business and includes original invoices, bills, and cancelled checks, assuming they are available. A mere presentation of financial statements will not suffice. Historically, accounting typically took place at the dissolution of a partnership because that was the time when it became important to determine who owed whom after settlement of all accounts (see UPA § 43). UPA in § 22 expanded the right to an accounting to allow it whenever circumstances "render it just and reasonable." RUPA § 405 also makes accounting available during the term of the partnership as well as upon dissolution.

§ 81. Indemnity and Contribution Rights of Partners

UPA. Section 18(b) of UPA states that "the partnership must indemnify every partner in respect of payments made and personal liabilities reasonably incurred by him in the ordinary and proper conduct of its business, or for the preservation of its business or property." This partner's right is similar to the indemnity rights of agents (see § 8 of this book) and reflects the same policy ("as the profits of the business will be [the partnership's], so should be the expenses"). The right to indemnity under UPA § 18 is qualified by "reasonably incurred" and in the "proper" conduct of the business, similar to the right of an agent to indemnity described in § 8. With regard to contribution rights, if the partnership is insolvent and unable to indemnify a partner, §§ 18(a) and 40(d) of UPA state that each partner shall contribute the amount necessary to satisfy the liabilities of the firm, which would include a partner's indemnity rights, "according to his share in the profits."

Partners usually pay for partnership obligations out of partnership funds. Because of this, indemnity rights under UPA § 18 are not often utilized as a practical matter. Perhaps they are most frequently used when one partner is sued under joint and several tort liability for a partnership obligation, pays the judgment, and then seeks indemnity. Even this would be rare because under modern rules of procedure the sole defendant partner can cross-claim against his fellow partners in the same suit on the basis of his indemnity right.

A specialized indemnity right exists under UPA § 38(2), describing the rights of a wrongfully dissolving partner. Section 38(2)(b) states that the continuing partners must "indemnify him against all present or future partnership liabilities." Present liabilities doubtless would be taken into account when calculating the net value of the interest of the wrongfully dissolving partner, and it seems sensible to indemnify him against future liabilities because he will no longer be a partner, sharing control and profits. Of course, notice of dissolution also should be promptly given to the appropriate parties (see Chapter 13), reducing the risk of future liabilities.

RUPA. RUPA broadens indemnity rights in its § 401(c) by deleting the words "reasonably" and "proper." No explanation for the deletion is given in the comments to § 401, but the reasoning apparently is that most partners understand that losses caused by a partner's negligence should be shared equally, just like other losses of the firm, rather than be borne solely by the negligent partner.

§ 82. Suits Among Partners

An accounting traditionally has been required when partners sue each other over matters relating to the partnership business on the reasoning that only with an accounting can one determine who really owes what to whom. Piecemeal litigation over particular claims does not take into account an overall review of the business and may later require adjustment. Also, perhaps it is thought that if the partners could not get along well enough to settle particular matters without litigation, they would be better off dissolving (where an accounting would be automatic) rather than wasting judicial time over particularized disputes.

This limitation on suits among partners has been fairly strictly applied in most litigation under UPA. Courts early carved out exceptions, such as when only one transaction is involved that is sufficiently isolated it can be decided without a full review of partnership accounts or when the issue is predominately personal between the partners. In addition, there seems to be general relaxation of the rule today, evidenced by § 405 of RUPA, stating that, "A partner may maintain an action against the partnership or another partner for legal or equitable relief." Comment 2 to § 405 states that, "Under RUPA an accounting is not a prerequisite to the availability of the other remedies a partner may have against the partnership or the other partners." One wonders, however, how claims of mismanagement, for example, can be resolved without an overall look at the partnership affairs, since they go to the heart of the conduct of the partnership business.

§ 83. Suits by and Against a Partnership

Under the common law aggregate theory, a partnership cannot sue or be sued because it is not a "person" and only legal persons can be named as parties to litigation. With some exceptions, suits by a partnership had to be brought in the names of all partners and all partners had to be joined as defendants in litigation.

UPA does not have a provision on this matter on the reasoning that it is procedural in nature. A large number of states have passed legislation allowing suit against a partnership in its own name, with the judgment binding the joint property of all partners and the individual property of partners named and served with process.

This problem does not exist under RUPA because of the entity status of a partnership. See § 307, stating, "A partnership may sue or be sued in the name of the partnership."

§ 84. The Interest of a Partner; Transfer of the Interest

UPA. Section 24(2) of UPA defines as one of the three property rights of a partner "his interest in the partnership," which is defined in UPA § 26 as "his share of the profits and surplus." This is the only one of the three property rights that a partner can transfer on his own initiative (UPA § 27 provides for this), unless the partnership agreement prohibits its transfer. Also, this is the only partnership right that the partner's individual creditors can reach. UPA § 28.

As noted in § 67 of this book, UPA § 25(2)(b) prohibits transfer of a partner's right in specific partnership property unless all partners join in the transfer. Also, UPA § 18(g) states that, subject to agreement, "No person can become a member without the consent of all the partners." This in effect prohibits transfer of management rights. This prohibition is easy to understand in view of the risks posed by misuse of the general agency powers of a partner and the liability of each partner for the misconduct of fellow partners. Thus there is no free transferability of a partner's full ownership interest in a partnership.

As noted above, unless otherwise agreed, UPA § 27(1) permits a partner to assign "his interest" in the partnership, meaning his economic interest. The transferor remains a partner because the rest of his rights have not been transferred, but his economic incentive to work for the firm may be adversely affected by the transfer. Because of this, UPA § 31(1)(c) grants the other partners dissolution rights, even during a term partnership, when a partner has assigned his interest.

RUPA. RUPA also contemplates transfer of the economic interest of a partner. The counterpart to UPA § 26 is RUPA § 502, stating, "The only transferable interest of a partner in the partnership is the partner's share of the profits and losses of the partnership and the partner's right to receive distributions. The interest is personal property." The counterpart to UPA § 27 is RUPA § 503, providing that the interest defined in § 502 is transferable, subject to agreement. The concerns of the other partners following a transfer, other than for security purposes, of all or substantially all of a partner's economic interest are addressed in RUPA § 601(4)(ii), which grants the other partners the right to expel the transferor upon their unanimous vote.

§ 85. Claims by Creditors of the Partnership

A. Rights Against Partnership Assets

The aggregate theory of partnership, which dominated the common law, complicated the assertion of rights against partnership assets by partnership creditors. Because a partnership was not an entity, it could not be sued. Thus, in the absence of a statute authorizing suits against a partnership and execution against its assets, a creditor had to sue the individual partners and reach the partnership assets by virtue of a partner's right to have partnership assets applied to the payment of partnership debts. This right was called the partner's equity because it was first recognized in England's court of equity.

This cumbersome process could not survive. It was changed in UPA by recognizing that partnership property could be attached for a partnership debt (§ 25(2)(c)) and by declaring that a partner's right in specific partnership property is not assignable unless the rights of all partners are assigned (§ 25(2)(b)). These changes recognize that partnership creditors have the right to have partnership property applied to the payment of firm debts while still maintaining a formal gesture toward the aggregate theory. The rights of partnership creditors when the partnership sells or merges into a new partnership are covered in § 90 F of this book.

RUPA, which expressly adopts the entity theory, defines a creditor's rights more simply. It denies that individual partners are co-owners of partnership property (§ 501), it states that a partnership may be sued in the partnership name, and it declares that "Property acquired by a partnership is property of the partnership and not of the partners individually." (§ 203)

B. Rights Against the Personal Assets of Individual Partners

The personal liability of partners for the debts of a partnership is established in § 15 of UPA and § 306 of RUPA. (This assumes that a partnership has not filed a statement of qualification as an LLP. See § 61.) In the states that follow UPA, a creditor of a joint and several obligation (see § 72) can obtain a judgment against any partner it chooses and execute against the personal assets of the partner until satisfaction of the underlying claim is achieved. A partner who pays a firm obligation is entitled to indemnity under UPA § 18(b), which softens the impact of this rule. Some states insist on exhaustion of partnership assets prior to allowing creditors to resort to personal assets. This latter line of authority is even stronger when the liability is joint in nature (involving contractual obligations).

RUPA in § 307(d) has adopted the view expressed above. Subsection (d) of 307 states that a judgment creditor "may not levy execution against the assets of a partner to satisfy a judgment based on a claim against the partnership unless a judgment on the same claim has been obtained against the partnership and a writ of execution on the judgment has been returned unsatisfied in whole or in part." RUPA provides an exception allowing a court in the exercise of its equitable powers to grant permission to a creditor to first levy against personal assets. Also, a partner can agree to forego the protections of § 307(d). But the thrust of § 307 is to make partners more in the nature of guarantors than principal debtors on partnership debt, as acknowledged in the comments to § 307.

With regard to priority of creditors, § 40 of UPA mandates that partnership creditors have priority in partnership assets and individual creditors in the individual assets of partners. This is known as the "dual priorities" or "jingle" rule. It governs state insolvency and receivership proceedings. The rule for federal bankruptcy matters was changed by the Bankruptcy Reform Act of 1978, which partially repealed the dual priorities rule, making it possible for partnership creditors to share equally with individual creditors in claims against the personal assets of partners. The reasoning behind the change was that partnership creditors rely heavily on the solvency of individual partners when extending credit to a partnership. The priority of partnership creditors in partnership assets is retained in the bankruptcy act. With regard to RUPA, Comment 2 to its § 807 states, "RUPA in effect abolishes the 'dual priority' or 'jingle' rule."

§ 86.   Claims by Personal Creditors of a Partner Against the Partnership Interest of the Partner

The partnership interest of a partner sometimes can constitute a substantial part of his assets and thus be of real significance to his unpaid personal creditors. Because, as noted earlier (see § 67), § 25 of UPA protects partnership property from the claims of personal creditors, a remedy for creditors was provided under § 28 in the form of a charging order. A charging order is similar to garnishment of wages of an employee. Upon application by a judgment creditor, a court order "charges" the interest of a partner with the amount of the judgment, redirecting any future payments of profits or surplus to the judgment creditor until the judgment is paid. Thereafter the partner's rights to receive distributions from the partnership revives.

Section 28(2) provides that a creditor may foreclose on the interest of a partner. This remedy would be of interest to a creditor if it appears unlikely that distributions of income and surplus will satisfy the judgment in a reasonable period of time. Once a partner's interest is sold in a foreclosure sale, he is forever foreclosed from receiving any profits or surplus from the partnership even though, curiously, he remains a partner. Because of the drastic consequence of this remedy, courts have restricted exercise of the foreclosure right to circumstances where the creditor would not otherwise obtain payment of the debt within a reasonable time through ordinary partnership distributions.

The status of a purchaser of a partner's interest upon foreclosure is that of an assignee by operation of law. The rights of an assignee are described in UPA § 27. There is no right to demand information from the partners or to inspect the partnership books. The purchaser does not acquire managerial rights, which remain with the partner, but does acquire the right to dissolve a partnership at will under UPA § 32(2) or at the termination of the term of a term partnership. This right may encourage the other partners to purchase the interest at the foreclosure sale, or to redeem it before the sale, which they have the right to do under § 28(2).

RUPA § 504 adopts the charging order procedure. It makes only minor changes from UPA. Section 503 of RUPA describes the rights of an assignee of a partner's interest, called a "transferee," adopting the approach of UPA in all material respects.

CHAPTER 13

DISSOCIATION OF A PARTNER AND DISSOLUTION OF A PARTNERSHIP

The title of this chapter draws a distinction between dissociation of a partner and dissolution of a partnership. The concept of "dissociation" was introduced into partnership law by RUPA. It is part of the reformulation of the underlying theory of partnership law by those drafting RUPA, with the goal of stabilizing the partnership form of doing business. Dissociation does not always or even usually result in dissolution of a RUPA partnership. This is a sharp departure from the theory underlying UPA, where any change in the membership of partners results in an automatic dissolution of the partnership, as developed below.

§ 87. Dissolution Under UPA

Dissolution is defined in § 29 of UPA as "the change in the relation of the partners caused by any partner ceasing to be associated in the carrying on

... of the business," such as the withdrawal, death, or bankruptcy of a partner. This language reflects the aggregate theory. It appears to make the existence of a business operating in partnership form highly fragile and likely to be discontinued at any time by, among other events, resignation or death of a partner. In reality, however, as noted earlier, termination of the *business* need not and usually does not automatically follow from dissolution of the *partnership*.

Termination of the business is avoided if there is planning ahead of time or if there is an agreement after dissolution to continue the business, although cooperation may not be as easy to come by in the latter situation because each partner has acquired on dissolution a liquidation right to sell the business and receive a cash payout (see immediately below). With regard to planning ahead, a partnership agreement can anticipate dissolution and provide for continuing the business and evaluating and distributing the departing partner's interest in a way that is convenient to the business (by payment over a period of time, for example) and fair to the partner. Under such circumstance the departing partner's liquidation right is waived by contract. Also, § 38(2) provides a statutory right to the remaining partners to continue the business when a partner wrongfully dissolves the partnership.

Liquidation right. As noted above, one of the major consequences of dissolution is that, unless otherwise agreed, it triggers a liquidation right in each partner of the firm, with the exception of the wrongfully dissolving partner of a term partnership. Liquidation rights are established in § 38(1) of UPA and in § 807(a) of RUPA. They give each partner the right to have the partnership property applied to discharge its liabilities and the surplus reduced to cash in order to pay the net amount owing to the respective partners. In effect, this gives each partner the right to force a sale of the business, the notion being that a sale is the best means of determining the fair market value of the assets and of generating the cash needed to pay the partners the value of their interests.

It is generally assumed that the estate of a deceased partner possesses liquidation rights. Several courts have placed a judicial gloss on § 38(1), however, denying the exercise of liquidation rights by estates when it is likely to cause particular hardship to the remaining partners. The issue is less likely to arise under RUPA because death does not cause dissolution.

Several courts have qualified the liquidation right under § 38(1) in view of the equities of the case before them. For example, in *Nicholes v. Hunt* (Or.1975), Hunt, who had established a small manufacturing business and carefully built it up over the years, needed capital and formed an at will partnership with Nicholes, a wealthy individual. Thereafter the firm dissolved and Nicholes sought a judicial sale under § 38(1) in an effort to obtain ownership of the assets by outbidding Hunt at the sale. The trial court refused to grant a judicial sale, instead evaluating Nicholes's interest, giving him a judgment for that amount, and distributing the assets to Hunt. This result was affirmed on appeal. It may be that a similar result would be reached under RUPA § 807(a). Despite this unusual case, however, unless there is agreement otherwise, the liquidation right is available automatically in almost all dissolution situations and can have a powerful impact on the relations among the partners at that stage for those who have not planned ahead of time.

Causes of dissolution under UPA. The causes of dissolution are set forth in § 31 of UPA, which is divided into three parts: (1) dissolution caused without violation of the partnership agreement, such as arrival of the agreed termination date, or by the will of any partner if no term was agreed upon, or by expulsion of a partner in accordance with a power conferred by the partnership agreement; (2) dissolution in violation of the partnership agreement by express will of any partner (this underscores the point that a partner under UPA always has the *power* to terminate the partnership, even though he or she may not have the contractual *right* to do so); and (3) four circumstances in which it does not seem to make any difference what the partnership agreement provides with respect to timing and existence of an event of dissolution. These circumstances are death or bankruptcy of a partner, dissolution by decree of court under § 32, and any event that makes it unlawful to carry on the business.

Dissolution by decree of court on application by a partner includes a finding by the court of incapacity or misconduct of another partner or a finding that it is not reasonably practicable to carry on the business with a particular partner. Dissolution by court decree also is provided upon application by a purchaser of a partner's interest by assignment or at foreclosure of a charging order. The purchaser's application can be made at any time if the partnership is at will or after the termination of a term partnership.

As noted, UPA draws a distinction between rightful and wrongful dissolution. A partner rightfully can dissolve an at will partnership at any time without incurring any liability even if the dissolution causes harm to his fellow partners by, for example, forcing a judicial sale under nonadvantageous circumstances. The policy underlying this right is referred to in the Comment to § 34, stating that a partner has the "right to terminate a relationship which must necessarily depend on mutual good will and confidence."

Page v. Page (Cal.1961), a well-known case, placed a limitation of good faith defined in economic terms on the exercise of the right to dissolve a partnership at will. In *Page* one partner was claiming that the other was trying to freeze him out and appropriate the business. After years of losses, the business had just started to turn the corner and make some money. The losses had been covered by loans from the partner who sought to dissolve the firm and who thus held a substantial amount of partnership debt that he could apply against the purchase price of the business. The partner seeking to dissolve the partnership brought a declaratory judgment action to have the partnership classified at will so that he could dissolve without contractual consequences. He is the plaintiff referred to in the quotation below. The court characterized the partnership as one at will. It then addressed the issue of good faith in the following terms:

> Plaintiff has the power to dissolve the partnership by express notice to defendant. If, however, it is proved that plaintiff acted in bad faith and violated his fiduciary duties by attempting to appropriate to his own use the new prosperity of the partnership without adequate compensation to his copartner, the dissolution would be wrongful and the plaintiff would be liable as provided by § 38(2) for violation of the implied agreement not to exclude defendant wrongfully from the partnership business opportunity.

Thus, we see again (see § 78 of this book) that good faith is satisfied in the ordinary case by adequately compensating a fellow partner when purchasing his interest.

Section 38(2) addresses wrongful dissolution, as noted in the above quotation from *Page*. A common use of § 38(2) is when a partnership is for a term and one partner dissolves prior to completion of the term. The dissolution breaches the partnership agreement and undermines the reliance the other partners may have made on the capital contribution and services of the withdrawing partner during the agreed term.

UPA § 38(2) addresses this problem by allowing the remaining partners to continue the business during the term by unanimous agreement, thus taking the liquidation right away from the departing partner under this circumstance. Also, the value of the good will of the business is not considered in determining the value of the interest of the departing partner. The buyout is defined in § 38(2)(b), stating that the parties continuing the business must pay (or secure payment by bond) to any partner who has caused wrongful dissolution "the value of his interest, less any damages recoverable [for breach of the agreement] and in like manner indemnify him against all present or future partnership liabilities."

A term for a partnership can be implied as well as express. This can catch people by surprise. An illustration of this is provided by *Owen v. Cohen* (Cal. 1941). The partners in *Owen* borrowed substantial amounts of money to launch a business with the understanding that the loans would be repaid from partnership profits. The court found that the partners had impliedly promised to continue the partnership for a term reasonably required to repay the loans.

The concept of an implied term is understandable as an abstract matter. Implied in fact terms are part of all contracts and the partnership agreement is a contract. Nevertheless, many courts require clear evidence before finding an implied term for a partnership. The requirement of clear evidence is sensible because the finding of an implied term interferes with a partner's choice to leave a marginal business and invest his money elsewhere. A partner should lose that choice and be bound to a term only if he has expressly agreed to it or the facts are compelling that a commitment for a term was impliedly understood by the parties.

As one can imagine, the disadvantage of being classified as a wrongfully dissolving partner has resulted in a fair amount of litigation over the grounds for dissolution. As noted earlier, § 32 provides for judicial dissolution upon a finding that a partner has engaged in misconduct or that it is not reasonably practicable to carry on the business with a particular partner, among other grounds.

Courts are reluctant to decree dissolution based on misconduct without serious misbehavior. As stated in *Potter v. Brown* (Pa.1938), "Differences and discord should be settled by the partners themselves by the application of mutual forbearance rather than by bills in equity for dissolution. Equity is not a referee of partnership quarrels." This language does not mean a court always will ignore the cumulative effect of even petty misbehavior, however. As stated in *Owen*, "an aggregate [of separately trivial acts] can destroy all the confidence and cooperation between the partners."

§ 88. Dissociation and Dissolution Under RUPA

RUPA defines dissolution differently than UPA, reducing the circumstances under which a partnership will dissolve. It substitutes "dissociation" for many (but not all) situations that would constitute dissolution under UPA. For example, unlike UPA, if a partner dies or becomes bankrupt, the partnership is not automatically dissolved, whether it is a partnership at will or for a term. Instead, the partner is "dissociated" under RUPA § 601. The partner (or his estate) is entitled to be paid for his interest, but not by exercising a liquidation right.

The dissociating partner's buyout rights are defined in considerable detail in RUPA § 701. As stated in Comment 1 to RUPA § 603, after a partner's dissociation, "the partner's interest in the partnership must be purchased pursuant to the buyout rules in Article 7 unless there is a dissolution and winding up of the partnership business under Article 8. Thus, a partner's dissociation will always result in either a buyout of the dissociated partner's interest or a dissolution and winding up of the business."

RUPA devotes three articles to breakup of personnel in a partnership. Article 6 covers all dissociations, including voluntary withdrawal of a partner, death, expulsion, and bankruptcy. Article 7 sets the standards for the buyout of a partner, providing for indemnification, valuation standards, and time periods for settling with the partnership. Article 8 covers dissolution and winding up of the business.

The dissolution provisions of RUPA are contained in § 801. They are complex and bear careful reading. (As noted earlier, RUPA is set forth as Appendix C to this book.) It is also necessary to read §§ 601 and 602 in conjunction with § 801 in order to get a full understanding of the provisions of § 801.

The word "dissolution" in RUPA is synonymous with termination of the business, a different meaning than it is given in UPA. Dissolution occurs under § 801 of RUPA (i) when a partnership is at will and a partner gives notice of intent to withdraw, (ii) when the term of a partnership expires, (iii) during the term of a partnership if, within 90 days after a partner's dissociation by death, bankruptcy, or wrongful dissociation, at least half of the remaining partners agree to wind up the business, (iv) upon judicial dissolution based on misconduct or a finding that it is not reasonably practicable to carry on the business in conformity with the partnership agreement, (v) upon application by a transferee of a partner's transferable interest, including the purchaser at foreclosure of a charging order, and (vi) upon any event that makes it unlawful to carry on the business.

A partner under RUPA does not have the power to dissolve a term partnership. This explains the use of the term "dissociating" partner in § 602 of RUPA, which deals with wrongful departures. Section 602(b) defines wrongful dissociation to include dissociating before the expiration of the partnership term. Section 602(c) states that a wrongfully dissociating partner is responsible for damages caused by the dissociation. The forfeiture of good will under UPA is implicitly rejected in RUPA. Section 701(h) states that the wrongfully dissociating partner is not entitled to payment of his interest until the end of the term unless a court finds that an earlier payment will not cause undue harm to the firm.

There is an exception under § 602(b)(2)(i) when a partner's withdrawal from a term partnership follows within 90 days after another partner's dissociation by death or bankruptcy or wrongful dissociation. Comment 2 to § 602 states that this exception "is intended to protect a partner's reactive withdrawal from a term partnership after the premature departure of another partner, such as the partnership's rainmaker or main supplier of capital." The partner who reactively withdraws following another partner's withdrawal will be bought out under § 701 as a rightfully dissociating partner.

Section 801(1) specifies as a default rule that a partner can dissolve an at will partnership at any time by giving notice to the partnership. In this respect RUPA retains one of the fundamental features of UPA. If, however, a partner dies or becomes bankrupt in a partnership at will the partnership continues automatically.

As stated in Comment 3 to § 801 of RUPA, "Section 801 continues two basic rules that have been the law for more than 75 years. First, it continues the UPA rule than any member of an *at-will* partnership has the right to force a liquidation. Second, by negative implication, it continues the rule that the partners who wish to continue the business of a *term* partnership can not be forced to liquidate the business by a partner who leaves early." One distinction between UPA and RUPA with regard to the latter point is that UPA requires unanimity for the partners to continue a term partnership whereas RUPA specifies that the partnership automatically continues unless at least half of the partners agree to wind up, providing more stability to the term partnership.

It is important to recognize that almost all of Article 8 is default in nature (§ 103(b) declares as mandatory only the provisions requiring winding up if the business becomes unlawful, or if judicial dissolution is decreed because of misconduct or a determination that it is not practicable to carry on the business, or on application by a transferee of a partner's transferable interest under certain circumstances). Thus, the partners can agree that the departure of a partner in an at will partnership will not constitute dissolution, depriving the departing partner of a liquidation right. (A useful way to express this would be to agree that the partnership will continue until a majority of partners vote to dissolve it.) Articles 6 and 7 also are default in nature, except § 103(b) specifies that an agreement cannot vary the power of a partner to dissociate at any time under § 602(a) nor can it vary the power of a court to expel a partner under § 601(5), dealing with misconduct or material breach of the partnership agreement.

§ 89. Termination Of Authority; Notice of Dissociation and Dissolution

A. Termination of Authority

UPA. Dissolution "terminates all authority of any partner to act for the partnership" except "so far as may be necessary to wind up partnership affairs or to complete transactions begun but not then finished." UPA § 33. If dissolution is caused by the act of a partner, an unknowing fellow partner who contracts for new business thereafter can call upon her fellow partners for contribution. UPA § 34.

RUPA. RUPA §§ 804 and 806 state the same rule for dissolution as UPA § 33 but in a more oblique manner. Section 806(b) states that a partner who, with knowledge of the dissolution, incurs a partnership liability "by an act that is not appropriate for winding up the partnership business is liable to the partnership for any damage arising from the liability."

B.   Notice of Dissociation and Dissolution

UPA. Section 35 of UPA addresses, among other things, the lingering apparent authority of a partner following dissolution to bind the partnership to an act unrelated to winding up or completing unfinished business. It distinguishes between third parties who extended credit to the partnership prior to dissolution and those who merely had known of the partnership prior to dissolution. Those who extended credit are entitled to more individualized notice before lingering apparent authority is cut off. Those who merely knew of the partnership are held to notice by publication in a newspaper of general circulation in each place the partnership business was carried on.

RUPA. With regard to dissociation that does not result in dissolution, RUPA §§ 702 addresses the lingering apparent authority of the dissociated partner, setting a two-year limit on the partnership's exposure to liability unless a statement of dissociation (RUPA § 704) is filed. All persons are on constructive notice of the dissociation 90 days after a statement is filed. Section 703 states that the dissociated partner remains liable as a partner for transactions entered into by the partnership for two years after the dissociation to persons who do not have knowledge or notice of the dissociation. Again, filing a statement of dissociation can reduce this period to 90 days. The ability to file a statement and cut off liability after 90 days is an innovation in RUPA, as is the two-year cut off period even if no statement is filed.

With regard to dissolution under RUPA, § 804 is the counterpart to UPA § 35. The distinction drawn in UPA between former creditors and other persons who knew of the partnership is rejected in RUPA. See Comment to § 804: "RUPA eschews these cumbersome notice provisions in favor of the general apparent authority rule of § 301, subject to the effect of a filed or recorded statement of dissolution under § 805." As noted in the quote, RUPA provides for the filing of a statement of dissolution in § 805, triggering a 90 day cut off period. The statement can be filed by any partner who has not wrongfully dissociated. Unlike dissociation, however, there is no two year cut off period if a statement is not filed. This difference between dissociation and dissolution is not explained in the comments.

§ 90. Continuing the Business

The remaining partners can unanimously agree, expressly or by conduct, to continue the business after dissolution even if there is no prior arrangement to do so. RUPA § 802(b) expressly provides that at any time after dissolution all of the partners (except a wrongfully dissociating partner) may waive the right to have the business wound up and under that circumstance the partnership "resumes carrying on its business as if dissolution had never occurred."

Whether the business is continued by prearrangement or by agreement after dissolution, one of the most important matters is providing for the evaluation and payout of the interest of the departing partner. With regard to evaluation, § 701(b) calls for evaluation of the interest of a dissociating partner "on the date of dissociation." Section 807(a), dealing with dissolution, calls for liquidation of the business and then distribution of surplus, which would place the valuation of the interest at a later date. This difference in timing may sometimes result in dispute among partners with regard to the proper characterization of the termination of their relationship. It is best to resolve the issue of evaluation and payout by agreement ahead of time, of course. In many partnerships a buy-sell agreement plays an important role in this context, as described immediately below.

A.   The Buy–Sell Agreement

Many partnership agreements provide that in the event of the death or withdrawal of a partner the remaining partners will purchase the interest of the departing partner. The agreements often include a process for appraising property owned by the firm, a formula for evaluating accounts receivable that takes into account the length of time each receivable has been outstanding, a payout term, and so forth. Life insurance often is purchased in order to fund the buyout if dissociation or dissolution is caused by death. Such provisions often are referred to as buy-sell agreements.

The buy-sell agreement anticipates and attempts to resolve conflicts likely to arise at the time of dissociation or dissolution. Its provisions are likely to be neutral and fair to the partners for the reason that each partner is in a dual role while drafting the agreement. As stated in *Seattle–First National Bank v. Marshall* (Wash.App.1982), "[Each partner] sees himself as the continuing partner; he also sees himself as the retired or deceased partner. As a potential continuing partner, he prefers a conservative valuation of the partnership. As a possible retired or deceased partner, he favors a more liberal valuation."

B.   Continuation Clauses

Some partnership agreements attempt to avoid the difficulties posed by dissolution under UPA by including a continuation clause denying dissolution upon the retirement or death of a partner. One can understand the desire to do this (although it is not a substitute for a buy-sell agreement, payout terms, and so forth), but the enforceability of a continuation clause is doubtful under UPA, which does not state "unless otherwise agreed" in front of its dissolution provisions in §§ 29, 31, and 32. This makes a partnership vulnerable to the argument that dissolution (upon withdrawal, say) took place under the statute even if it did not under the partnership agreement, and thus the provisions of UPA and not of the agreement control. By this argument the departing partner would attempt to avoid the enforceability of a long payout term, or a non-compete clause, or other terms in the agreement that she does not like.

The argument should not succeed. It is too formalistic and ignores the agreements relating to payout and so forth. But the remaining partners make themselves vulnerable to it by denying what a statute clearly declares. Perhaps the best approach under UPA would be to draft the partnership agreement in the alternative, drafting both a continuation clause and an alternative clause specifying the consequences of dissolution if it does take place despite the continuation clause.

RUPA. The formalistic argument made above and in a number of cases would not be available under RUPA. The dissolution provisions of § 801 are mere default rules in large part, as noted above, and thus there would be no question about the validity of a continuation clause.

C.   Liability of an Incoming Partner

Sections 17 and 41(7) of UPA specify that an incoming partner is liable for the existing debts of the firm but that such liability "shall be satisfied only out of partnership property" unless there is agreement to assume all or part of the existing debts. RUPA § 306(b) is similar.

Case authority is split on the issue whether an incoming partner becomes personally liable for continuing obligations of the firm. For example, assume that an incoming partner joins during the middle of a long-term lease. UPA § 17 and RUPA § 306(b) specify that there is no personal liability for past-due payments of rent, but does the incoming partner become personally liable for rental payments due once she commences possession under the lease? Or suppose a long-term loan with installment payments is entered into prior to admission to the partnership. Does the incoming partner become personally liable for installments due after her admission to the firm?

Arguments against personal liability point to the language of the statutes. Arguments in favor of liability point to the partner's use and enjoyment of the benefits of these long-term contracts. There is authority on both sides of this question. To the extent a bare majority rule can be identified, it seems to be on the side of personal liability for benefits received under continuing obligations. (This issue would not arise if the partnership is an LLP, absent a personal assumption of liability.)

D. Liability of a Withdrawing Partner

A withdrawing partner remains liable to the creditors who extended credit at the time the partner was a member of the firm, assuming the firm was not an LLP. UPA § 36(1); RUPA § 703. A creditor can agree to release the partner. Accidental release also is possible because both UPA and RUPA utilize suretyship concepts to define the relationship between the withdrawing partner and creditors. The withdrawing partner stands in the position of surety for the obligations of the firm, assuming that she has already accounted to her fellow partners for her share of outside debts. Thus, if the creditor and the remaining partners agree to a material alteration of the original debt without the consent of the withdrawing partner, she is released. See § 36(3) and 703(d).

E. Duties of Withdrawing Partner to Former Partners

What are the duties, if any, of a partner who withdraws and takes some of the ongoing business with her or otherwise thereafter competes with her former partners? In analyzing the rights and duties of the parties, it is important to know whether the fiduciary relationship ends immediately upon dissociation or dissolution. UPA specifies in its § 21 that the fiduciary relationship among partners covers the "formation, conduct, or liquidation" of the partnership. Although a partnership can be liquidated immediately upon dissolution (see § 91A of this book), the more usual situation contemplated by

UPA includes a period of winding up, when assets are sold, debts paid, and surplus distributed to the partners. During this time fiduciary duties continue and thus a partner taking *ongoing* business without consent is accountable to the partnership for the profits lost during the period of winding up. Subject to agreement, former partners are free to compete for *new* business, however, so long as confidential information is not being misused.

RUPA specifies in § 404(b)(3) that a partner's duty of loyalty is, among other things, limited to refraining from competing with the partnership "in the conduct of partnership business before dissolution of the partnership." Thus "a partner is free to compete immediately upon an event of dissolution, unless the partnership agreement provides otherwise." Comment 2 to § 404. The same standard applies to dissociation from a partnership: see § 603(b)(2).

This rule does not provide an easy answer to the issue posed above, however, because § 404(b)(1) and (2) provide that a partner is required to account for profits derived in the conduct and winding up of the partnership business and to refrain from dealing with the partnership in the conduct or winding up of the partnership business as or on behalf of an adverse party. It appears, therefore, that RUPA sees open competition during the winding up period as limited to new business only. Although the statutory scheme in RUPA is more complex, the RUPA and UPA standards turn out to be very similar in application.

F. Creditors' Claims

It is important to distinguish between existing creditors of a partnership at the time of dissociation or dissolution and new creditors of the business continued thereafter in partnership form.

(i) New Creditors

With regard to new creditors (and existing creditors engaging in new business with the partnership), the only matter of significance is notice of dissociation or dissolution. See § 89B, addressing this issue.

(ii) Existing Creditors

UPA. The critical concern for existing creditors is the right to make claims against the assets of the new partnership that is continuing the business. The rule at common law was that creditors of the former partnership did not have claims against the new partnership absent an assumption of the debts. Their claims were against the former partners and the equitable right of the partners to have the assets existing at the time of dissolution applied to pay the obligations of the partnership. This placed the creditors at a disadvantage to the extent that the new firm became indebted to new creditors.

UPA addresses this concern in its §§ 17 and 41, providing for continuity of obligation to creditors when there is some continuity of partners in the new partnership. The underlying principle is that all creditors of the business should have equal rights in the assets of the business, regardless of the time they became creditors and of the exact combination of persons then owning the business. This right against the assets of the new partnership ends when the new partnership has no partners in common with the partnership incurring the obligation. UPA § 41(4)(by necessary implication).

RUPA. The issue of successor liability is not significant under RUPA due to its adoption of the entity theory. In general, relationships between the partnership and its creditors are not affected by a change in membership of the partnership.

G.   Rights of the Estate of a Deceased Partner When the Business is Continued

UPA. The estate of a deceased partner is entitled to have the value of the deceased's interest determined as of the date of dissolution and receive payment in cash plus either interest from the date of dissolution to the date of payment or profits attributable to the use of the deceased's capital, at the choice of the estate. UPA § 42. The choice of interest or profits is designed to avoid unjust enrichment through use of deceased's capital without compensation and to encourage the remaining partners to promptly wind up the partnership affairs.

This right of an estate applies in most jurisdictions whether or not the estate consented to continuation of the business. Some courts, however, read UPA §§ 41(3) and 42 literally to allow the choice of profits only if the estate consents to the continuance of the business, waiving its liquidation right.

Consent by an estate to continuation of the business does not expose the estate to liability for new debts incurred by the business because the act of consent does not make the estate a partner. Instead, as stated in UPA § 42, the estate is "an ordinary creditor" of the partnership. That language would seem to grant the estate equal status with new creditors in claims against the assets of the firm. Some secondary authority states, however, that new creditors have priority over the claim of the consenting estate, as if the estate were a limited partner rather than an ordinary creditor (see Comment 3 to § 41). Of course, creditors whose claims arose prior to the death of the partner have priority if the partnership was not an LLP.

The above discussion of the rights of the estate of a deceased partner applies equally to a retired partner. Again, consent to continuance of the business can be construed as waiver of the retiring partner's liquidation right. See *Timmermann v. Timmermann* (Or.1975), where the court stated, "The facts clearly support the trial court's finding that plaintiff elected to be treated as a creditor under [UPA] § 42. Plaintiff is not entitled to withdraw from a failing partnership on the brink of insolvency, allow the other partners to continue the business for one and a half years, until the economic picture improves, and then force liquidation...."

RUPA. The above issues would arise in different form under RUPA because death of a partner is a dissociation and does not in itself cause dissolution. The rights of an estate thus are governed primarily by § 701. It is of interest that RUPA does not provide a choice of interest or profits to an estate, confining the estate to interest only. See § 701(b). The same rights and limitations apply to a retired partner unless the partner was a member of an at will partnership that had not altered the default rule of § 801(1).

H.   The Treatment of Good Will

Good will is defined in *In re Brown* (N.Y.1926) as follows: "Men will pay for any privilege that gives a reasonable expectancy of preference in the race of competition. Such expectancy may come from succession in place or name or otherwise to a business that has won the favor of its customers. It is then known as good will...." See also, Bromberg and Ribstein on Partnership 7:123–24:

> Goodwill has a variety of meanings but is generally used in partnership cases to refer to the going concern value of the business, as opposed to the breakup or liquidation value of its separate assets.... Goodwill in this sense includes favorable relationships with customers, employment relationships, credit rating, and other aspects of relationships with suppliers, the value of an assembled organization of property, equipment, and personnel, and such relatively objective components as trade name and customer records.

> Good will is presumptively an asset of a partnership. There is authority that refuses to recognize this presumption if the business is personal or professional, like a music group or a professional

practice, on the reasoning that professional skills and qualifications are incapable of transfer. This distinction is breaking down in modern law. See *Dawson v. White & Case* (N.Y. 1996), stating: "To the extent that dictum in [a prior case] stands for the proposition that a professional business, as a matter of law, cannot have any goodwill apart from the goodwill of its constituent members, we note that this rationale has been rejected by the Court in a different context [enforcing sale of goodwill in a dentistry practice] and has been superseded by the economic realities of the contemporary practice of law, illustrated by attorney advertising, internationalization of law firms, and other professional developments."

Well-drafted partnership agreements address the issue of good will, usually providing a method of evaluation of this intangible asset if they choose to include it in the valuation of a partner's interest. Clauses recognizing and evaluating good will typically are accompanied by covenants not to compete. Also, the treatment of good will can have income tax consequences.

§ 91. Winding Up; Liquidation; Terminating the Business

This section addresses winding up and liquidation of a dissolved partnership, as distinguished from the separate matter discussed above of continuing the business without liquidation. Also, the topic of termination of the business will be addressed.

A. Winding Up and Liquidation

The phrase "winding up" is defined as follows: "Winding up the partnership business entails selling its assets, paying its debts, and distributing the net balance, if any, to the partners in cash according to their interests." (Comment 2, RUPA § 801.) It is customary to think of winding up as involving liquidation of debts and then settlement of accounts among partners, as the quotation indicates. The comment to UPA § 29 appears to support this view by stating: "In this act dissolution designates the point in time when the partners cease to carry on the business together; termination is the point in time when all partnership affairs are wound up; winding up, the process of settling partnership affairs after dissolution."

The phrase "winding up" is used in a different sense when a partnership business continues after dissolution without liquidation of all debts. See, for example, the language of *Wilzig v. Sisselman* (N.J.Super.1982), stating that an agreement for continuing the business is "in effect a type of winding up without the necessity of discontinuing the day-to-day business.... In this case the formation of the new partnership and assumption of liabilities of the old constituted the automatic winding up of the affairs of its predecessor." Also, *Ellebracht v. Siebring* (W.D.Mo.1981), contains language stating that termination of partnership affairs "can occur contemporaneously with dissolution."

From the perspective of these courts, the former partnership has been dissolved, accounts among partners have been settled, and the rights of creditors attach to the new partnership. There is nothing left of the former partnership to be concerned about. This seems sensible. Nevertheless, the more usual use of the phrase "winding up" contemplates liquidation of debts and it will be so used in the remainder of these materials.

Dissolution requires the remaining partners to wind up partnership affairs unless the partnership agreement provides otherwise or there has been an effective consent by the withdrawing partner or estate of a deceased partner to continuation of the business. Section 38(1) of UPA has been so interpreted. And RUPA § 801(1) states that, when a partnership is dissolved, "its business must be wound up."

Section 37 of UPA focuses on the right to wind up, stating that, subject to agreement, "the partners who have not wrongfully dissolved" have the right to wind up; "provided, however, that any partner, his legal representative or his assignee, upon cause shown, may obtain winding up by the court." Section 803 of RUPA is the counterpart to § 37. It defines the right to wind up in similar terms, adding language describing some of the powers of the person winding up the business.

Section 30 of UPA provides that, "On dissolution the partnership is not terminated, but continues until the winding up of partnership affairs is completed." RUPA § 802(a) encompasses the same concept. Among other things, this means that partners continue to represent the partnership when completing unfinished business. Also, fiduciary duties among partners continue with regard to unfinished business. For example, in *Resnick v. Kaplan* (Md. App.1981), Resnick, a partner in a law firm, took 150 contingent fee cases with him upon withdrawing from the firm. He claimed he could keep the fees earned thereafter, with a quantum meruit payment to his former partners for work done prior to dissolution, on the ground that the clients were now his and had signed separate representation agreements with him. There was no language in the partnership agreement addressing this situation. The court rejected Resnick's argument and required him to allocate the fees earned on those cases to his former partners according to the percentage granted each partner under the partnership agreement. The fees were assets of the firm and Resnick was entitled to receive only his partnership interest in them.

The argument that Resnick entered into new contractual relationships with the clients carried no weight because the relationship at issue was that of Resnick and his former partners, not Resnick and the 150 clients. Resnick was finishing uncompleted business that was the business of the firm.

The court buttressed its opinion by pointing to UPA § 18(f), stating that no partner is entitled to remuneration for acting in the partnership business "except that a surviving partner is entitled to reasonable compensation for his services in winding up the partnership affairs." Since withdrawal, not death, was involved in the *Resnick* case, by negative implication no compensation for concluding the 150 cases was allowed. This principle applied to the remaining partners as well, who had to share with Resnick the fees they generated from the cases they retained. RUPA § 401(h) is the counterpart to UPA § 18(f), except that it does not confine compensation for winding up to surviving partners, which would allow Resnick to claim that he was entitled to compensation for winding up the 150 cases. He still could not claim ownership of the accounts, however, and would be subject to a corresponding claim by his remaining partners to compensation for the work they did in settling the cases they retained.

Resnick was cited and distinguished in *Marr v. Langhoff* (Md.1991). In this case a law partner, Langhoff, left a law firm and took a lucrative case with him. The two remaining partners, citing *Resnick*, recovered over $800,000 at trial as their share of the contingent fee Langhoff received from the case. (*Marr* involved a professional corporation but the court resolved the dispute by applying partnership law, an approach that often is taken in professional corporation cases.) The trial court decision was reversed on appeal on the ground that just prior to leaving, Langhoff and one of the two remaining partners (Bennett) had in a brief, oral conversation ("Whatever is yours is yours, and whatever is ours is ours.") extinguished any continuing duty of loyalty Langhoff owed to his remaining partners. The court stated, "We construe the Langhoff–Bennett contract to have effected an immediate winding up of [the firm].... Faced with dissolution, Bennett agreed with Langhoff to eliminate a period of winding up and to cut directly to termination of the partnership. The Langhoff–Bennett contract substituted for the fiduciary duty."

B. Termination

(i) Settlement of Accounts

UPA. The order of distribution of assets is specified by UPA § 40(b). Creditors outside the partnership are paid first, then debts owed to partners other than for capital contributions or profits are paid, then capital is returned, and finally the remaining balance, if any, is distributed as profits (surplus). If the partnership property is insufficient to repay obligations, the loss is to be shared by the solvent partners in the proportions in which they share profits. UPA §§ 18(a), 40(d).

RUPA. Section 807 of RUPA is the counterpart to § 40. It does not subordinate inside debt (partners as creditors of the firm) to outside debt, however. And § 807 in effect abolishes the "dual priority" rule in UPA § 40(h) and (i) that mandates priority for partnership creditors in partnership assets and for personal creditors in personal assets (see Comment 2 to § 807). In all other significant respects §§ 40 and 807 are in agreement.

(ii) Claims Among Partners: The Losing Business

Section 18(a) of UPA states: "Each partner ... must contribute toward the losses, whether of capital or otherwise, sustained by the partnership according to his share in the profits." This default rule poses a vexing problem when the partners have unequal capital accounts or when one partner has contributed all the money and the other only labor in a two-person partnership. The venture fails and the money partner sues the services partner for one-half her capital loss. By a literal reading of the language of § 18(a), the money partner should prevail, absent agreement otherwise.

This result has disturbed some commentators, who feel that the services partner has lost the value of his services as well. Unless it was agreed that the services would constitute a capital contribution, however, the language of § 18(f) that no partner "is entitled to remuneration for acting in the partnership business" is construed by some courts to destroy the inference that services constitute capital. *Richert v. Handly* (Wash.1958), is clear authority in support of this analysis. There is a conflicting line of authority denying a claim by the money partner for sharing her losses unless the services partner was paid for his services, in which event sharing is required.

RUPA § 401(b) continues the rule of § 18(a). Comment 3 to § 401 acknowledges that it adopts the *Richert* rule and that this "may seem unfair," but continues on to state that:

In entering a partnership with such a capital structure, the partners should foresee that application of the default rule may bring about unusual results and take advantage of their power to vary by agreement the allocation of capital losses. On the other hand, as a practical matter, the working partner's obligation to contribute anything beyond his original investment may be illusory. The partner who contributes little or no capital may be without resources to share losses and is, in that case, execution proof. (The last two sentences were contained in Comment 3 to the 1993 version of RUPA but were not carried forward in the current version of RUPA.)

It is useful to note that the money partner lost the opportunity cost of the money during the time the partnership was active. The opportunity cost usually would be measured by lost interest that the money otherwise could have generated had it not been invested in the partnership. This loss in some situations conceivably could equal the loss of time of the services partner, which may help explain the *Richert* rule.

CHAPTER 14

THE LIMITED PARTNERSHIP

§ 92. Introduction

The limited partnership is a form of doing business made available by statute. A limited partnership is created by filing with the state a certificate for a partnership consisting of at least one general partner and one limited partner. It allows an investor who is a limited partner to participate in profits in an ownership capacity in a partnership without personal liability for the obligations of the business.

A limited partnership differs from a general partnership in a number of ways beyond the filing requirement and the liability protection for limited partners. Under its default rules, limited partners do not have an equal right to management, profits are shared according to capital contributions instead of equally, limited partners do not have agency powers, and the limited partnership is harder to dissolve, as developed below.

Prior to the LLP and the LLC, the limited partnership was the only flexible and convenient form of doing business that allowed an investor the combined benefits of profits, ownership status, limited liability, and the advantage of partnership taxation. The limited partnership satisfied this need for many years and it remains in significant use today. The most recent figures available from the Internal Revenue Service show that in 2001 there were 369,000 limited partnerships in this country, with 7,000,000 partners. The great bulk of the limited partnerships are in real estate and holding and investment companies. While the number of limited partnerships is less than one-half of the number of LLCs, the number of limited partnerships has grown from 271,000 in 1991. (http://www.irs.gov/pub/irs-soi/01partnr.pdf). Internal Revenue Service, Statistics of Income Bulletin 52, Figure G (fall 1999).

The limited partnership remains viable even after the appearance of the LLP and LLC in part because of its clear and well-defined distinction between the roles of the partners. The general partners run the business and the limited partners occupy a passive role in the usual case, making the limited partnership "hard-wired" in the sense that the distinct roles of general and limited partners are clearly defined in the statute. That feature makes it a favorite, among other things, for estate planning, allowing a family to include children in a partnership without sharing control with them and without granting them agency powers. There are other ways of achieving this objective, such as creating an LLC with two classes of members, only one of which enjoys managerial powers. Nevertheless, there is a comfort level with the limited partnership. It has been a prominent part of the law for over 100 years, generating a considerable body of precedent on many issues.

LLLP. The acronym "LLLP" stands for limited liability limited partnership. The LLLP extends limited liability to the general partners of a limited partnership. This feature allows the owners to avoid the inconvenience of creating and operating a corporate general partner in order to ensure limited liability for all owners, which many limited partnerships do today. The LLLP may play a significant role in the continued use of the limited partnership because it extends limited liability in a convenient way to all owners of the business.

Legislation making the LLLP available is recent and has been adopted in 17 jurisdictions to date. It makes limited liability for general partners available merely by filing a certificate, allowing the general partners of limited partnerships to enjoy the same immunity from liability for the obligations of the business as partners in an LLP, members of an LLC, and shareholders in a corporation. Borrowing from the LLP and the LLC, the state statutes providing for the LLLP have special name requirements, usually requiring that the initials "LLLP" or some close approximation thereof be part of the firm name in order to alert people that they are dealing with a limited liability entity.

§ 93. The Uniform Acts

ULPA. The first Uniform Limited Partnership Act (ULPA) was promulgated by the National Conference of Commissioners on Uniform State Laws (NCCUSL) in 1916. At one time it was adopted in all states except Louisiana. It was designed to replace the scattered state statutes that were in existence at the time. Uniformity was considered desirable. Also, the state statutes were generally narrow in language and strictly construed by courts, making the status of being a limited partner hazardous. The threat to a limited partner of unwittingly falling into general partner status was ever present.

ULPA addressed some of these concerns in a short, tightly drafted act, but it was strict about limiting the amount of control a limited partner could safely engage in and had rigid and burdensome requirements about what must be included in the certificate filed with the state in order to create a limited partnership. ULPA is still law in several states that did not displace it when they adopted RULPA (see below). Those states apply ULPA to limited partnerships that were formed prior to the enactment of RULPA and that have not subsequently elected to be governed by the revised act.

RULPA (1976). In 1976 NCCUSL promulgated a revised limited partnership act in order to modernize the prior law, clarify ambiguities, and fill gaps by adding more detailed language. The revision was largely in response to the increasingly frequent use of limited partnerships for large-scale economic enterprises such as commercial real estate and oil and gas exploration, drilling, and production. Limited partnerships were effective tax shelter vehicles due to the pass-through nature of partnership taxation, allowing tax losses generated by interest expense, depreciation, and depletion allowances to be passed directly through to the limited partners. ULPA needed modernization in order to make the limited partnership a more convenient vehicle for these large-scale projects containing many limited partners. Among other things, RULPA (1976) added a list of "safe harbors" for limited partners who exercise some control. Also, the partnership agreement was emphasized as the primary organizational and governing document of a limited partnership. RULPA (1976) has been adopted in nearly all states.

The 1985 Amendments to RULPA (1976). In 1985 NCCUSL promulgated substantial amendments to the 1976 act, further increasing the flexibility and ease of use of the limited partnership by, for example, greatly simplifying the filing and amending requirements and further reducing the risks to limited partners who want to be active in the business. Forty-four states have adopted the 1985 amendments or significant portions of those amendments.

The 1976 Act with the 1985 amendments will be referred to in this book as RULPA. The 1976 Act without amendments will be referred to as RULPA (1976). These materials will focus primarily on

RULPA, which is governing law in almost all the states.

Re-RULPA. In August, 2001, the National Conference of Commissioners on Uniform State Laws approved a new act to govern limited partnerships. Although simply entitled "Uniform Limited Partnership Act (2001)," this book will refer to the act as "Re–RULPA," as it is known in much of the scholarly comment and to differentiate it from prior uniform laws relating to limited partnerships. The fact that three uniform laws relating to limited partnerships were approved by NCCUSL in the span of 25 years, while the original act stood for sixty years, speaks to the continuing importance of, and interest in, limited partnerships as a form of business. Re–RULPA makes several important changes to RULPA, including the following:

- *De-linking*. Re–RULPA de-links limited partnership law from UPA. Section 1105 of RULPA provides that, "in any case not provided for in this [Act] the provisions of the Uniform Partnership Act shall govern." This linkage caused considerable confusion and was one of the primary motivating forces behind the Re–RULPA project. Because Re–RULPA is now a stand-alone act governing limited partnerships, it is considerably longer than its predecessor acts.

- *Limited liability for the general partner*. Re–RULPA recognizes the growing popularity of the limited liability limited partnership (LLLP), that is, a limited partnership in which neither the general partners nor the limited partners are liable for partnership obligations. LLLPs are, thus, to limited partnerships what an LLP is to a general partnership. Re–RULPA allows a limited partnership to elect LLLP status through a simple statement in the certificate of limited partnership. See §§ 102(9), 201(a)(4) and 404(c).

- *Liability Shield for Limited Partners.* Under RULPA and ULPA, if the limited partner engages in certain activities on behalf of the partnership, the limited partner runs the risk of being treated as a general partner for liability purposes (although those two acts differ on just what activities are sufficient to result in a loss of protection for the limited partner). Section 303 of Re–RULPA abandons that approach and provides, simply, that a limited partner is not liable for the obligations of the limited partnership, "even if the limited partner participates in the management and control of the limited partnership."

As Re–RULPA has been approved so recently by NCCULS and, at this writing, has been adopted by only a handful of states, this book will emphasize ULPA and RULPA. References will be made to Re–RULPA where Re–RULPA makes a significant change in the law.

§ 94. Securities Law, Tax, and Rollup Issues

The use of the limited partnership to raise capital on a large-scale basis can create complex tax and securities law problems. Although such problems are beyond the scope of this book, it may prove useful to refer briefly to several important matters that occur frequently.

Securities law issues. The interest of a limited partner is regarded as a "security" under applicable federal and state law under many circumstances, due to the passive role the typical limited partner plays in the business. Unless an exemption applies, or the limited partners take an active role in the management of the business, if a limited partnership is large enough it may be necessary to register its ownership interests (or "units") as securities with the federal Securities and Exchange Commission and/or with state securities commissioners. This can be time consuming and costly, but the failure to identify securities law issues can pose very substantial problems for the parties involved.

Taxation issues. In 1986 Congress passed the Tax Reform Act, which restricted the use of tax shelters by, among other things, mandating that passive losses can be offset only against passive income. Since limited partners are deemed to engage in a passive activity, they cannot use partnership losses to reduce their active income. Also, in 1988 Congress enacted legislation mandating that "a publicly traded partnership shall be treated as a corporation" unless 90% of its income is passive income, such as income from rent, interest, dividends, or sale of property. In addition to these specific measures, there are various provisions in the Tax Code that provide different treatment for limited partners than for general partners.

Rollups. The changes in taxation noted above, plus the sharp real estate slump of the 1980s, created severe financial difficulties for many limited partnerships. This resulted in reorganizations on a large scale, labelled "rollups," described below.

In a rollup transaction, limited partnerships are combined or reorganized and new securities are issued to the partners. The typical rollup involves finite-life limited partnerships, which are merged or reorganized into a new partnership, corporation, or real estate investment trust. The successor entity whose securities the limited partners receive has different compensation arrangements with the general partner and different policies for reinvestment and distribution of earnings and proceeds from asset sales than did the original limited partnership entities. ...[M]any rollup proponents have been the limited partnership's general partner. ...[A] rollup raises numerous complex questions about valuation of the assets and entities involved. DeMott, 70 Wash. U. L. Rev. 617.

Rollups have sometimes created their own problems, including a suspicion that limited partners were not treated fairly on evaluation and other issues. This controversy resulted in more federal legislation, the Limited Partnership Roll-up Reform Act of 1993, mandating extensive disclosures, among other things.

§ 95. Organization of the Limited Partnership

A limited partnership is formed by filing a certificate of limited partnership with the secretary of state of the state chosen by the general partner or partners. Usually the state chosen is the state in which the firm plans to do business but a partnership can do business outside of the state of its organization, as many partnerships do. The firm will have to register in the other states as a "foreign limited partnership" (RULPA §§ 101(4) and 902). In its state of organization the firm is defined in RULPA § 101(7) as a "domestic limited partnership."

The 1985 amendments to RULPA (1976) greatly simplify what is required to be in the certificate, mandating in § 201 only that the certificate set forth the name of the limited partnership, the name and address of an agent for service of process, the name and business address of each general partner, and the latest date on which the partnership is to dissolve. This is dramatically different from the requirements of the 1976 act which, among other things, requires that the names and addresses of all limited partners be set forth in the certificate and that the amount and kind of the capital contribution of each partner, including all limited partners, be described. The philosophy behind this change in 1985 is expressed in the Comments to § 201:

> This is in recognition that the partnership agreement, not the certificate of limited partnership, has become the authoritative and comprehensive

document for most limited partnerships, and that creditors and potential creditors of the partnership do and should refer to the partnership agreement and to other information furnished to them directly by the partnership and by others, not to the certificate, to obtain facts concerning the capital and finances of the partnership and other matters of concern.

Although RULPA does not require a written partnership agreement, most partnerships have one. As the Comment quoted above suggests, it is the partnership agreement that sets forth the details of capitalization, distribution rights, contribution commitments, allocation of management powers, and other matters of importance. The certificate is a public document and thus usually contains only the minimum required by the statute. The filing of the certificate brings the partnership into existence (unless the certificate specifies a later date) as a separate legal entity.

Section 304 of RULPA addresses the situation in which a filing is defective and a limited partnership is never effectively organized. Failing to file the certificate at all is a problem, of course, and so is filing it in the wrong place. Section 304 protects a limited partner from liability under such circumstances if the limited partner believed in good faith that he or she was a limited partner and either withdraws from future equity participation in the enterprise or causes an appropriate certificate to be filed. Also, liability is limited to creditors who actually believed that the limited partner was a general partner at the time credit was extended, a strict standard of reliance.

§ 96. Linkage

As noted above, RULPA provides expressly for linkage to UPA as a source of law for cases not covered in RULPA. RULPA § 1105 states: "In any case not provided for in this Act the provisions of the Uniform Partnership Act govern." The adoption of RUPA in a particular state under a statute where it completely displaces UPA (this is true in many but not all states) poses a problem because of the specific reference to UPA in § 1105. This is a technical issue that, once recognized, is easily resolved at the legislative level. Linkage for ULPA is provided in § 6(2) of UPA, which states, "this act shall apply to limited partnerships except in so far as the statutes relating to such partnerships are inconsistent herewith." Linkage is an important matter because some partnership issues are not covered in the limited partnership acts. (Re–RULPA is a "stand alone" statute. It incorporates all partnership concepts and thus is "de-linked" from the general partnership act.)

§ 97. The General Partner in a Limited Partnership

A. Fiduciary Duties

A general partner of a limited partnership "has the rights and powers and is subject to the restrictions [and liabilities] of a partner in a partnership without limited partners." RULPA § 403. Thus the provisions of UPA or RUPA apply to general partners, including fiduciary duties, personal liability for partnership obligations (unless the state of origin has made the LLLP available), agency powers, and managerial rights.

The general partner manages the business in the typical limited partnership. Management responsibility intensifies the fiduciary duties of the general partner. In *Bassan v. Investment Exch. Corp.* (Wash.1974), for example, the court stated: "The articles give the general partner the authority to conduct 'any and all of the business of the Partnership.' Once the limited partner has joined the partnership he has no effective voice in the decision-making process. He must, then, be able to rely on the highest standard of conduct from the general partner." Analogously, the court in *Pohl v. National Benefits Consultants, Inc.* (7th Cir.1992), stressed this duty in the context of the nonsupervising principal: "A fiduciary is an agent who is required to treat his principal with utmost loyalty and care— treat him, indeed, as if the principal were himself. The reason for the duty is clearest when the agent has a broad discretion the exercise of which the principal cannot feasibly supervise, so that the principal is at the agent's mercy."

Can general partners tailor their fiduciary duties in the limited partnership agreement in a way that will allow them to engage in conduct and take some benefits that the law otherwise would not tolerate? Courts divide on this issue. Compare *Riviera Congress Associates v. Yassky* (N.Y.1966):

The plaintiffs [limited partners] charge a breach of fiduciary duty by the general partners in that they were assertedly guilty of self-dealing and, on the surface, it is difficult to dispute the fact of such self-dealing since they leased the motel [the main partnership asset] to their own thinly capitalized corporation and then consented to successive assignments of the lease to other business entities which they owned or controlled. Ordinarily, such self-dealing would render the defendants incapable, as general partners, ... from releasing themselves from liability.... However, partners may include in the partnership articles practically "any agreement they want" and, if the asserted self-dealing was actually contemplated and authorized, it would not, ipso facto, be impermissible and deemed wrongful.

with *Appletree Square I Limited Partnership v. Investmark, Inc.* (Minn.App.1993): "[W]hile partners are free to vary many aspects of their relationship, they are not free to destroy its fiduciary character. To hold that partners may replace their broad duty of disclosure with a narrow duty to render information upon demand would destroy the fiduciary character of their relationship...."

The trend in the law, at least statutorily, clearly is to broaden the contractual flexibility that parties have to reduce or eliminate fiduciary duties. See § 76, where the Delaware provision allowing the elimination of fiduciary duties in the context of a general partnership, is quoted. Delaware has adopted similar provisions for limited partnerships and LLCs. In addition, Delaware statutes also contain this provision limiting the liability of a partner (and, for LLCs, a member) under certain circumstances:

> (d) To the extent that, at law or in equity, a partner or other person has duties (including fiduciary duties) and liabilities relating thereto to a limited partnership or to another partner or to another person that is a party to or is otherwise bound by a partnership agreement, (1) any such partner or other person acting under the partnership agreement shall not be liable to the limited partnership or to any such other partner or to any such other person for the partner's or other person's good faith reliance on the provisions of the partnership agreement, and (2) the partner's or other person's duties and liabilities may be expanded or restricted by provisions in the partnership agreement. 6 Del. C. § 17–1101(d).

Because many publicly-held partnerships are organized under Delaware law, and because a provision similar to § 17–1101 is in the Delaware LLC Act and in other statutes in other jurisdictions (e.g., Washington, RCWA 25.15.040; Massachusetts, M.G.L.A. 156C § 63), judicial interpretation of this section is important. The Chancery Court of Delaware, which is the most important court in the United States in terms of corporate law and, probably, in terms of partnership law as well (at least with regard to publicly-held partnerships), recently had an occasion to consider the meaning of this section, and opted for a narrow interpretation of it.

In *Gotham Partners, L.P v. Hallwood Realty Partners, L.P.* (Del.Ch. 2001), the Delaware Chancery Court held that the above-quoted provision only protects the general partner when the partnership provision in question was "ambiguous." The court thus interpreted the statute narrowly, and went on to find that the provision in question was not ambiguous and that the general partner's interpretation of it was in error.

B.   Withdrawal and Removal of General Partner

Unlike limited partners, a general partner in a limited partnership has a right to withdraw at any time by giving written notice to the other partners (RULPA § 602). The withdrawal does not necessarily cause dissolution, however. Section 801(4) of RULPA (there is no material difference between the 1976 act and the 1985 amendments in this section, except for internal renumbering) deals with this issue. Dissolution does not take place if there is at least one other general partner and the agreement permits the business to be continued by that partner and he does so.

In addition, the partnership is not required to dissolve even if the above situation does not exist if all of the partners, general and limited, agree in writing to continue the business and to appoint one or more additional general partners within 90 days after the withdrawal. If the vote is not unanimous, however, the partnership must dissolve. It is said that the purpose of this section "is to give each limited partner, who has no voice in the operation of the partnership business, the opportunity to prevent his investment from falling into the hands of an unknown or unwanted general partner." *Wasserman v. Wasserman* (Mass.App.1979).

Section 801(4) seems to require unanimity even if the partnership agreement has a contrary provision calling for less than a unanimous vote on this issue, which would make § 801(4) a mandatory provision of the act. This requirement could create problems when limited partners seek to remove a sole general partner pursuant to the terms of the partnership agreement granting such a power, but the general partner is also a limited partner and votes to block his removal and the choice of any successor partner. See *Obert v. Environmental Research and Development Corp.* (Wash.App.1988)(rev'd on other grounds), discussing this issue and resolving that § 801(4) is a mandatory provision.

Can a general partner who is engaging in misconduct be removed by the limited partners if nothing is said in the partnership agreement about removal? If the agreement does not contain an expulsion provision, the only recourse for the limited partners (and other general partners if there is more than one in the firm) is to seek dissolution based on the misconduct. Section 802, the judicial dissolution provision of RULPA, does not contain the detail one sees in UPA § 32(1)(c) and (d) and in RUPA § 601(5) (i)-(iii) addressing misconduct by a partner. Section 802 instead confines judicial dissolution to one circumstance: "whenever it is not reasonably practicable to carry on the business in conformity with the partnership agreement." Although this language does not foreclose dissolution because of misconduct, perhaps in this instance courts would find it convenient to utilize the greater detail in the general partnership acts through the linkage concept.

§ 98. Rights and Obligations of Limited Partners

The control issue. As noted above, ULPA adopted a strict position on the exercise of control by limited partners. Its § 7 stated: "A limited partner shall not become liable as a general partner unless, in addition to the exercise of his rights and powers as a limited partner, he takes part in the control of the business." Lawyers worried about the potentially broad reach of § 7, although most of the authority holding limited partners liable under this section involved substantial exercise of control. In *Holzman v. De Escamilla* (Cal.App. 1948), for example, the limited partners in a farming partnership were active in dictating the crops to be planted, had authority to withdraw all partnership funds from its bank without the knowledge or consent of the general partner, replaced the general partner as manager of the farm, and selected his successor. Also, the general partner had no authority to sign checks without the signature of one of the limited partners. The limited partners were held liable under § 7.

Control alone created liability under § 7. There was no additional requirement of creditor reliance on an impression that the limited partner was a general partner. Creditor reliance was protected under § 16 of UPA in any event (see § 65 of this book, discussing partner liability by estoppel) because, as noted earlier, UPA is linked to ULPA via § 6(2) of UPA.

The 1976 version of the uniform act returned to the control issue, describing it in the Prefatory Note as "the single most difficult issue facing lawyers who use the limited partnership." RULPA (1976) rewrote § 7, renumbered as § 303, and created a list of "safe harbors" for limited partners, describing acts that were declared not to constitute participating in control, such as being an agent or employee of the limited partnership or of a general partner, voting on the sale or exchange of all or substantially all of the assets of the partnership, voting on the removal of a general partner, and so forth.

In addition, § 303 added a reliance element, requiring a creditor to establish actual knowledge of the limited partner's participation in control unless the limited partner's control was "substantially the same as the exercise of the powers of a general partner." The "unless" clause left an opening for creditors to evade the reliance element and left lawyers with the worrisome task of trying to figure out exactly what acts of control were substantially the same as the exercise of the powers of a general partner. Nevertheless, the scope of liability was reduced under RULPA (1976), with the safe harbors proving particularly helpful.

In 1985 the control issue was revisited and § 303 redrafted to make even more secure the position of the controlling limited partner. The phrase "substantially the same as the exercise of the powers of a general partner" was deleted and the creditor reliance test applied to all situations. Also, the standard for reliance was tightened from requiring that the creditor prove actual knowledge of the participation in control to requiring that the creditor prove that he "reasonably believed, based upon the limited partner's conduct, that the limited partner is a general partner."

The combination of these two changes, plus an expansion of the safe harbors to include, among other things, a limited partner being an officer, director, or shareholder of a corporate general partner of the limited partnership, voting to admit a general partner, or requesting a meeting of partners, means that a careful limited partner can play a dominant role in the business without incurring liability as a general partner. This flexibility constitutes a major change in direction and philosophy from the original act.

As noted above, Re–RULPA has gone to the ultimate in this regard. It simply provides that a limited partner is not liable for the obligations of the limited partnership, "even if the limited partner participates in the management and control of the limited partnership." Although Re–RULPA has only been enacted in four states to date, a number of states have enacted legislation allowing for the formation of LLLPs, which provides the same sort of liability protection for limited partners as for general partners. Where such a statute or Re–RULPA applies, a limited partner would no longer need to worry about creditors relying on his exercise of control. Presumably this is true even if the creditors thought the limited partner was a general partner, due to the limited liability status of general partners in an LLLP.

Rights of limited partners. In addition to whatever rights may be granted by the partnership agreement, limited partners have a right under RULPA § 305 to inspect and copy partnership records and make reasonable demands for information about the business. As noted above, they have a vote under certain circumstances to avoid dissolution after withdrawal of a general partner. Also, they have the right to bring derivative suits on behalf of the partnership if the general partners have refused or are not likely to bring the action themselves (RULPA § 1001).

Obligations of limited partners. In general, in the default mode limited partners face far fewer obligations than general partners because they play a passive role. To the extent they become active in the business, however, they necessarily assume duties of care and loyalty relating to their agency and managerial roles. Also, see *KE Property Mgt. v. 275 Madison Mgt. Corp.* (Del. Ch. 1993), stating: "To the extent that a partnership agreement empowers a limited partner with discretion to take actions affecting the governance of the limited partnership [like removal of a general partner], the limited partner may be subject to the obligations of a fiduciary, including the obligation to act in good faith as to the other partners."

In addition, even if inactive, a duty of good faith should apply to a limited partner who receives confidential information about the business. The duty would encompass not revealing the information to others who could do the business harm and not using it against the business to advance his own personal, competitive interests. Also, obligations attach to a limited partner who receives distributions to the disadvantage of creditors of the firm, as discussed below in § 100.

§ 99. Exit Rights of Limited Partners

RULPA § 603 provides limited partners a withdrawal right upon six months' written notice to each general partner. This is a default right, however. As a practical matter, nearly all limited partnership agreements restrict limited partner withdrawals, some of them denying withdrawal completely during the life of the firm in order to keep their capital in the firm. In addition, some states have amended RULPA and deleted the default six month withdrawal privilege. This was done for federal transfer tax reasons relating to minority discounts for valuation purposes. Also, if the partnership is a term partnership, § 603 states that a limited partner has no right of withdrawal during the term.

§ **100.** Distributions

Unlike the default rule in UPA specifying that distributions of profits are equal for each partner, RULPA's default rule in §§ 503 and 504 is that distributions are allocated "on the basis of the value of the contributions made by each partner," including limited partners. (As a practical matter, the allocation of distributions almost always will be established in the partnership agreement.)

RULPA places restrictions on distributions in its §§ 607 and 608. Section 607 places a solvency limitation on distributions to partners. Section § 608 mandates the return of contributions that were received even while the firm was solvent if they are needed to pay creditors who extended credit during the period the contribution was held by the partnership. This exposure to liability is only up to one year from the date of the distribution for rightful distributions. If the distribution was made in violation of the partnership agreement, however, or if it left the partnership insolvent, the period of liability to return it is six years from the date of the distribution.

The policy lying behind these restrictions probably is that this protection of creditors is the price one must pay for limited liability. Similar restrictions apply to the LLC (see Chapter 15) and to LLPs in most states.

§ **101.** Transfers of Interest

RULPA § 702 states that, subject to agreement, a "partnership interest" is assignable in whole or in part. The phrase "partnership interest" is defined in § 101(10) to mean "a partner's share of the profits and losses of a limited partnership and the right to receive distributions of partnership assets." The transferee is not entitled to exercise any of the rights of a partner in the absence of consent of all the partners or authorization as prescribed in the partnership agreement. Unless the agreement provides otherwise, a partner ceases to be a partner upon assignment of all his partnership interest.

§ 102. Dissolution

A limited partnership dissolves less readily than a general partnership. Dissolution is covered in RULPA §§ 801 and 802. Section 801 deals with nonjudicial dissolution. It provides that a limited partnership is dissolved (i) at the time specified in the certificate or (ii) upon the happening of events specified in writing in the partnership agreement or (iii) upon written consent of all partners or (iv) when a general partner withdraws unless there is at least one other general partner and the agreement permits the business to be carried on by that partner. Alternatively, the partnership is not dissolved if, within 90 days after the withdrawal of a general partner, all partners agree in writing to continue the business and to the appointment of one or more additional general partners. As noted earlier, § 802 provides for judicial dissolution upon application by or for a partner "whenever it is not reasonably practicable to carry on the business in conformity with the partnership agreement."

If dissolution does occur, a process of winding up and termination takes place. Section 803 deals with winding up in language similar to UPA § 37 and RUPA § 807(a). Unless otherwise provided in the agreement, "the general partners who have not wrongfully dissolved the partnership or, if none, the limited partners, may wind up the limited partnership's affairs." RULPA § 803. A court may wind up "upon application of any partner." Id.

Distribution of assets is prescribed in RULPA § 804, with creditors, including partners who are creditors, receiving first priority, then accrued distributions, then return of contributions. Finally, the remaining assets are distributed according to the partnership interests in the proportions the partners share in distributions.

CHAPTER 15

THE LIMITED LIABILITY COMPANY

§ 103. Introduction

The limited liability company (LLC) is a relatively new form of doing business that offers investors who make a proper filing with the state freedom from personal liability for the obligations of the business, flexibility of management, control of the business in an ownership capacity, and the tax advantage of partnership status. This was an extraordinary combination of attractive options for investors when the LLC first appeared on the scene in a Wyoming statute in 1977, patterned on a European model. Eleven years later the IRS issued a revenue ruling approving partnership taxation for the LLC. Thereafter enabling legislation for the LLC was rapidly adopted by all of the states, with considerable variation from state to state. Most states adopted enabling legislation in 1991 or 1992, and at this point there are relatively few judicial precedents on the LLC.

The owners of an LLC, called members, enjoy limited liability similar to shareholders of a corporation in that no member of an LLC is personally liable for its obligations. Among other things, this means that no member is exposed to vicarious liability for the torts of other members or of employees of the LLC. Only liability for personal misconduct or on a personal guaranty of entity obligations exists in the LLC setting, similar to the LLP, the LLLP, and the corporation.

The LLC is a separate entity, capable of suing and being sued and of holding property. It is a flexible form of doing business. Management of an LLC bears none of the formalities of the corporate form unless the owners choose to introduce formalities. Similar to partners, the owners of an LLC can structure management as they wish. Nearly all states provide for a choice of management upon forming an LLC. It can be member-managed and thus very similar in informality and flexibility to a partnership, or it can be manager-managed by persons who can be but do not have to be members, where the owners who are not also managers play a largely passive role, similar to limited partners in a limited partnership.

The LLC is viewed by some investors as superior to the limited partnership because a member can exercise control without the risk of personal liability for the debts of the business, a status that the limited partner does not enjoy with complete safety even today in some jurisdictions. Also, in the LLC all owners enjoy limited liability, as contrasted with the limited partnership where the general partners are liable for all obligations of the partnership. (The recent creation of the LLLP (see § 92) overcomes these limitations in the 17 states that have made it available, however.)

The LLC is viewed as an improvement over the general partnership because the owners are not personally liable for the obligations of the business. The fact that, unlike the general partnership, documents have to be prepared and filed in order to create an LLC is of little concern to the sophisticated investor. (The recent creation of the LLP in all 50 states (see § 61) now neutralizes the concern about personal liability.) Also, a number of states allow LLCs to be organized for nonbusiness purposes, such as co-ownership of a vacation cabin. This is not possible in partnership form because the statutory definition of a partnership requires co-ownership of "a business for profit." (See § 60.)

The LLC is an improvement over the corporation in some situations because it can be run more informally and the double taxation of operating in corporate form is avoided. It is regarded as an improvement over the Subchapter S corporation, which avoids corporate taxation, because its organization and operation are far less restricted.

The combination of control, limited liability, and partnership tax status in the LLC is less extraordinary today due to the subsequent development of the LLP and the LLLP, which also offer control, limited liability, and partnership tax status. Also, a few states impose franchise or other taxes on LLCs that they do not levy on partnerships. Nevertheless, it is important to understand the LLC, which is the preferred entity of many attorneys for small businesses, in part because of the flexibility they provide.

A large number of businesses operate as LLCs today. As of 2001, the most recent data available, there were more than 800,000 LLCs in this country, substantially more than the number of limited partnerships (369,000) and roughly equal to the number of general partnerships (815,000). (http:// www.irs.gov/pub/irs-soi/01partnr.pdf).

§ 104. Taxation and Securities Law Issues

The Kintner Regulations. In order to understand the reasoning behind provisions relating to dissolution and transferability that still exist in a few LLC statutes and in some LLC operating agreements, it might prove helpful to take a brief look at the tax system that existed before January 1, 1997, when the check-the-box regulations became effective. For many years the Kintner regulations of the Internal Revenue Service (IRS) determined when an unincorporated business organization was taxable as a partnership. As noted earlier, this is important because of the flow-through feature of partnership taxation. Briefly, the Kintner regulations applied a four-part test that looked at four fundamental characteristics of a corporation to determine whether an entity should be taxed as a corporation rather than a partnership. It would be taxed as a corporation if it had at least three of the following four characteristics: limited liability, centralized management, continuity of life, and free transferability of ownership interests.

For years a substantial part of the transactional practice of law involved careful drafting and planning to ensure that an unincorporated organization lacked at least two of the four characteristics of a corporation and thus would be taxed as a partnership. The organizers of an LLC give away one of the four characteristics right at the start: limited liability. That prompted a search to ensure that an LLC lacked two of the remaining three characteristics: centralized management, continuity of life, or free transferability of ownership interests.

Nearly all of the early LLC legislation was tailored to qualify LLCs for partnership tax status under the four-part test used by the IRS at that time. Also, some of the early legislation (including the Wyoming statute) was "bulletproof," removing the possibility of attorney error. These statutes mandated ready dissolution, required unanimous consent for continuation of an LLC, and declared membership interests nontransferable without unanimous consent of all other members, thus avoiding the corporate characteristics of continuity of life and free transferability of interests.

The Check-the-Box Regulations. As noted above, on January 1, 1997, the IRS put into effect the "check-the-box" regulations. These regulations allow owners of unincorporated business organizations to elect partnership treatment even if their business organization would have been classified as a corporation under the Kintner regulations. Taxpayers are also free to elect treatment as an association taxable as a corporation. If the taxpayer does not specify otherwise, a domestic unincorporated organization of two or more owners is automatically qualified as a partnership for tax purposes. Also, the regulations clarify the status of the one-member LLC, disregarding it as an entity separate from its owner unless the owner elects treatment of the LLC as a corporation. Accordingly, the one-member LLC can offer limited liability and yet be treated as a sole proprietorship (if the member is an individual) or an unincorporated division (if the member is a corporation).

The check-the-box regulations have had a major impact on business organization and planning, greatly simplifying the process for all concerned. Many states subsequently have amended their LLC statutes to remove mandatory dissolution and transferability provisions, allowing flexibility of drafting for the LLC by making most provisions default in nature.

Securities law issues. An important issue is whether a membership interest in an LLC is a security under federal and state laws. If so, unless an exemption applies, the LLC may have to go through expensive and time-consuming registration and disclosure processes before selling interests to others. A major factor to consider in deciding this issue is whether the members rely upon the efforts of others to generate profits. If they do not, then the interests are likely not securities. Thus, in a member-managed LLC, in which the management rights of all members are equal as in a partnership, the securities laws usually are not of major concern. If, however, an LLC is manager-managed and some or all of the members play a passive role, like limited partners in a limited partnership, it is necessary to take a close look at the likely impact of the securities laws.

§ 105. Uniform Limited Liability Company Act (1995)

A Uniform Limited Liability Company Act ("ULLCA") was promulgated by NCCUSL in 1995 and amended thereafter to take into account the check-the-box regulations. It has been adopted in eight states and the Virgin Islands to date (July 2005) and has influenced amendments to legislation in other states. It is patterned largely upon RUPA. ULLCA is set forth in Appendix D to this book.

Nearly all states now allow persons to craft an LLC according to their own wishes. ULLCA also is strongly default in tone. It contains a few mandatory provisions, collected in one section of the Act, and declares all other provisions in the Act default in nature. The list of mandatory provisions is in § 103. They are closely patterned upon RUPA § 103, perhaps in part because the essence of the LLC, especially its flexibility of management, operation, and capital structure, resembles the partnership.

The mandatory provisions in ULLCA § 103 include provisions that the operating agreement for an LLC cannot (i) unreasonably restrict a member's access to books and records, (ii) vary the right to expel a member upon a judicial determination of wrongdoing, or (iii) vary the requirement to wind up the business if an event makes it unlawful to carry on the business or if a court finds that it is not reasonably practicable to carry on the business in conformity with the articles and operating agreement or if the managers or members in control are acting in a manner that is illegal, oppressive, fraudulent, or unfairly prejudicial to the petitioning member. The latter limitation, dealing with manager misbehavior, is not taken from RUPA and instead has corporate law overtones. ULLCA § 103 also declares its fiduciary duties nonwaivable, in language closely patterned on RUPA § 103.

§ 106. Organizational Matters

It is necessary to file a document with the state in order to create an LLC. Although the details vary considerably among the states, in many states one or more persons (called "members") file articles of organization with the state, containing at a minimum provisions describing the name and identification of the firm as a limited liability company, the address of the principal place of business or registered office, and the name and address of the registered agent for service of process. The act of filing creates the LLC, unless a delayed effective date is specified in the articles.

ULLCA specifies that one or more persons may organize an LLC, making it clear that an LLC can consist of only one person. A number of states initially required that LLCs have at least two members on the assumption that in order to qualify for partnership taxation it was necessary to have an "association of two or more persons." Many of those states recently have amended their statutes to include a provision similar to ULLCA, in part for reasons of flexibility and in part because the IRS will recognize one member LLCs as sole proprietorships for taxation purposes. Today the one-member LLC is possible in nearly all states.

As noted above, owners of an LLC are referred to as "members." An LLC also can have "managers." The internal organizing document of an LLC is referred to almost everywhere as an "operating agreement."

The operating agreement is the primary document for nearly all LLCs. With few exceptions, most states allow members to define their relationship and operate the business as they wish and usually these decisions are reflected in the operating agreement. In many respects the operating agreement is the functional equivalent of the partnership agreement in a partnership. It defines the managerial responsibilities of the parties, governance of the LLC, capital accounts, compensation, distributions, admission and withdrawal of members, buyout arrangements, and other matters central to the business. An operating agreement is not required in most states, just as a partnership agreement is not required, but it is highly advisable for an LLC to have a written agreement.

On other matters, the name of an LLC must contain the initials "LLC" or some equivalent in order to alert persons that they are dealing with a limited liability entity. In most states LLCs must file annual reports with the state, on pain of administrative dissolution if they fail to do so. A few states place restrictions on the kind of business in which an LLC can engage.

§ 107. Piercing the Veil of an LLC

The issue of whether and when the protective shield of an LLC can be pierced and the members held individually liable for the obligations of the business is significant. It is a matter of special concern when one is operating under an entity that is new in the law, due to the understandable fear of persons forming and operating the entity that it will not stand up to attack in a close case. Some LLC statutes have provisions specifically focusing on this issue. See, for example, Colo. Rev. Stat. § 7–80–107, stating, "In any case in which a party seeks to hold the members of a limited liability company personally responsible for the alleged improper actions of the limited liability company, the court shall apply the case law which interprets the conditions and circumstances under which the corporate veil of a corporation may be pierced under Colorado law."

In general, a corporate veil is pierced only when the separate corporate entity is not respected by its owners and the corporate form is being used to further a fraudulent or inequitable purpose. Evidence of lack of respect for the corporate entity ordinarily consists of commingling the assets of the corporation with those of other individuals or entities, failing to adopt bylaws, failing to appoint officers, and failing to keep corporate records. Because an LLC is not restrained by the formalities that apply to corporations, the veil piercing jurisprudence developed in corporate law does not translate easily to LLC law. In fact, courts have focused more on the possibility of fraud or injustice and less on following formalities in deciding whether to "pierce the veil" of an LLC. See *Kaycee Land and Livestock v. Flahive* (Wyo. 2002).

§ 108. Management

In most state statutes the management default rule is the member-managed LLC. This rule is consistent with the idea that the LLC resembles a partnership. With regard to default management rights of members, many state statutes do not contain the equivalent of UPA § 18(e) or RUPA § 401(f) ("Each partner has equal rights in the management and conduct of the partnership business"), although ULLCA specifically addresses the issue in its § 404(a)(1) in terms almost identical to RUPA § 401(f).

With regard to default voting rights of members, state LLC statutes divide. Some states allocate voting power in proportion to contributions made and not returned, that is, pro rata by financial interest.

Other states allocate voting rights on a per capita basis, like partnership law. ULLCA, with its close analogy to partnership law, adopts the per capita approach as a default rule.

ULLCA and many state statutes distinguish between member-managed and manager-managed LLCs. In nearly half the states the decision to have a manager-managed LLC must be set forth in the articles of organization. Manager-managed LLCs can be created under all state legislation today.

Most statutes limit the right of non-managing members in a manager-managed LLC to act in the business. ULLCA § 301(a) states that in a manager-managed company, "A member is not an agent of the company solely by reason of being a member." This rule has the planning and tactical advantage of stripping away apparent authority from members who are not involved in management, something that cannot be done in a general partnership due to the statutory conferral of agency status upon all partners (see § 70 of this book). In this sense the nonmanager members in a manager-managed LLC resemble limited partners in a limited partnership. If an LLC is member-managed, however, under most statutes each member has agency powers, including apparent authority, similar to a partner in a partnership.

§ 109. Indemnity and Contribution Rights of Members

Most state statutes do not specifically address the matter of indemnity rights of members. ULLCA, however, covers this issue in its § 403(a), stating, "A limited liability company shall reimburse a member for payments made and indemnify a member for liabilities incurred by the member in the ordinary course of the business of the company or for the preservation of its business or property." This provision closely resembles the indemnity rights of partners under RUPA.

Contribution rights are not so central to the LLC because there is no personal liability for LLC obligations, unlike the general partnership. Liabilities and losses incurred when a member acts as an agent of the LLC are handled as they would be for any other agent of the firm (see § 8 of this book).

§ 110. Fiduciary Duties of Members

Fiduciary duties accompany positions of trust. The broader the conferral of trust, the broader the fiduciary duty. This concept plays a role in business primarily with regard to the entrustment of managerial rights and duties. Accordingly, it would stand to reason that a member in a manager-managed LLC who is not a manager ordinarily would not have any fiduciary duties, as he or she is not being placed in a position of trust. This distinction is reflected in § 404 of ULLCA, which distinguishes between member-managed and manager-managed LLCs, and in § 409. Section 409(h) of ULLCA states that in a manager-managed company "a member who is not also a manager owes no duties to the company or to the other members solely by reason of being a member." It is presumed that such member will be inactive in the business, much like a limited partner in the typical limited partnership (see § 92 of this book).

Members are subject to fiduciary duties in member-managed LLCs because they likely will be active in the business. UCCLA § 409 addresses the topic of fiduciary duties for members under such circumstances in language very similar to § 404 of RUPA. This parallel treatment may reflect the notion that the member-managed LLC is functionally similar to a partnership. Section 409 confines fiduciary duties to those of loyalty and care, defines the standard of care as gross negligence, and makes fiduciary duties mandatory, all similar to RUPA.

Not all states make fiduciary duties in the LLC mandatory. In Delaware, for example, parties may, by agreement, eliminate or reduce their common law and statutory fiduciary duties. (See §§ 76 and 97 of this book.)

§ 111. Distributions

As a default rule, in many states members receive distributions pro rata based on the contributions they have made to the LLC, similar to the default rule in limited partnerships. By contrast, the default rule in partnership law calls for equal distribution of profits, presumably on the theory that each partner has equal management rights and is contributing equally to the production of profits. ULLCA § 405 adopts the partnership approach, prescribing distribution in equal shares and explaining this as follows in the Comment to § 405:

Recognizing the informality of many limited liability companies, this section creates a simple default rule regarding interim distributions. ...The rule assumes that profits will be divided equally. ...In the simple case where the members make equal contributions of property or equal contributions of services, those assumptions avoid the necessity of maintaining a complex capital account. Where some members contribute services and others property, the unanimous vote necessary to approve interim distributions [see ULLCA § 404(c)(6)] protects against unwanted distributions of contributions to service contributors.

Similar to the limited partnership (see § 100), nearly all state LLC statutes and ULLCA contain restrictions on distributions to members. The restrictions focus on insolvency. Many states place a time limitation on the liability of a member to return a contribution. ULLCA § 407(d) requires that any proceeding under its unlawful distribution section must commence within two years after the distribution.

§ 112.   Transfer of Interests

All state statutes and ULLCA provide that a transfer of a member's interest transfers only his financial right to profits and losses and the right to participate in distributions. The full ownership interest of a member, which includes governance rights (such as the right to vote on new members), cannot be transferred without the consent of the other members. In most states this is now a default rule, following the adoption of the check-the-box regulations. ULLCA § 503(a) requires the consent of all members to a transfer of full ownership interest but allows this to be modified or eliminated in the operating agreement.

No member has a right to transfer any of the property of the business without the authorization of others. Individual members do not have an ownership interest in the property of the LLC. Instead, the LLC as an entity owns the property of the business.

§ 113. Exit Privileges

State statutes vary on the issue of exit privileges for members of an LLC. Some states allow withdrawal at will upon giving notice, others prohibit it before the expiration of a term or undertaking. Some say a member has the power to withdraw but is liable for any damages caused by premature withdrawal. In some states the withdrawing member is entitled to return of his contribution. In others he is treated as a mere assignee and must await the return of contributions to all members. In nearly all states these are default rules, subject to the agreement of the members.

There are conflicting interests on this issue. On the one hand, the unexpected withdrawal of a member may cause a crisis of shortage of capital for the business and thus the other members would like to keep a member in as long as the business is operating. On the other hand, the withdrawing member does not want to keep his capital in a business that may be going nowhere and wants to be able to leave at will and invest his money elsewhere. What is the best way to handle this? By way of analogy, the entity offering the maximum freedom of individual choice under these circumstances is the general partnership under UPA, which allows a partner to withdraw at will. Withdrawal triggers dissolution of the firm and gives the withdrawing partner a liquidation right to sell the firm assets and get paid out in cash. At the opposite extreme, in deference to federal tax rules relating to discount valuations for transfer tax purposes, some limited partnership and LLC statutes have recently been amended to deny any default right of exit altogether.

Perhaps the best way to handle this problem is to recognize the choices made in the operating agreement with regard to exit privileges and if the agreement does not address this issue, to allow a member to withdraw at will. This is the approach taken in §§ 601 and 602 of ULLCA, which provide that a member can withdraw and force the purchase of his distributional interest under § 701, unless otherwise provided in the operating agreement. This approach protects the contract among the members, yet allows movement of capital when there is no agreement otherwise.

§ 114. Dissolution

Many state LLC statutes initially provided for dissolution of an LLC under circumstances that seem borrowed from partnership law, including the withdrawal, bankruptcy, or death of a member. The goal was to avoid the corporate characteristic of continuity of life, which is now no longer a matter of concern. Although some states still have those provisions in their law, many states are amending their statutes to enhance the stability of the LLC form of doing business by taking away those unpredictable and uncertain causes of dissolution. Along those lines, ULLCA was amended recently to confine the events of dissolution to the following: (1) those specified in the operating agreement, (2) consent of the members by a percentage specified in the agreement, (3) the occurrence of an event that makes it unlawful to carry on the business, and (4) a judicial decree based on misconduct or frustration of the business purpose of the LLC.

APPENDIX A

UNIFORM PARTNERSHIP
ACT (1914)

Editor's note: The text of the Uniform Partnership Act (1914) ("UPA") contained below is taken from volume 6 of Uniform Laws Annotated, Master Edition, Uniform Partnership Act (1995) and is reproduced with permission of the publishers. At one time UPA was adopted in all states except Louisiana. It is still governing law in about half of the states, identified below. The other half of the states have adopted the revised Uniform Partnership Act (1997) ("RUPA"). They are identified in the Editor's Note to RUPA in Appendix C.

In a few states, such as Colorado, RUPA was adopted without repealing UPA, which remains as governing law for partnerships formed prior to the effective date of RUPA unless the partners of a firm elect to be governed by RUPA. Thus Colorado is contained both in the list of states below and in the list of states identified as adopting RUPA. Also, some of the states listed below have adopted RUPA but postponed the repeal of UPA until a date beyond the date of this book (e.g., Oregon, which has a 2003 date for repeal of UPA), and thus are listed below because at present UPA still is effective law in those states. They also are listed in Appendix C, where the effective date of RUPA is identified.

The information contained below on adoptions of UPA is drawn from the 2000 Cumulative Annual Pocket Part to the 1995 revision of volume 6. The date following each state is the date UPA was adopted in the state.

UPA was approved by the National Conference of Commissioners on Uniform State Laws on October 14, 1914, and adopted in the following jurisdictions: Alabama (1972), Alaska (1917), Arkansas (1941), Colorado (1931), Delaware (1947), Georgia (1985), Idaho (1920), Illinois (1917), Indiana (1950), Iowa (1971), Kentucky (1954), Maine (1973), Massachusetts (1923), Michigan (1917), Minnesota (1921), Mississippi (1977), Missouri (1949), Nebraska (1943), Nevada (1931), New Hampshire (1973), New Jersey (1919), New York (1919), North Carolina (1941), Ohio (1949), Oregon (1939), Pennsylvania (1915), Rhode Island (1957), South Carolina (1950), South Dakota (1923), Tennessee (1917), and Wisconsin (1915).

Table of Sections

PART I

PRELIMINARY PROVISIONS

PART II

NATURE OF PARTNERSHIP

PART III

RELATIONS OF PARTNERS TO PERSONS DEALING WITH THE PARTNERSHIP

PART IV

RELATIONS OF PARTNERS TO ONE ANOTHER

PART I

PRELIMINARY PROVISIONS

§ 1. Name of Act

This act may be cited as Uniform Partnership Act.

§ 2. Definition of Terms

In this act, "Court" includes every court and judge having jurisdiction in the case.

"Business" includes every trade, occupation, or profession.

"Person" includes individuals, partnerships, corporations, and other associations.

"Bankrupt" includes bankrupt under the Federal Bankruptcy Act or insolvent under any state insolvent act.

"Conveyance" includes every assignment, lease, mortgage, or encumbrance.

"Real property" includes land and any interest or estate in land.

§ 3. Interpretation of Knowledge and Notice

(1) A person has "knowledge" of a fact within the meaning of this act not only when he has actual knowledge thereof, but also when he has knowledge of such other facts as in the circumstances shows bad faith.

(2) A person has "notice" of a fact within the meaning of this act when the person who claims the benefit of the notice:

(a) States the fact to such person, or

(b) Delivers through the mail, or by other means of communication, a written statement of the fact to such person or to a proper person at his place of business or residence.

§ 4. Rules of Construction

(1) The rule that statutes in derogation of the common law are to be strictly construed shall have no application to this act.

(2) The law of estoppel shall apply under this act.

(3) The law of agency shall apply under this act.

(4) This act shall be so interpreted and construed as to effect its general purpose to make uniform the law of those states which enact it.

(5) This act shall not be construed so as to impair the obligations of any contract existing when the act goes into effect, nor to affect any action or proceedings begun or right accrued before this act takes effect.

§ 5. Rules for Cases Not Provided for in This Act

In any case not provided for in this act the rules of law and equity, including the law merchant, shall govern.

PART II

NATURE OF PARTNERSHIP

§ 6. Partnership Defined

(1) A partnership is an association of two or more persons to carry on as co-owners a business for profit.

(2) But any association formed under any other statute of this state, or any statute adopted by authority, other than the authority of this state, is not a partnership under this act, unless such association would have been a partnership in this state prior to the adoption of this act; but this act shall apply to limited partnerships except in so far as the statutes relating to such partnerships are inconsistent herewith.

§ 7. Rules for Determining the Existence of a Partnership

In determining whether a partnership exists, these rules shall apply:

(1) Except as provided by section 16 persons who are not partners as to each other are not partners as to third persons.

(2) Joint tenancy, tenancy in common, tenancy by the entireties, joint property, common property, or part ownership does not of itself establish a partnership, whether such co-owners do or do not share any profits made by the use of the property.

(3) The sharing of gross returns does not of itself establish a partnership, whether or not the persons sharing them have a joint or common right or interest in any property from which the returns are derived.

(4) The receipt by a person of a share of the profits of a business is prima facie evidence that he is a partner in the business, but no such inference shall be drawn if such profits were received in payment:

(a) As a debt by installments or otherwise,

(b) As wages of an employee or rent to a landlord,

(c) As an annuity to a widow or representative of a deceased partner,

(d) As interest on a loan, though the amount of payment vary with the profits of the business,

(e) As the consideration for the sale of a goodwill of a business or other property by installments or otherwise.

§ 8. Partnership Property

(1) All property originally brought into the partnership stock or subsequently acquired by purchase

or otherwise, on account of the partnership, is partnership property.

(2) Unless the contrary intention appears, property acquired with partnership funds is partnership property.

(3) Any estate in real property may be acquired in the partnership name. Title so acquired can be conveyed only in the partnership name.

(4) A conveyance to a partnership in the partnership name, though without words of inheritance, passes the entire estate of the grantor unless a contrary intent appears.

PART III

RELATIONS OF PARTNERS TO PERSONS DEALING WITH THE PARTNERSHIP

§ 9. Partner Agent of Partnership as to Partnership Business

(1) Every partner is an agent of the partnership for the purpose of its business, and the act of every partner, including the execution in the partnership name of any instrument, for apparently carrying on in the usual way the business of the partnership of which he is a member binds the partnership, unless the partner so acting has in fact no authority to act for the partnership in the particular matter, and the person with whom he is dealing has knowledge of the fact that he has no such authority.

(2) An act of a partner which is not apparently for the carrying on of the business of the partner-

ship in the usual way does not bind the partnership unless authorized by the other partners.

(3) Unless authorized by the other partners or unless they have abandoned the business, one or more but less than all the partners have no authority to:

(a) Assign the partnership property in trust for creditors or on the assignee's promise to pay the debts of the partnership,

(b) Dispose of the good-will of the business,

(c) Do any other act which would make it impossible to carry on the ordinary business of a partnership,

(d) Confess a judgment,

(e) Submit a partnership claim or liability to arbitration or reference.

(4) No act of a partner in contravention of a restriction on authority shall bind the partnership to persons having knowledge of the restriction.

§ 10. Conveyance of Real Property of the Partnership

(1) Where title to real property is in the partnership name, any partner may convey title to such property by a conveyance executed in the partnership name; but the partnership may recover such property unless the partner's act binds the partnership under the provisions of paragraph (1) of section 9, or unless such property has been conveyed by the grantee or a person claiming through such

grantee to a holder for value without knowledge that the partner, in making the conveyance, has exceeded his authority.

(2) Where title to real property is in the name of the partnership, a conveyance executed by a partner, in his own name, passes the equitable interest of the partnership, provided the act is one within the authority of the partner under the provisions of paragraph (1) of section 9.

(3) Where title to real property is in the name of one or more but not all the partners, and the record does not disclose the right of the partnership, the partners in whose name the title stands may convey title to such property, but the partnership may recover such property if the partners' act does not bind the partnership under the provisions of paragraph (1) of section 9, unless the purchaser or his assignee, is a holder for value, without knowledge.

(4) Where the title to real property is in the name of one or more or all the partners, or in a third person in trust for the partnership, a conveyance executed by a partner in the partnership name, or in his own name, passes the equitable interest of the partnership, provided the act is one within the authority of the partner under the provisions of paragraph (1) of section 9.

(5) Where the title to real property is in the names of all the partners, a conveyance executed by all the partners passes all their rights in such property.

§ 11. Partnership Bound by Admission of Partner

An admission or representation made by any partner concerning partnership affairs within the scope of his authority as conferred by this act is evidence against the partnership.

§ 12. Partnership Charged With Knowledge of or Notice to Partner

Notice to any partner of any matter relating to partnership affairs, and the knowledge of the partner acting in the particular matter, acquired while a partner or then present to his mind, and the knowledge of any other partner who reasonably could and should have communicated it to the acting partner, operate as notice to or knowledge of the partnership, except in the case of a fraud on the partnership committed by or with the consent of that partner.

§ 13. Partnership Bound by Partner's Wrongful Act

Where, by any wrongful act or omission of any partner acting in the ordinary course of the business of the partnership or with the authority of his co-partners, loss or injury is caused to any person, not being a partner in the partnership, or any penalty is incurred, the partnership is liable therefor to the same extent as the partner so acting or omitting to act.

§ 14. Partnership Bound by Partner's Breach of Trust

The partnership is bound to make good the loss:

(a) Where one partner acting within the scope of his apparent authority receives money or property of a third person and misapplies it; and

(b) Where the partnership in the course of its business receives money or property of a third person and the money or property so received is misapplied by any partner while it is in the custody of the partnership.

§ 15. Nature of Partner's Liability

All partners are liable

(a) Jointly and severally for everything chargeable to the partnership under sections 13 and 14.

(b) Jointly for all other debts and obligations of the partnership; but any partner may enter into a separate obligation to perform a partnership contract.

§ 16. Partner by Estoppel

(1) When a person, by words spoken or written or by conduct, represents himself, or consents to another representing him to any one, as a partner in an existing partnership or with one or more persons not actual partners, he is liable to any such person to whom such representation has been made, who has, on the faith of such representation, given credit to the actual or apparent partnership, and if he has made such representation or consented to its being

made in a public manner he is liable to such person, whether the representation has or has not been made or communicated to such person so giving credit by or with the knowledge of the apparent partner making the representation or consenting to its being made.

(a) When a partnership liability results, he is liable as though he were an actual member of the partnership.

(b) When no partnership liability results, he is liable jointly with the other persons, if any, so consenting to the contract or representation as to incur liability, otherwise separately.

(2) When a person has been thus represented to be a partner in an existing partnership, or with one or more persons not actual partners, he is an agent of the persons consenting to such representation to bind them to the same extent and in the same manner as though he were a partner in fact, with respect to persons who rely upon the representation. Where all the members of the existing partnership consent to the representation, a partnership act or obligation results; but in all other cases it is the joint act or obligation of the person acting and the persons consenting to the representation.

§ 17. Liability of Incoming Partner

A person admitted as a partner into an existing partnership is liable for all the obligations of the partnership arising before his admission as though he had been a partner when such obligations were incurred, except that this liability shall be satisfied only out of partnership property.

PART IV

RELATIONS OF PARTNERS TO ONE ANOTHER

§ 18. Rules Determining Rights and Duties of Partners

The rights and duties of the partners in relation to the partnership shall be determined, subject to any agreement between them, by the following rules:

(a) Each partner shall be repaid his contributions, whether by way of capital or advances to the partnership property and share equally in the profits and surplus remaining after all liabilities, including those to partners, are satisfied; and must contribute towards the losses, whether of capital or otherwise, sustained by the partnership according to his share in the profits.

(b) The partnership must indemnify every partner in respect of payments made and personal liabilities reasonably incurred by him in the ordinary and proper conduct of its business, or for the preservation of its business or property.

(c) A partner, who in aid of the partnership makes any payment or advance beyond the amount of capital which he agreed to contribute, shall be paid interest from the date of the payment or advance.

(d) A partner shall receive interest on the capital contributed by him only from the date when repayment should be made.

(e) All partners have equal rights in the management and conduct of the partnership business.

(f) No partner is entitled to remuneration for acting in the partnership business, except that a surviving partner is entitled to reasonable compensation for his services in winding up the partnership affairs.

(g) No person can become a member of a partnership without the consent of all the partners.

(h) Any difference arising as to ordinary matters connected with the partnership business may be decided by a majority of the partners; but no act in contravention of any agreement between the partners may be done rightfully without the consent of all the partners.

§ 19. Partnership Books

The partnership books shall be kept, subject to any agreement between the partners, at the principal place of business of the partnership, and every partner shall at all times have access to and may inspect and copy any of them.

§ 20. Duty of Partners to Render Information

Partners shall render on demand true and full information of all things affecting the partnership

to any partner or the legal representative of any
deceased partner or partner under legal disability.

§ 21. Partner Accountable as a Fiduciary

(1) Every partner must account to the partnership for any benefit, and hold as trustee for it any
profits derived by him without the consent of the
other partners from any transaction connected with
the formation, conduct, or liquidation of the partnership or from any use by him of its property.

(2) This section applies also to the representatives of a deceased partner engaged in the liquidation of the affairs of the partnership as the personal representatives of the last surviving partner.

§ 22. Right to an Account

Any partner shall have the right to a formal
account as to partnership affairs:

(a) If he is wrongfully excluded from the partnership business or possession of its property by his co-
partners,

(b) If the right exists under the terms of any
agreement,

(c) As provided by section 21,

(d) Whenever other circumstances render it just
and reasonable.

§ 23. Continuation of Partnership Beyond Fixed Term

(1) When a partnership for a fixed term or particular undertaking is continued after the termination

of such term or particular undertaking without any express agreement, the rights and duties of the partners remain the same as they were at such termination, so far as is consistent with a partnership at will.

(2) A continuation of the business by the partners or such of them as habitually acted therein during the term, without any settlement or liquidation of the partnership affairs, is prima facie evidence of a continuation of the partnership.

PART V

PROPERTY RIGHTS OF A PARTNER

§ 24. Extent of Property Rights of a Partner

The property rights of a partner are (1) his rights in specific partnership property, (2) his interest in the partnership, and (3) his right to participate in the management.

§ 25. Nature of a Partner's Right in Specific Partnership Property

(1) A partner is co-owner with his partners of specific partnership property holding as a tenant in partnership.

(2) The incidents of this tenancy are such that:

(a) A partner, subject to the provisions of this act and to any agreement between the partners, has an equal right with his partners to possess specific partnership property for partnership purposes; but he has no right to possess such property for any other purpose without the consent of his partners.

(b) A partner's right in specific partnership property is not assignable except in connection with the assignment of rights of all the partners in the same property.

(c) A partner's right in specific partnership property is not subject to attachment or execution, except on a claim against the partnership. When partnership property is attached for a partnership debt the partners, or any of them, or the representatives of a deceased partner, cannot claim any right under the homestead or exemption laws.

(d) On the death of a partner his right in specific partnership property vests in the surviving partner or partners, except where the deceased was the last surviving partner, when his right in such property vests in his legal representative. Such surviving partner or partners, or the legal representative of the last surviving partner, has no right to possess the partnership property for any but a partnership purpose.

(e) A partner's right in specific partnership property is not subject to dower, curtesy, or allowances to widows, heirs, or next of kin.

§ 26. Nature of Partner's Interest in the Partnership

A partner's interest in the partnership is his share of the profits and surplus, and the same is personal property.

§ 27.   Assignment of Partner's Interest

(1) A conveyance by a partner of his interest in the partnership does not of itself dissolve the partnership, nor, as against the other partners in the absence of agreement, entitle the assignee, during the continuance of the partnership, to interfere in the management or administration of the partnership business or affairs, or to require any information or account of partnership transactions, or to inspect the partnership books; but it merely entitles the assignee to receive in accordance with his contract the profits to which the assigning partner would otherwise be entitled.

(2) In case of a dissolution of the partnership, the assignee is entitled to receive his assignor's interest and may require an account from the date only of the last account agreed to by all the partners.

§ 28.   Partner's Interest Subject to Charging Order

(1) On due application to a competent court by any judgment creditor of a partner, the court which entered the judgment, order, or decree, or any other court, may charge the interest of the debtor partner with payment of the unsatisfied amount of such judgment debt with interest thereon; and may then or later appoint a receiver of his share of the profits, and of any other money due or to fall due to him in respect of the partnership, and make all other orders, directions, accounts and inquiries which the debtor partner might have made, or which the circumstances of the case may require.

(2) The interest charged may be redeemed at any time before foreclosure, or in case of a sale being directed by the court may be purchased without thereby causing a dissolution:

(a) With separate property, by any one or more of the partners, or

(b) With partnership property, by any one or more of the partners with the consent of all the partners whose interests are not so charged or sold.

(3) Nothing in this act shall be held to deprive a partner of his right, if any, under the exemption laws, as regards his interest in the partnership.

PART VI

DISSOLUTION AND WINDING UP

§ 29. Dissolution Defined

The dissolution of a partnership is the change in the relation of the partners caused by any partner ceasing to be associated in the carrying on as distinguished from the winding up of the business.

§ 30. Partnership Not Terminated by Dissolution

On dissolution the partnership is not terminated, but continues until the winding up of partnership affairs is completed.

§ 31. Causes of Dissolution

Dissolution is caused:

(1) Without violation of the agreement between the partners,

(a) By the termination of the definite term or particular undertaking specified in the agreement,

(b) By the express will of any partner when no definite term or particular undertaking is specified,

(c) By the express will of all the partners who have not assigned their interests or suffered them to be charged for their separate debts, either before or after the termination of any specified term or particular undertaking,

(d) By the expulsion of any partner from the business bona fide in accordance with such a power conferred by the agreement between the partners;

(2) In contravention of the agreement between the partners, where the circumstances do not permit a dissolution under any other provision of this section, by the express will of any partner at any time;

(3) By any event which makes it unlawful for the business of the partnership to be carried on or for the members to carry it on in partnership;

(4) By the death of any partner;

(5) By the bankruptcy of any partner or the partnership;

(6) By decree of court under section 32.

§ 32. Dissolution by Decree of Court

(1) On application by or for a partner the court shall decree a dissolution whenever:

(a) A partner has been declared a lunatic in any judicial proceeding or is shown to be of unsound mind,

(b) A partner becomes in any other way incapable of performing his part of the partnership contract,

(c) A partner has been guilty of such conduct as tends to affect prejudicially the carrying on of the business,

(d) A partner wilfully or persistently commits a breach of the partnership agreement, or otherwise so conducts himself in matters relating to the partnership business that it is not reasonably practicable to carry on the business in partnership with him,

(e) The business of the partnership can only be carried on at a loss,

(f) Other circumstances render a dissolution equitable.

(2) On the application of the purchaser of a partner's interest under sections 28 or 29 [should read 27 or 28]:

(a) After the termination of the specified term or particular undertaking,

(b) At any time if the partnership was a partnership at will when the interest was assigned or when the charging order was issued.

§ 33. General Effect of Dissolution on Authority of Partner

Except so far as may be necessary to wind up partnership affairs or to complete transactions begun but not then finished, dissolution terminates all authority of any partner to act for the partnership,

(1) With respect to the partners,

(a) When the dissolution is not by the act, bankruptcy or death of a partner; or

(b) When the dissolution is by such act, bankruptcy or death of a partner, in cases where section 34 so requires.

(2) With respect to persons not partners, as declared in section 35.

§ 34. Right of Partner to Contribution From Co-partners After Dissolution

Where the dissolution is caused by the act, death or bankruptcy of a partner, each partner is liable to his co-partners for his share of any liability created by any partner acting for the partnership as if the partnership had not been dissolved unless

(a) The dissolution being by act of any partner, the partner acting for the partnership had knowledge of the dissolution, or

(b) The dissolution being by the death or bankruptcy of a partner, the partner acting for the partnership had knowledge or notice of the death or bankruptcy.

§ 35. Power of Partner to Bind Partnership to Third Persons After Dissolution

(1) After dissolution a partner can bind the partnership except as provided in Paragraph (3).

(a) By any act appropriate for winding up partnership affairs or completing transactions unfinished at dissolution;

(b) By any transaction which would bind the partnership if dissolution had not taken place, provided the other party to the transaction

(I) Had extended credit to the partnership prior to dissolution and had no knowledge or notice of the dissolution; or

(II) Though he had not so extended credit, had nevertheless known of the partnership prior to dissolution, and, having no knowledge or notice of dissolution, the fact of dissolution had not been advertised in a newspaper of general circulation in the place (or in each place if more than one) at which the partnership business was regularly carried on.

(2) The liability of a partner under Paragraph (1b) shall be satisfied out of partnership assets alone when such partner had been prior to dissolution

(a) Unknown as a partner to the person with whom the contract is made; and

(b) So far unknown and inactive in partnership affairs that the business reputation of the partnership could not be said to have been in any degree due to his connection with it.

(3) The partnership is in no case bound by any act of a partner after dissolution

(a) Where the partnership is dissolved because it is unlawful to carry on the business, unless the act is appropriate for winding up partnership affairs; or

(b) Where the partner has become bankrupt; or

(c) Where the partner has no authority to wind up partnership affairs; except by a transaction with one who

(I) Had extended credit to the partnership prior to dissolution and had no knowledge or notice of his want of authority; or

(II) Had not extended credit to the partnership prior to dissolution, and, having no knowledge or notice of his want of authority, the fact of his want of authority has not been advertised in the manner provided for advertising the fact of dissolution in Paragraph (1bII).

(4) Nothing in this section shall affect the liability under Section 16 of any person who after dissolution represents himself or consents to another representing him as a partner in a partnership engaged in carrying on business.

§ 36. Effect of Dissolution on Partner's Existing Liability

(1) The dissolution of the partnership does not of itself discharge the existing liability of any partner.

(2) A partner is discharged from any existing liability upon dissolution of the partnership by an

agreement to that effect between himself, the partnership creditor and the person or partnership continuing the business; and such agreement may be inferred from the course of dealing between the creditor having knowledge of the dissolution and the person or partnership continuing the business.

(3) Where a person agrees to assume the existing obligations of a dissolved partnership, the partners whose obligations have been assumed shall be discharged from any liability to any creditor of the partnership who, knowing of the agreement, consents to a material alteration in the nature or time of payment of such obligations.

(4) The individual property of a deceased partner shall be liable for all obligations of the partnership incurred while he was a partner but subject to the prior payment of his separate debts.

§ 37. Right to Wind Up

Unless otherwise agreed the partners who have not wrongfully dissolved the partnership or the legal representative of the last surviving partner, not bankrupt, has the right to wind up the partnership affairs; provided, however, that any partner, his legal representative or his assignee, upon cause shown, may obtain winding up by the court.

§ 38. Rights of Partners to Application of Partnership Property

(1) When dissolution is caused in any way, except in contravention of the partnership agreement, each

partner, as against his co-partners and all persons claiming through them in respect of their interests in the partnership, unless otherwise agreed, may have the partnership property applied to discharge its liabilities, and the surplus applied to pay in cash the net amount owing to the respective partners. But if dissolution is caused by expulsion of a partner, bona fide under the partnership agreement and if the expelled partner is discharged from all partnership liabilities, either by payment or agreement under section 36(2), he shall receive in cash only the net amount due him from the partnership.

(2) When dissolution is caused in contravention of the partnership agreement the rights of the partners shall be as follows:

(a) Each partner who has not caused dissolution wrongfully shall have,

I.   All the rights specified in paragraph (1) of this section, and

II.   The right, as against each partner who has caused the dissolution wrongfully, to damages for breach of the agreement.

(b) The partners who have not caused the dissolution wrongfully, if they all desire to continue the business in the same name, either by themselves or jointly with others, may do so, during the agreed term for the partnership and for that purpose may possess the partnership property, provided they secure the payment by bond approved by the court, or pay to any partner who has caused the dissolution wrongfully, the value of his interest in the partnership at the dissolution, less any damages recoverable under clause (2a II) of this section, and in like manner indemnify him against all present or future partnership liabilities.

(c) A partner who has caused the dissolution wrongfully shall have:

I.   If the business is not continued under the provisions of paragraph (2b) all the rights of a partner under paragraph (1), subject to clause (2a II), of this section,

II.   If the business is continued under paragraph (2b) of this section the right as against his co-partners and all claiming through them in respect of their interests in the partnership, to have the value of his interest in the partnership, less any damages caused to his co-partners by the dissolution, ascertained and paid to him in cash, or the payment secured by bond approved by the court, and to be released from all existing liabilities of the partnership; but in ascertaining the value of the partner's interest the value of the good-will of the business shall not be considered.

§ 39.   Rights Where Partnership is Dissolved for Fraud or Misrepresentation

Where a partnership contract is rescinded on the ground of the fraud or misrepresentation of one of the parties thereto, the party entitled to rescind is, without prejudice to any other right, entitled,

(a) To a lien on, or a right of retention of, the surplus of the partnership property after satisfying the partnership liabilities to third persons for any sum of money paid by him for the purchase of an interest in the partnership and for any capital or advances contributed by him; and

(b) To stand, after all liabilities to third persons have been satisfied, in the place of the creditors of the partnership for any payments made by him in respect of the partnership liabilities; and

(c) To be indemnified by the person guilty of the fraud or making the representation against all debts and liabilities of the partnership.

§ 40. Rules for Distribution

In settling accounts between the partners after dissolution, the following rules shall be observed, subject to any agreement to the contrary:

(a) The assets of the partnership are:

I.   The partnership property,

II.   The contributions of the partners necessary for the payment of all the liabilities specified in clause (b) of this paragraph.

(b) The liabilities of the partnership shall rank in order of payment, as follows:

I.   Those owing to creditors other than partners,

II.   Those owing to partners other than for capital and profits,

III.   Those owing to partners in respect of capital,

IV.   Those owing to partners in respect of profits.

(c) The assets shall be applied in order of their declaration in clause (a) of this paragraph to the satisfaction of the liabilities.

(d) The partners shall contribute, as provided by section 18(a) the amount necessary to satisfy the liabilities; but if any, but not all, of the partners are insolvent, or, not being subject to process, refuse to contribute, the other partners shall contribute their share of the liabilities, and, in the relative proportions in which they share the profits, the additional amount necessary to pay the liabilities.

(e) An assignee for the benefit of creditors or any person appointed by the court shall have the right to enforce the contributions specified in clause (d) of this paragraph.

(f) Any partner or his legal representative shall have the right to enforce the contributions specified in clause (d) of this paragraph, to the extent of the amount which he has paid in excess of his share of the liability.

(g) The individual property of a deceased partner shall be liable for the contributions specified in clause (d) of this paragraph.

(h) When partnership property and the individual properties of the partners are in possession of a court for distribution, partnership creditors shall have priority on partnership property and separate creditors on individual property, saving the rights of lien or secured creditors as heretofore.

(i) Where a partner has become bankrupt or his estate is insolvent the claims against his separate property shall rank in the following order:

> I.   Those owing to separate creditors,
>
> II. Those owing to partnership creditors,
>
> III. Those owing to partners by way of contribution.

§ 41. Liability of Persons Continuing the Business in Certain Cases

(1) When any new partner is admitted into an existing partnership, or when any partner retires and assigns (or the representative of the deceased partner assigns) his rights in partnership property to two or more of the partners, or to one or more of the partners and one or more third persons, if the business is continued without liquidation of the partnership affairs, creditors of the first or dissolved partnership are also creditors of the partnership so continuing the business.

(2) When all but one partner retire and assign (or the representative of a deceased partner assigns)

their rights in partnership property to the remaining partner, who continues the business without liquidation of partnership affairs, either alone or with others, creditors of the dissolved partnership are also creditors of the person or partnership so continuing the business.

(3) When any partner retires or dies and the business of the dissolved partnership is continued as set forth in paragraphs (1) and (2) of this section, with the consent of the retired partners or the representative of the deceased partner, but without any assignment of his right in partnership property, rights of creditors of the dissolved partnership and of the creditors of the person or partnership continuing the business shall be as if such assignment had been made.

(4) When all the partners or their representatives assign their rights in partnership property to one or more third persons who promise to pay the debts and who continue the business of the dissolved partnership, creditors of the dissolved partnership are also creditors of the person or partnership continuing the business.

(5) When any partner wrongfully causes a dissolution and the remaining partners continue the business under the provisions of section 38(2b), either alone or with others, and without liquidation of the partnership affairs, creditors of the dissolved partnership are also creditors of the person or partnership continuing the business.

(6) When a partner is expelled and the remaining partners continue the business either alone or with others, without liquidation of the partnership affairs, creditors of the dissolved partnership are also creditors of the person or partnership continuing the business.

(7) The liability of a third person becoming a partner in the partnership continuing the business, under this section, to the creditors of the dissolved partnership shall be satisfied out of partnership property only.

(8) When the business of a partnership after dissolution is continued under any conditions set forth in this section the creditors of the dissolved partnership, as against the separate creditors of the retiring or deceased partner or the representative of the deceased partner, have a prior right to any claim of the retired partner or the representative of the deceased partner against the person or partnership continuing the business, on account of the retired or deceased partner's interest in the dissolved partnership or on account of any consideration promised for such interest or for his right in partnership property.

(9) Nothing in this section shall be held to modify any right of creditors to set aside any assignment on the ground of fraud.

(10) The use by the person or partnership continuing the business of the partnership name, or the name of a deceased partner as part thereof, shall not of itself make the individual property of

the deceased partner liable for any debts contracted by such person or partnership.

§ 42. Rights of Retiring or Estate of Deceased Partner When the Business Is Continued

When any partner retires or dies, and the business is continued under any of the conditions set forth in section 41 (1, 2, 3, 5, 6), or section 38(2b) without any settlement of accounts as between him or his estate and the person or partnership continuing the business, unless otherwise agreed, he or his legal representative as against such persons or partnership may have the value of his interest at the date of dissolution ascertained, and shall receive as an ordinary creditor an amount equal to the value of his interest in the dissolved partnership with interest, or, at his option or at the option of his legal representative, in lieu of interest, the profits attributable to the use of his right in the property of the dissolved partnership; provided that the creditors of the dissolved partnership as against the separate creditors, or the representative of the retired or deceased partner, shall have priority on any claim arising under this section, as provided by section 41(8) of this act.

§ 43. Accrual of Actions

The right to an account of his interest shall accrue to any partner, or his legal representative, as against the winding up partners or the surviving partners or the person or partnership continuing the business, at the date of dissolution, in the absence of any agreement to the contrary.

PART VII

MISCELLANEOUS PROVISIONS

§ 44. When Act Takes Effect

This act shall take effect on the _____ day of _____ one thousand nine hundred and _____.

§ 45. Legislation Repealed

All acts or parts of acts inconsistent with this act are hereby repealed.

APPENDIX B

CONVERSION TABLE

UPA TO RUPA

UPA	RUPA
1	1002
2	101
3	102
4(2) and (3)	104(a)
4(4)	1001
4(5)	1007
5	104(a)
6	202
7	202
8	203, 204
9	301
10	302
11	none
12	102(f)
13	305(a)
14	305(b)
15	306(a)
16	308
17	306(b)
18	401
19	403(a) and (b)
20	403(c)

380

UPA	RUPA
21	404
22	405(b)
23	406
24	none
25	501
26	502
27	503
28	504
29	801 (see also 601)
30	802
31	801 (see also 601, 602)
32	801(5)(6)(see also 601(5)(7))
33	804(1)(see also 603(b)(1))
34	806 (see also 702(b))
35	804 (see also 702(a))
36	703
37	803
38	602(c), 701, 807(a)
39	none
40	807
41	705 (re 41(10))
42	701(b) and (i)
43	405
44	1004
45	1005

CONVERSION TABLE

RUPA TO UPA

RUPA	UPA
101	2
102	3, 12
103	none
104	5
105	none
106	none

<u>RUPA</u>	<u>UPA</u>
107	none
201	none
202	6, 7
203	8(1), 25
204	8
301	9
302	10
303	none
304	none
305	13, 14
306	15, 17
307	none
308	16
401	18
402	38(1)
403	19, 20
404	21
405(a)	none
405(b)	22, 43
406	23
501	24, 25
502	26
503	27, 32(2)
504	28
601	see 31, 32
602	see 31(2), 38(2)
603	none
701	38, 42
702	34, 35
703	35, 36
704	none
705	41(10)
801	29, 31, 32
802	30
803	37
804	33, 35
805	none
806	33(1), 34

RUPA	UPA
807	38(1), 40
901	none
902	none
903	none
904	none
905	none
906	none
907	none
908	none
1001	4(4)
1002	1
1003	none
1004	44
1005	45
1006	none
1007	none

APPENDIX C

UNIFORM PARTNERSHIP ACT (1997)

Editor's note: The revised Uniform Partnership Act (1997) ("RUPA") is reproduced below. The text includes amendments enacted in 1996 incorporating limited liability partnership provisions and in 1997 modifying the dissolution provisions in response to the check-the-box regulations adopted by the Internal Revenue Service.

RUPA has been adopted in 28 jurisdictions as of the date of this writing (August 2000). The data set forth below is based on the 2000 Cumulative Annual Pocket Part to 6 Uniform Laws Annotated 1 (1995), as updated through August 2000 by information supplied by the National Conference of Commissioners on Uniform State Laws ("NCCUSL") at www.nccusl.org. The date set forth immediately after each jurisdiction is the effective date of the Act. In some jurisdictions (e.g., Colorado) UPA remains effective law for all partnerships formed prior to the effective date of RUPA unless the partners of a firm elect to be governed by RUPA. In other jurisdictions UPA remains effective law until a certain date (e.g., until 2003 in Oregon) and then is repealed. In all other jurisdictions UPA is repealed upon the adoption of RUPA, although it will continue to govern disputes that arise prior to the effective date of RUPA.

RUPA has been adopted in the following jurisdictions: Alabama (1997), Arizona (1996), Arkansas (2000), California (1997), Colorado (1998), Connecticut (1997), Delaware (2000), District of Columbia (1997), Florida (1996), Hawaii (2000), Idaho (2001), Iowa (1999), Kansas (1999), Maryland (1998), Minnesota (1999), Montana (1993), Nebraska (1998), New Mexico (1997), North Dakota (1996); Oklahoma (1997), Oregon (1998), Texas (1994); Vermont (1999), Virgin Islands (1998), Virginia (1997), Washington (1999), West Virginia (1995); and Wyoming (1994).

UNIFORM PARTNERSHIP ACT– QUICK CHRONOLOGY

1914–Original Uniform Partnership Act

1992–Promulgation of Uniform Partnership Act (1992)

1993–Amendments to 1992 Act, becomes Uniform Partnership Act (1993)

1994–Amendments to 1993 Act, becomes Uniform Partnership Act (1994)

1996–Amendments to 1994 act, becomes Uniform Partnership Act (1996)

1997–Amendments to 1996 act, becomes Uniform Partnership Act (1997)

Table of Sections

ARTICLE 1

GENERAL PROVISIONS

ARTICLE 2

NATURE OF PARTNERSHIP

ARTICLE 9

CONVERSIONS AND MERGERS

ARTICLE 10

MISCELLANEOUS PROVISIONS

[ARTICLE] 1

GENERAL PROVISIONS

§ 101. Definitions.

In this [Act]:

(1) "Business" includes every trade, occupation, and profession.

(2) "Debtor in bankruptcy" means a person who is the subject of:

(i) an order for relief under Title 11 of the United States Code or a comparable order under a successor statute of general application; or

(ii) a comparable order under federal, state, or foreign law governing insolvency.

(3) "Distribution" means a transfer of money or other property from a partnership to a partner in the partner's capacity as a partner or to the partner's transferee.

(4) "Foreign limited liability partnership" means a partnership that:

(i) is formed under laws other than the laws of this State; and

(ii) has the status of a limited liability partnership under those laws.

(5) "Limited liability partnership" means a partnership that has filed a statement of qualification under Section 1001 and does not have a similar statement in effect in any other jurisdiction.

(6) "Partnership" means an association of two or more persons to carry on as co-owners a business for profit formed under Section 202, predecessor law, or comparable law of another jurisdiction.

(7) "Partnership agreement" means the agreement, whether written, oral, or implied, among the partners concerning the partnership, including amendments to the partnership agreement.

(8) "Partnership at will" means a partnership in which the partners have not agreed to remain partners until the expiration of a definite term or the completion of a particular undertaking.

(9) "Partnership interest" or "partner's interest in the partnership" means all of a partner's inter-

ests in the partnership, including the partner's transferable interest and all management and other rights.

(10) "Person" means an individual, corporation, business trust, estate, trust, partnership, association, joint venture, government, governmental subdivision, agency, or instrumentality, or any other legal or commercial entity.

(11) "Property" means all property, real, personal, or mixed, tangible or intangible, or any interest therein.

(12) "State" means a State of the United States, the District of Columbia, the Commonwealth of Puerto Rico, or any territory or insular possession subject to the jurisdiction of the United States.

(13) "Statement" means a statement of partnership authority under Section 303, a statement of denial under Section 304, a statement of dissociation under Section 704, a statement of dissolution under Section 805, a statement of merger under Section 907, a statement of qualification under Section 1001, a statement of foreign qualification under Section 1102, or an amendment or cancellation of any of the foregoing.

(14) "Transfer" includes an assignment, conveyance, lease, mortgage, deed, and encumbrance.

§ 102. Knowledge and Notice

(a) A person knows a fact if the person has actual knowledge of it.

(b) A person has notice of a fact if the person:

    (1) knows of it;

    (2) has received a notification of it; or

    (3) has reason to know it exists from all of the facts known to the person at the time in question.

(c) A person notifies or gives a notification to another by taking steps reasonably required to inform the other person in ordinary course, whether or not the other person learns of it.

(d) A person receives a notification when the notification:

    (1) comes to the person's attention; or

    (2) is duly delivered at the person's place of business or at any other place held out by the person as a place for receiving communications.

(e) Except as otherwise provided in subsection (f), a person other than an individual knows, has notice, or receives a notification of a fact for purposes of a particular transaction when the individual conducting the transaction knows, has notice, or receives a notification of the fact, or in any event when the fact would have been brought to the individual's attention if the person had exercised reasonable diligence. The person exercises reasonable diligence if it maintains reasonable routines for communicating significant information to the individual conducting the transaction and there is reasonable compliance with the routines. Reasonable diligence does not require an individual acting for the person to communicate information unless the communication is part of the individual's regular duties or the individual has reason to know of the transaction and that the transaction would be materially affected by the information.

(f) A partner's knowledge, notice, or receipt of a notification of a fact relating to the partnership is effective immediately as knowledge by, notice to, or receipt of a notification by the partnership, except in the case of a fraud on the partnership committed by or with the consent of that partner.

§ 103. Effect of Partnership Agreement; Nonwaivable Provisions

(a) Except as otherwise provided in subsection (b), relations among the partners and between the partners and the partnership are governed by the partnership agreement. To the extent the partnership agreement does not otherwise provide, this [Act] governs relations among the partners and between the partners and the partnership.

(b) The partnership agreement may not:

(1) vary the rights and duties under Section 105 except to eliminate the duty to provide copies of statements to all of the partners;

(2) unreasonably restrict the right of access to books and records under Section 403(b);

(3) eliminate the duty of loyalty under Section 404(b) or 603(b)(3), but:

(i) the partnership agreement may identify specific types or categories of activities that do not violate the duty of loyalty, if not manifestly unreasonable; or

(ii) all of the partners or a number or percentage specified in the partnership agreement may authorize or ratify, after full disclosure of all material facts, a specific act or transaction that otherwise would violate the duty of loyalty;

(4) unreasonably reduce the duty of care under Section 404(c) or 603(b)(3);

(5) eliminate the obligation of good faith and fair dealing under Section 404(d), but the partnership agreement may prescribe the standards by which the performance of the obligation is to be measured, if the standards are not manifestly unreasonable;

(6) vary the power to dissociate as a partner under Section 602(a), except to require the notice under Section 601(1) to be in writing;

(7) vary the right of a court to expel a partner in the events specified in Section 601(5);

(8) vary the requirement to wind up the partnership business in cases specified in Section 801(4), (5), or (6);

(9) vary the law applicable to a limited liability partnership under Section 106(b); or

(10) restrict rights of third parties under this [Act].

§ 104. Supplemental Principles of Law

(a) Unless displaced by particular provisions of this [Act], the principles of law and equity supplement this [Act].

(b) If an obligation to pay interest arises under this [Act] and the rate is not specified, the rate is that specified in [applicable statute].

§ 105. Execution, Filing, and Recording of Statements

(a) A statement may be filed in the office of [the Secretary of State]. A certified copy of a statement that is filed in an office in another State may be filed in the office of [the Secretary of State]. Either filing has the effect provided in this [Act] with respect to partnership property located in or transactions that occur in this State.

(b) A certified copy of a statement that has been filed in the office of the [Secretary of State] and recorded in the office for recording transfers of real property has the effect provided for recorded statements in this [Act]. A recorded statement that is not a certified copy of a statement filed in the office of the [Secretary of State] does not have the effect provided for recorded statements in this [Act].

(c) A statement filed by a partnership must be executed by at least two partners. Other statements must be executed by a partner or other person authorized by this [Act]. An individual who executes a statement as, or on behalf of, a partner or other person named as a partner in a statement shall personally declare under penalty of perjury that the contents of the statement are accurate.

(d) A person authorized by this [Act] to file a statement may amend or cancel the statement by filing an amendment or cancellation that names the partnership, identifies the statement, and states the substance of the amendment or cancellation.

(e) A person who files a statement pursuant to this section shall promptly send a copy of the statement to every nonfiling partner and to any other person named as a partner in the statement. Failure to send a copy of a statement to a partner or other person does not limit the effectiveness of the statement as to a person not a partner.

(f) The [Secretary of State] may collect a fee for filing or providing a certified copy of a statement. The [officer responsible for] recording transfers of real property may collect a fee for recording a statement.

§ 106. Governing Law

(a) Except as otherwise provided in subsection (b), the law of the jurisdiction in which a partnership has its chief executive office governs relations among the partners and between the partners and the partnership.

(b) The law of this State governs relations among the partners and between the partners and the partnership and the liability of partners for an obligation of a limited liability partnership.

§ 107. Partnership Subject to Amendment or Repeal of [Act]

A partnership governed by this [Act] is subject to any amendment to or repeal of this [Act].

[ARTICLE 2]

NATURE OF PARTNERSHIP

§ 201. Partnership as Entity

(a) A partnership is an entity distinct from its partners.

(b) A limited liability partnership continues to be the same entity that existed before the filing of a statement of qualification under Section 1001.

§ 202. Formation of Partnership

(a) Except as otherwise provided in subsection (b), the association of two or more persons to carry on as co-owners a business for profit forms a partnership, whether or not the persons intend to form a partnership.

(b) An association formed under a statute other than this [Act], a predecessor statute, or a comparable statute of another jurisdiction is not a partnership under this [Act].

(c) In determining whether a partnership is formed, the following rules apply:

(1) Joint tenancy, tenancy in common, tenancy by the entireties, joint property, common property, or part ownership does not by itself establish a partnership, even if the co-owners share profits made by the use of the property.

(2) The sharing of gross returns does not by itself establish a partnership, even if the persons

sharing them have a joint or common right or interest in property from which the returns are derived.

(3) A person who receives a share of the profits of a business is presumed to be a partner in the business, unless the profits were received in payment:

(i) of a debt by installments or otherwise;

(ii) for services as an independent contractor or of wages or other compensation to an employee;

(iii) of rent;

(iv) of an annuity or other retirement or health benefit to a beneficiary, representative, or designee of a deceased or retired partner;

(v) of interest or other charge on a loan, even if the amount of payment varies with the profits of the business, including a direct or indirect present or future ownership of the collateral, or rights to income, proceeds, or increase in value derived from the collateral; or

(vi) for the sale of the goodwill of a business or other property by installments or otherwise.

§ 203. Partnership Property

Property acquired by a partnership is property of the partnership and not of the partners individually.

§ 204. When Property is Partnership Property

(a) Property is partnership property if acquired in the name of:

(1) the partnership; or

(2) one or more partners with an indication in the instrument transferring title to the property of the person's capacity as a partner or of the existence of a partnership but without an indication of the name of the partnership.

(b) Property is acquired in the name of the partnership by a transfer to:

(1) the partnership in its name; or

(2) one or more partners in their capacity as partners in the partnership, if the name of the partnership is indicated in the instrument transferring title to the property.

(c) Property is presumed to be partnership property if purchased with partnership assets, even if not acquired in the name of the partnership or of one or more partners with an indication in the instrument transferring title to the property of the person's capacity as a partner or of the existence of a partnership.

(d) Property acquired in the name of one or more of the partners, without an indication in the instrument transferring title to the property of the person's capacity as a partner or of the existence of a partnership and without use of partnership assets is presumed to be separate property, even if used for partnership purposes.

[ARTICLE] 3

RELATIONS OF PARTNERS TO PERSONS DEALING WITH PARTNERSHIP

§ 301. Partner Agent of Partnership

Subject to the effect of a statement of partnership authority under Section 303:

(1) Each partner is an agent of the partnership for the purpose of its business. An act of a partner, including the execution of an instrument in the partnership name, for apparently carrying on in the ordinary course the partnership business or business of the kind carried on by the partnership binds the partnership, unless the partner had no authority to act for the partnership in the particular matter and the person with whom the partner was dealing knew or had received a notification that the partner lacked authority.

(2) An act of a partner which is not apparently for carrying on in the ordinary course the partnership business or business of the kind carried on by the partnership binds the partnership only if the act was authorized by the other partners.

§ 302. Transfer of Partnership Property

(a) Partnership property may be transferred as follows:

(1) Subject to the effect of a statement of partnership authority under Section 303, partnership property held in the name of the partnership may be transferred by an instrument of transfer executed by a partner in the partnership name.

(2) Partnership property held in the name of one or more partners with an indication in the instrument transferring the property to them of their capacity as partners or of the existence of a partnership, but without an indication of the name of the partnership, may be transferred by an instrument of transfer executed by the persons in whose name the property is held.

(3) Partnership property held in the name of one or more persons other than the partnership, without an indication in the instrument transferring the property to them of their capacity as partners or of the existence of a partnership, may be transferred by an instrument of transfer executed by the persons in whose name the property is held.

(b) A partnership may recover partnership property from a transferee only if it proves that execution of the instrument of initial transfer did not bind the partnership under Section 301 and:

(1) as to a subsequent transferee who gave value for property transferred under subsection (a)(1) and (2), proves that the subsequent transferee knew or had received a notification that the person who executed the instrument of initial

transfer lacked authority to bind the partnership; or

(2) as to a transferee who gave value for property transferred under subsection (a)(3), proves that the transferee knew or had received a notification that the property was partnership property and that the person who executed the instrument of initial transfer lacked authority to bind the partnership.

(c) A partnership may not recover partnership property from a subsequent transferee if the partnership would not have been entitled to recover the property, under subsection (b), from any earlier transferee of the property.

(d) If a person holds all of the partners' interests in the partnership, all of the partnership property vests in that person. The person may execute a document in the name of the partnership to evidence vesting of the property in that person and may file or record the document.

§ 303. Statement of Partnership Authority

(a) A partnership may file a statement of partnership authority, which:

(1) must include:

(i) the name of the partnership;

(ii) the street address of its chief executive office and of one office in this State, if there is one;

(iii) the names and mailing addresses of all of the partners or of an agent appointed and maintained by the partnership for the purpose of subsection (b); and

(iv) the names of the partners authorized to execute an instrument transferring real property held in the name of the partnership; and

(2) may state the authority, or limitations on the authority, of some or all of the partners to enter into other transactions on behalf of the partnership and any other matter.

(b) If a statement of partnership authority names an agent, the agent shall maintain a list of the names and mailing addresses of all of the partners and make it available to any person on request for good cause shown.

(c) If a filed statement of partnership authority is executed pursuant to Section 105(c) and states the name of the partnership but does not contain all of the other information required by subsection (a), the statement nevertheless operates with respect to a person not a partner as provided in subsections (d) and (e).

(d) Except as otherwise provided in subsection (g), a filed statement of partnership authority supplements the authority of a partner to enter into transactions on behalf of the partnership as follows:

(1) Except for transfers of real property, a grant of authority contained in a filed statement of partnership authority is conclusive in favor of a

person who gives value without knowledge to the contrary, so long as and to the extent that a limitation on that authority is not then contained in another filed statement. A filed cancellation of a limitation on authority revives the previous grant of authority.

(2) A grant of authority to transfer real property held in the name of the partnership contained in a certified copy of a filed statement of partnership authority recorded in the office for recording transfers of that real property is conclusive in favor of a person who gives value without knowledge to the contrary, so long as and to the extent that a certified copy of a filed statement containing a limitation on that authority is not then of record in the office for recording transfers of that real property. The recording in the office for recording transfers of that real property of a certified copy of a filed cancellation of a limitation on authority revives the previous grant of authority.

(e) A person not a partner is deemed to know of a limitation on the authority of a partner to transfer real property held in the name of the partnership if a certified copy of the filed statement containing the limitation on authority is of record in the office for recording transfers of that real property.

(f) Except as otherwise provided in subsections (d) and (e) and Sections 704 and 805, a person not a partner is not deemed to know of a limitation on the authority of a partner merely because the limitation is contained in a filed statement.

(g) Unless earlier canceled, a filed statement of partnership authority is canceled by operation of law five years after the date on which the statement, or the most recent amendment, was filed with the [Secretary of State].

§ 304. Statement of Denial

A partner or other person named as a partner in a filed statement of partnership authority or in a list maintained by an agent pursuant to Section 303(b) may file a statement of denial stating the name of the partnership and the fact that is being denied, which may include denial of a person's authority or status as a partner. A statement of denial is a limitation on authority as provided in Section 303(d) and (e).

§ 305. Partnership Liable for Partner's Actionable Conduct

(a) A partnership is liable for loss or injury caused to a person, or for a penalty incurred, as a result of a wrongful act or omission, or other actionable conduct, of a partner acting in the ordinary course of business of the partnership or with authority of the partnership.

(b) If, in the course of the partnership's business or while acting with authority of the partnership, a partner receives or causes the partnership to receive money or property of a person not a partner, and the money or property is misapplied by a partner, the partnership is liable for the loss.

§ 306. Partner's Liability

(a) Except as otherwise provided in subsections (b) and (c), all partners are liable jointly and severally for all obligations of the partnership unless otherwise agreed by the claimant or provided by law.

(b) A person admitted as a partner into an existing partnership is not personally liable for any partnership obligation incurred before the person's admission as a partner.

(c) An obligation of a partnership incurred while the partnership is a limited liability partnership, whether arising in contract, tort, or otherwise, is solely the obligation of the partnership. A partner is not personally liable, directly or indirectly, by way of contribution or otherwise, for such a partnership obligation solely by reason of being or so acting as a partner. This subsection applies notwithstanding anything inconsistent in the partnership agreement that existed immediately before the vote required to become a limited liability partnership under Section 1001(b).

§ 307. Actions by and Against Partnership and Partners

(a) A partnership may sue and be sued in the name of the partnership.

(b) An action may be brought against the partnership and, to the extent not inconsistent with Section 306, any or all of the partners in the same action or in separate actions.

(c) A judgment against a partnership is not by itself a judgment against a partner. A judgment against a partnership may not be satisfied from a partner's assets unless there is also a judgment against the partner.

(d) A judgment creditor of a partner may not levy execution against the assets of the partner to satisfy a judgment based on a claim against the partnership unless the partner is personally liable for the claim under Section 306 and:

(1) a judgment based on the same claim has been obtained against the partnership and a writ of execution on the judgment has been returned unsatisfied in whole or in part;

(2) the partnership is a debtor in bankruptcy;

(3) the partner has agreed that the creditor need not exhaust partnership assets;

(4) a court grants permission to the judgment creditor to levy execution against the assets of a partner based on a finding that partnership assets subject to execution are clearly insufficient to satisfy the judgment, that exhaustion of partnership assets is excessively burdensome, or that the grant of permission is an appropriate exercise of the court's equitable powers; or

(5) liability is imposed on the partner by law or contract independent of the existence of the partnership.

(e) This section applies to any partnership liability or obligation resulting from a representation by a partner or purported partner under Section 308.

§ 308. Liability of Purported Partner

(a) If a person, by words or conduct, purports to be a partner, or consents to being represented by another as a partner, in a partnership or with one or more persons not partners, the purported partner is liable to a person to whom the representation is made, if that person, relying on the representation, enters into a transaction with the actual or purported partnership. If the representation, either by the purported partner or by a person with the purported partner's consent, is made in a public manner, the purported partner is liable to a person who relies upon the purported partnership even if the purported partner is not aware of being held out as a partner to the claimant. If partnership liability results, the purported partner is liable with respect to that liability as if the purported partner were a partner. If no partnership liability results, the purported partner is liable with respect to that liability jointly and severally with any other person consenting to the representation.

(b) If a person is thus represented to be a partner in an existing partnership, or with one or more persons not partners, the purported partner is an agent of persons consenting to the representation to bind them to the same extent and in the same manner as if the purported partner were a partner, with respect to persons who enter into transactions in reliance upon the representation. If all of the partners of the existing partnership consent to the representation, a partnership act or obligation results. If fewer than all of the partners of the existing partnership consent to the representation, the person acting and the partners consenting to the representation are jointly and severally liable.

(c) A person is not liable as a partner merely because the person is named by another in a statement of partnership authority.

(d) A person does not continue to be liable as a partner merely because of a failure to file a statement of dissociation or to amend a statement of partnership authority to indicate the partner's dissociation from the partnership.

(e) Except as otherwise provided in subsections (a) and (b), persons who are not partners as to each other are not liable as partners to other persons.

[ARTICLE] 4

RELATIONS OF PARTNERS TO EACH OTHER AND TO PARTNERSHIP

§ 401. Partner's Rights and Duties

(a) Each partner is deemed to have an account that is:

(1) credited with an amount equal to the money plus the value of any other property, net of the

amount of any liabilities, the partner contributes to the partnership and the partner's share of the partnership profits; and

(2) charged with an amount equal to the money plus the value of any other property, net of the amount of any liabilities, distributed by the partnership to the partner and the partner's share of the partnership losses.

(b) Each partner is entitled to an equal share of the partnership profits and is chargeable with a share of the partnership losses in proportion to the partner's share of the profits.

(c) A partnership shall reimburse a partner for payments made and indemnify a partner for liabilities incurred by the partner in the ordinary course of the business of the partnership or for the preservation of its business or property.

(d) A partnership shall reimburse a partner for an advance to the partnership beyond the amount of capital the partner agreed to contribute.

(e) A payment or advance made by a partner which gives rise to a partnership obligation under subsection (c) or (d) constitutes a loan to the partnership which accrues interest from the date of the payment or advance.

(f) Each partner has equal rights in the management and conduct of the partnership business.

(g) A partner may use or possess partnership property only on behalf of the partnership.

(h) A partner is not entitled to remuneration for services performed for the partnership except for reasonable compensation for services rendered in winding up the business of the partnership.

(i) A person may become a partner only with the consent of all of the partners.

(j) A difference arising as to a matter in the ordinary course of business of a partnership may be decided by a majority of the partners. An act outside the ordinary course of business of a partnership and an amendment to the partnership agreement may be undertaken only with the consent of all of the partners.

(k) This section does not affect the obligations of a partnership to other persons under Section 301.

§ 402. Distributions in Kind

A partner has no right to receive, and may not be required to accept, a distribution in kind.

§ 403. Partner's Rights and Duties With Respect to Information

(a) A partnership shall keep its books and records, if any, at its chief executive office.

(b) A partnership shall provide partners and their agents and attorneys access to its books and records. It shall provide former partners and their agents and attorneys access to books and records pertaining to the period during which they were partners. The right of access provides the opportunity to inspect and copy books and records during ordinary business hours. A partnership may impose a reasonable charge, covering the costs of labor and material, for copies of documents furnished.

(c) Each partner and the partnership shall furnish to a partner, and to the legal representative of a deceased partner or partner under legal disability:

(1) without demand, any information concerning the partnership's business and affairs reasonably required for the proper exercise of the partner's rights and duties under the partnership agreement or this [Act]; and

(2) on demand, any other information concerning the partnership's business and affairs, except to the extent the demand or the information demanded is unreasonable or otherwise improper under the circumstances.

§ 404. General Standards of Partner's Conduct

(a) The only fiduciary duties a partner owes to the partnership and the other partners are the duty of loyalty and the duty of care set forth in subsections (b) and (c).

(b) A partner's duty of loyalty to the partnership and the other partners is limited to the following:

(1) to account to the partnership and hold as trustee for it any property, profit, or benefit derived by the partner in the conduct and winding up of the partnership business or derived from a use by the partner of partnership property, in-

cluding the appropriation of a partnership opportunity;

(2) to refrain from dealing with the partnership in the conduct or winding up of the partnership business as or on behalf of a party having an interest adverse to the partnership; and

(3) to refrain from competing with the partnership in the conduct of the partnership business before the dissolution of the partnership.

(c) A partner's duty of care to the partnership and the other partners in the conduct and winding up of the partnership business is limited to refraining from engaging in grossly negligent or reckless conduct, intentional misconduct, or a knowing violation of law.

(d) A partner shall discharge the duties to the partnership and the other partners under this [Act] or under the partnership agreement and exercise any rights consistently with the obligation of good faith and fair dealing.

(e) A partner does not violate a duty or obligation under this [Act] or under the partnership agreement merely because the partner's conduct furthers the partner's own interest.

(f) A partner may lend money to and transact other business with the partnership, and as to each loan or transaction the rights and obligations of the partner are the same as those of a person who is not a partner, subject to other applicable law.

(g) This section applies to a person winding up the partnership business as the personal or legal representative of the last surviving partner as if the person were a partner.

§ 405. Actions by Partnership and Partners

(a) A partnership may maintain an action against a partner for a breach of the partnership agreement, or for the violation of a duty to the partnership, causing harm to the partnership.

(b) A partner may maintain an action against the partnership or another partner for legal or equitable relief, with or without an accounting as to partnership business, to:

(1) enforce the partner's rights under the partnership agreement;

(2) enforce the partner's rights under this [Act], including:

(i) the partner's rights under Sections 401, 403, or 404;

(ii) the partner's right on dissociation to have the partner's interest in the partnership purchased pursuant to Section 701 or enforce any other right under [Article] 6 or 7; or

(iii) the partner's right to compel a dissolution and winding up of the partnership business under Section 801 or enforce any other right under [Article] 8; or

(3) enforce the rights and otherwise protect the interests of the partner, including rights and interests arising independently of the partnership relationship.

(c) The accrual of, and any time limitation on, a right of action for a remedy under this section is governed by other law. A right to an accounting upon a dissolution and winding up does not revive a claim barred by law.

§ 406. Continuation of Partnership Beyond Definite Term or Particular Undertaking

(a) If a partnership for a definite term or particular undertaking is continued, without an express agreement, after the expiration of the term or completion of the undertaking, the rights and duties of the partners remain the same as they were at the expiration or completion, so far as is consistent with a partnership at will.

(b) If the partners, or those of them who habitually acted in the business during the term or undertaking, continue the business without any settlement or liquidation of the partnership, they are presumed to have agreed that the partnership will continue.

[ARTICLE] 5

TRANSFEREES AND CREDITORS OF PARTNER

§ 501. Partner Not Co–Owner of Partnership Property

A partner is not a co-owner of partnership property and has no interest in partnership property which can be transferred, either voluntarily or involuntarily.

§ 502. Partner's Transferable Interest in Partnership

The only transferable interest of a partner in the partnership is the partner's share of the profits and losses of the partnership and the partner's right to receive distributions. The interest is personal property.

§ 503. Transfer of Partner's Transferable Interest

(a) A transfer, in whole or in part, of a partner's transferable interest in the partnership:

(1) is permissible;

(2) does not by itself cause the partner's dissociation or a dissolution and winding up of the partnership business; and

(3) does not, as against the other partners or the partnership, entitle the transferee, during the continuance of the partnership, to participate in the management or conduct of the partnership business, to require access to information concerning partnership transactions, or to inspect or copy the partnership books or records.

(b) A transferee of a partner's transferable interest in the partnership has a right:

(1) to receive, in accordance with the transfer, distributions to which the transferor would otherwise be entitled;

(2) to receive upon the dissolution and winding up of the partnership business, in accordance with the transfer, the net amount otherwise distributable to the transferor; and

(3) to seek under Section 801(6) a judicial determination that it is equitable to wind up the partnership business.

(c) In a dissolution and winding up, a transferee is entitled to an account of partnership transactions only from the date of the latest account agreed to by all of the partners.

(d) Upon transfer, the transferor retains the rights and duties of a partner other than the interest in distributions transferred.

(e) A partnership need not give effect to a transferee's rights under this section until it has notice of the transfer.

(f) A transfer of a partner's transferable interest in the partnership in violation of a restriction on transfer contained in the partnership agreement is ineffective as to a person having notice of the restriction at the time of transfer.

§ 504. Partner's Transferable Interest Subject to Charging Order

(a) On application by a judgment creditor of a partner or of a partner's transferee, a court having jurisdiction may charge the transferable interest of the judgment debtor to satisfy the judgment. The court may appoint a receiver of the share of the distributions due or to become due to the judgment debtor in respect of the partnership and make all other orders, directions, accounts, and inquiries the judgment debtor might have made or which the circumstances of the case may require.

(b) A charging order constitutes a lien on the judgment debtor's transferable interest in the partnership. The court may order a foreclosure of the interest subject to the charging order at any time. The purchaser at the foreclosure sale has the rights of a transferee.

(c) At any time before foreclosure, an interest charged may be redeemed:

(1) by the judgment debtor;

(2) with property other than partnership property, by one or more of the other partners; or

(3) with partnership property, by one or more of the other partners with the consent of all of the partners whose interests are not so charged.

(d) This [Act] does not deprive a partner of a right under exemption laws with respect to the partner's interest in the partnership.

(e) This section provides the exclusive remedy by which a judgment creditor of a partner or partner's transferee may satisfy a judgment out of the judgment debtor's transferable interest in the partnership.

[ARTICLE] 6

PARTNER'S DISSOCIATION

§ 601. Events Causing Partner's Dissociation

A partner is dissociated from a partnership upon the occurrence of any of the following events:

(1) the partnership's having notice of the partner's express will to withdraw as a partner or on a later date specified by the partner;

(2) an event agreed to in the partnership agreement as causing the partner's dissociation;

(3) the partner's expulsion pursuant to the partnership agreement;

(4) the partner's expulsion by the unanimous vote of the other partners if:

(i) it is unlawful to carry on the partnership business with that partner;

(ii) there has been a transfer of all or substantially all of that partner's transferable interest in the partnership, other than a transfer for security purposes, or a court order charging the partner's interest, which has not been foreclosed;

(iii) within 90 days after the partnership notifies a corporate partner that it will be expelled because it has filed a certificate of dissolution or the equivalent, its charter has been revoked, or its right to conduct business has been suspended by the jurisdiction of its incorporation, there is no revocation of the certificate of dissolution or no reinstatement of its charter or its right to conduct business; or

(iv) a partnership that is a partner has been dissolved and its business is being wound up;

(5) on application by the partnership or another partner, the partner's expulsion by judicial determination because:

(i) the partner engaged in wrongful conduct that adversely and materially affected the partnership business;

(ii) the partner willfully or persistently committed a material breach of the partnership agreement or of a duty owed to the partnership or the other partners under Section 404; or

(iii) the partner engaged in conduct relating to the partnership business which makes it not reasonably practicable to carry on the business in partnership with the partner;

(6) the partner's:

(i) becoming a debtor in bankruptcy;

(ii) executing an assignment for the benefit of creditors;

(iii) seeking, consenting to, or acquiescing in the appointment of a trustee, receiver, or liquidator of that partner or of all or substantially all of that partner's property; or

(iv) failing, within 90 days after the appointment, to have vacated or stayed the appointment of a trustee, receiver, or liquidator of the partner or of all or substantially all of the partner's property obtained without the partner's consent or acquiescence, or failing within 90 days after the expiration of a stay to have the appointment vacated;

(7) in the case of a partner who is an individual:

(i) the partner's death;

(ii) the appointment of a guardian or general conservator for the partner; or

(iii) a judicial determination that the partner has otherwise become incapable of performing the partner's duties under the partnership agreement;

(8) in the case of a partner that is a trust or is acting as a partner by virtue of being a trustee of a trust, distribution of the trust's entire transferable interest in the partnership, but not merely by reason of the substitution of a successor trustee;

(9) in the case of a partner that is an estate or is acting as a partner by virtue of being a personal representative of an estate, distribution of the estate's entire transferable interest in the partnership, but not merely by reason of the substitution of a successor personal representative; or

(10) termination of a partner who is not an individual, partnership, corporation, trust, or estate.

§ 602. Partner's Power to Dissociate; Wrongful Dissociation

(a) A partner has the power to dissociate at any time, rightfully or wrongfully, by express will pursuant to Section 601(1).

(b) A partner's dissociation is wrongful only if:

(1) it is in breach of an express provision of the partnership agreement; or

(2) in the case of a partnership for a definite term or particular undertaking, before the expiration of the term or the completion of the undertaking:

(i) the partner withdraws by express will, unless the withdrawal follows within 90 days after another partner's dissociation by death or otherwise under Section 601(6) through (10) or wrongful dissociation under this subsection;

(ii) the partner is expelled by judicial determination under Section 601(5);

(iii) the partner is dissociated by becoming a debtor in bankruptcy; or

(iv) in the case of a partner who is not an individual, trust other than a business trust, or estate, the partner is expelled or otherwise dissociated because it willfully dissolved or terminated.

(c) A partner who wrongfully dissociates is liable to the partnership and to the other partners for damages caused by the dissociation. The liability is in addition to any other obligation of the partner to the partnership or to the other partners.

§ 603. Effect of Partner's Dissociation

(a) If a partner's dissociation results in a dissolution and winding up of the partnership business, [Article] 8 applies; otherwise, [Article] 7 applies.

(b) Upon a partner's dissociation:

(1) the partner's right to participate in the management and conduct of the partnership business terminates, except as otherwise provided in Section 803;

(2) the partner's duty of loyalty under Section 404(b)(3) terminates; and

(3) the partner's duty of loyalty under Section 404(b)(1) and (2) and duty of care under Section 404(c) continue only with regard to matters arising and events occurring before the partner's dissociation, unless the partner participates in winding up the partnership's business pursuant to Section 803.

[ARTICLE] 7

PARTNER'S DISSOCIATION WHEN BUSINESS NOT WOUND UP

§ 701. Purchase of Dissociated Partner's Interest

(a) If a partner is dissociated from a partnership without resulting in a dissolution and winding up of the partnership business under Section 801, the partnership shall cause the dissociated partner's interest in the partnership to be purchased for a buyout price determined pursuant to subsection (b).

(b) The buyout price of a dissociated partner's interest is the amount that would have been distributable to the dissociating partner under Section 807(b) if, on the date of dissociation, the assets of the partnership were sold at a price equal to the greater of the liquidation value or the value based on a sale of the entire business as a going concern without the dissociated partner and the partnership were wound up as of that date. Interest must be paid from the date of dissociation to the date of payment.

(c) Damages for wrongful dissociation under Section 602(b), and all other amounts owing, whether or not presently due, from the dissociated partner to the partnership, must be offset against the buyout price. Interest must be paid from the date the amount owed becomes due to the date of payment.

(d) A partnership shall indemnify a dissociated partner whose interest is being purchased against all partnership liabilities, whether incurred before or after the dissociation, except liabilities incurred by an act of the dissociated partner under Section 702.

(e) If no agreement for the purchase of a dissociated partner's interest is reached within 120 days after a written demand for payment, the partnership shall pay, or cause to be paid, in cash to the dissociated partner the amount the partnership estimates to be the buyout price and accrued interest, reduced by any offsets and accrued interest under subsection (c).

(f) If a deferred payment is authorized under subsection (h), the partnership may tender a written offer to pay the amount it estimates to be the buyout price and accrued interest, reduced by any offsets under subsection (c), stating the time of payment, the amount and type of security for payment, and the other terms and conditions of the obligation.

(g) The payment or tender required by subsection (e) or (f) must be accompanied by the following:

(1) a statement of partnership assets and liabilities as of the date of dissociation;

(2) the latest available partnership balance sheet and income statement, if any;

(3) an explanation of how the estimated amount of the payment was calculated; and

(4) written notice that the payment is in full satisfaction of the obligation to purchase unless, within 120 days after the written notice, the dissociated partner commences an action to determine the buyout price, any offsets under subsection (c), or other terms of the obligation to purchase.

(h) A partner who wrongfully dissociates before the expiration of a definite term or the completion of a particular undertaking is not entitled to payment of any portion of the buyout price until the expiration of the term or completion of the undertaking, unless the partner establishes to the satisfaction of the court that earlier payment will not cause undue hardship to the business of the partnership. A deferred payment must be adequately secured and bear interest.

(i) A dissociated partner may maintain an action against the partnership, pursuant to Section 405(b)(2)(ii), to determine the buyout price of that partner's interest, any offsets under subsection (c), or other terms of the obligation to purchase. The action must be commenced within 120 days after the partnership has tendered payment or an offer to pay or within one year after written demand for payment if no payment or offer to pay is tendered. The court shall determine the buyout price of the dissociated partner's interest, any offset due under subsection (c), and accrued interest, and enter judgment for any additional payment or refund. If deferred payment is authorized under subsection (h), the court shall also determine the security for payment and other terms of the obligation to purchase. The court may assess reasonable attorney's fees and the fees and expenses of appraisers or other experts for a party to the action, in amounts the court finds equitable, against a party that the court finds acted arbitrarily, vexatiously, or not in good faith. The finding may be based on the partnership's failure to tender payment or an offer to pay or to comply with subsection (g).

§ 702. Dissociated Partner's Power to Bind and Liability to Partnership

(a) For two years after a partner dissociates without resulting in a dissolution and winding up of the partnership business, the partnership, including a surviving partnership under [Article] 9, is bound by an act of the dissociated partner which would have bound the partnership under Section 301 before dissociation only if at the time of entering into the transaction the other party:

(1) reasonably believed that the dissociated partner was then a partner;

(2) did not have notice of the partner's dissociation; and

(3) is not deemed to have had knowledge under Section 303(e) or notice under Section 704(c).

(b) A dissociated partner is liable to the partnership for any damage caused to the partnership arising from an obligation incurred by the dissociated partner after dissociation for which the partnership is liable under subsection (a).

§ 703. Dissociated Partner's Liability to Other Persons

(a) A partner's dissociation does not of itself discharge the partner's liability for a partnership obligation incurred before dissociation. A dissociated partner is not liable for a partnership obligation incurred after dissociation, except as otherwise provided in subsection (b).

(b) A partner who dissociates without resulting in a dissolution and winding up of the partnership business is liable as a partner to the other party in a transaction entered into by the partnership, or a surviving partnership under [Article] 9, within two years after the partner's dissociation, only if the partner is liable for the obligation under Section

306 and at the time of entering into the transaction the other party:

(1) reasonably believed that the dissociated partner was then a partner;

(2) did not have notice of the partner's dissociation; and

(3) is not deemed to have had knowledge under Section 303(e) or notice under Section 704(c).

(c) By agreement with the partnership creditor and the partners continuing the business, a dissociated partner may be released from liability for a partnership obligation.

(d) A dissociated partner is released from liability for a partnership obligation if a partnership creditor, with notice of the partner's dissociation but without the partner's consent, agrees to a material alteration in the nature or time of payment of a partnership obligation.

§ 704. Statement of Dissociation

(a) A dissociated partner or the partnership may file a statement of dissociation stating the name of the partnership and that the partner is dissociated from the partnership.

(b) A statement of dissociation is a limitation on the authority of a dissociated partner for the purposes of Section 303(d) and (e).

(c) For the purposes of Sections 702(a)(3) and 703(b)(3), a person not a partner is deemed to have notice of the dissociation 90 days after the statement of dissociation is filed.

§ 705. Continued Use of Partnership Name

Continued use of a partnership name, or a dissociated partner's name as part thereof, by partners continuing the business does not of itself make the dissociated partner liable for an obligation of the partners or the partnership continuing the business.

[ARTICLE] 8

WINDING UP PARTNERSHIP BUSINESS

§ 801. Events Causing Dissolution and Winding Up of Partnership Business

A partnership is dissolved, and its business must be wound up, only upon the occurrence of any of the following events:

(1) in a partnership at will, the partnership's having notice from a partner, other than a partner who is dissociated under Section 601(2) through (10), of that partner's express will to withdraw as a partner, or on a later date specified by the partner;

(2) in a partnership for a definite term or particular undertaking:

(i) within 90 days after a partner's dissociation by death or otherwise under Section 601(6) through (10) or wrongful dissociation under Section 602(b), the express will of at least half of the remaining partners to wind up the partnership business, for which purpose a partner's rightful dissociation pursuant to Section 602(b)(2)(i) constitutes the expression of that partner's will to wind up the partnership business;

(ii) the express will of all of the partners to wind up the partnership business; or

(iii) the expiration of the term or the completion of the undertaking;

(3) an event agreed to in the partnership agreement resulting in the winding up of the partnership business;

(4) an event that makes it unlawful for all or substantially all of the business of the partnership to be continued, but a cure of illegality within 90 days after notice to the partnership of the event is effective retroactively to the date of the event for purposes of this section;

(5) on application by a partner, a judicial determination that:

(i) the economic purpose of the partnership is likely to be unreasonably frustrated;

(ii) another partner has engaged in conduct relating to the partnership business which makes it not reasonably practicable to carry on the business in partnership with that partner; or

(iii) It is not otherwise reasonably practicable to carry on the partnership business in conformity with the partnership agreement; or

(6) on application by a transferee of a partner's transferable interest, a judicial determination that it is equitable to wind up the partnership business:

(i) after the expiration of the term or completion of the undertaking, if the partnership was for a definite term or particular undertaking at the time of the transfer or entry of the charging order that gave rise to the transfer; or

(ii) at any time, if the partnership was a partnership at will at the time of the transfer or entry of the charging order that gave rise to the transfer.

§ 802. Partnership Continues After Dissolution

(a) Subject to subsection (b), a partnership continues after dissolution only for the purpose of winding up its business. The partnership is terminated when the winding up of its business is completed.

(b) At any time after the dissolution of a partnership and before the winding up of its business is completed, all of the partners, including any dissociating partner other than a wrongfully dissociating partner, may waive the right to have the partnership's business wound up and the partnership terminated. In that event:

(1) the partnership resumes carrying on its business as if dissolution had never occurred, and any liability incurred by the partnership or a partner after the dissolution and before the waiv-

er is determined as if dissolution had never occurred; and

(2) the rights of a third party accruing under Section 804(1) or arising out of conduct in reliance on the dissolution before the third party knew or received a notification of the waiver may not be adversely affected.

§ 803. Right to Wind up Partnership Business

(a) After dissolution, a partner who has not wrongfully dissociated may participate in winding up the partnership's business, but on application of any partner, partner's legal representative, or transferee, the [designate the appropriate court], for good cause shown, may order judicial supervision of the winding up.

(b) The legal representative of the last surviving partner may wind up a partnership's business.

(c) A person winding up a partnership's business may preserve the partnership business or property as a going concern for a reasonable time, prosecute and defend actions and proceedings, whether civil, criminal, or administrative, settle and close the partnership's business, dispose of and transfer the partnership's property, discharge the partnership's liabilities, distribute the assets of the partnership pursuant to Section 807, settle disputes by mediation or arbitration, and perform other necessary acts.

§ 804. Partner's Power to Bind Partnership After Dissolution

Subject to Section 805, a partnership is bound by a partner's act after dissolution that:

(1) is appropriate for winding up the partnership business; or

(2) would have bound the partnership under Section 301 before dissolution, if the other party to the transaction did not have notice of the dissolution.

§ 805. Statement of Dissolution

(a) After dissolution, a partner who has not wrongfully dissociated may file a statement of dissolution stating the name of the partnership and that the partnership has dissolved and is winding up its business.

(b) A statement of dissolution cancels a filed statement of partnership authority for the purposes of Section 303(d) and is a limitation on authority for the purposes of Section 303(e).

(c) For the purposes of Sections 301 and 804, a person not a partner is deemed to have notice of the dissolution and the limitation on the partners' authority as a result of the statement of dissolution 90 days after it is filed.

(d) After filing and, if appropriate, recording a statement of dissolution, a dissolved partnership may file and, if appropriate, record a statement of partnership authority which will operate with respect to a person not a partner as provided in

Section 303(d) and (e) in any transaction, whether or not the transaction is appropriate for winding up the partnership business.

§ 806. Partner's Liability to Other Partners After Dissolution

(a) Except as otherwise provided in subsection (b) and Section 306, after dissolution a partner is liable to the other partners for the partner's share of any partnership liability incurred under Section 804.

(b) A partner who, with knowledge of the dissolution, incurs a partnership liability under Section 804(2) by an act that is not appropriate for winding up the partnership business is liable to the partnership for any damage caused to the partnership arising from the liability.

§ 807. Settlement of Accounts and Contributions Among Partners

(a) In winding up a partnership's business, the assets of the partnership, including the contributions of the partners required by this section, must be applied to discharge its obligations to creditors, including, to the extent permitted by law, partners who are creditors. Any surplus must be applied to pay in cash the net amount distributable to partners in accordance with their right to distributions under subsection (b).

(b) Each partner is entitled to a settlement of all partnership accounts upon winding up the partnership business. In settling accounts among the partners, the profits and losses that result from the liquidation of the partnership assets must be credited and charged to the partners' accounts. The partnership shall make a distribution to a partner in an amount equal to any excess of the credits over the charges in the partner's account. A partner shall contribute to the partnership an amount equal to any excess of the charges over the credits in the partner's account but excluding from the calculation charges attributable to an obligation for which the partner is not personally liable under Section 306.

(c) If a partner fails to contribute the full amount required under subsection (b), all of the other partners shall contribute, in the proportions in which those partners share partnership losses, the additional amount necessary to satisfy the partnership obligations for which they are personally liable under Section 306. A partner or partner's legal representative may recover from the other partners any contributions the partner makes to the extent the amount contributed exceeds that partner's share of the partnership obligations for which the partner is personally liable under Section 306.

(d) After the settlement of accounts, each partner shall contribute, in the proportion in which the partner shares partnership losses, the amount necessary to satisfy partnership obligations that were not known at the time of the settlement and for which the partner is personally liable under Section 306.

(e) The estate of a deceased partner is liable for the partner's obligation to contribute to the partnership.

(f) An assignee for the benefit of creditors of a partnership or a partner, or a person appointed by a court to represent creditors of a partnership or a partner, may enforce a partner's obligation to contribute to the partnership.

[ARTICLE] 9

CONVERSIONS AND MERGERS

§ 901. Definitions

In this [article]:

(1) "General partner" means a partner in a partnership and a general partner in a limited partnership.

(2) "Limited partner" means a limited partner in a limited partnership.

(3) "Limited partnership" means a limited partnership created under the [State Limited Partnership Act], predecessor law, or comparable law of another jurisdiction.

(4) "Partner" includes both a general partner and a limited partner.

§ 902. Conversion of Partnership to Limited Partnership

(a) A partnership may be converted to a limited partnership pursuant to this section.

(b) The terms and conditions of a conversion of a partnership to a limited partnership must be approved by all of the partners or by a number or percentage specified for conversion in the partnership agreement.

(c) After the conversion is approved by the partners, the partnership shall file a certificate of limited partnership in the jurisdiction in which the limited partnership is to be formed. The certificate must include:

(1) a statement that the partnership was converted to a limited partnership from a partnership;

(2) its former name; and

(3) a statement of the number of votes cast by the partners for and against the conversion and, if the vote is less than unanimous, the number or percentage required to approve the conversion under the partnership agreement.

(d) The conversion takes effect when the certificate of limited partnership is filed or at any later date specified in the certificate.

(e) A general partner who becomes a limited partner as a result of the conversion remains liable as a general partner for an obligation incurred by the partnership before the conversion takes effect. If the other party to a transaction with the limited partnership reasonably believes when entering the transaction that the limited partner is a general partner, the limited partner is liable for an obligation incurred by the limited partnership within 90 days after the conversion takes effect. The limited partner's liability for all other obligations of the limited partnership incurred after the conversion takes effect is that of a limited partner as provided in the [State Limited Partnership Act].

§ 903. Conversion of Limited Partnership to Partnership

(a) A limited partnership may be converted to a partnership pursuant to this section.

(b) Notwithstanding a provision to the contrary in a limited partnership agreement, the terms and conditions of a conversion of a limited partnership to a partnership must be approved by all of the partners.

(c) After the conversion is approved by the partners, the limited partnership shall cancel its certificate of limited partnership.

(d) The conversion takes effect when the certificate of limited partnership is canceled.

(e) A limited partner who becomes a general partner as a result of the conversion remains liable only as a limited partner for an obligation incurred by the limited partnership before the conversion takes effect. Except as otherwise provided in Section 306, the partner is liable as a general partner for an obligation of the partnership incurred after the conversion takes effect.

§ 904. Effect of Conversion; Entity Unchanged

(a) A partnership or limited partnership that has been converted pursuant to this [article] is for all purposes the same entity that existed before the conversion.

(b) When a conversion takes effect:

(1) all property owned by the converting partnership or limited partnership remains vested in the converted entity;

(2) all obligations of the converting partnership or limited partnership continue as obligations of the converted entity; and

(3) an action or proceeding pending against the converting partnership or limited partnership may be continued as if the conversion had not occurred.

§ 905. Merger of Partnerships

(a) Pursuant to a plan of merger approved as provided in subsection (c), a partnership may be merged with one or more partnerships or limited partnerships.

(b) The plan of merger must set forth:

(1) the name of each partnership or limited partnership that is a party to the merger;

(2) the name of the surviving entity into which the other partnerships or limited partnerships will merge;

(3) whether the surviving entity is a partnership or a limited partnership and the status of each partner;

(4) the terms and conditions of the merger;

(5) the manner and basis of converting the interests of each party to the merger into interests or obligations of the surviving entity, or into money or other property in whole or part; and

(6) the street address of the surviving entity's chief executive office.

(c) The plan of merger must be approved:

(1) in the case of a partnership that is a party to the merger, by all of the partners, or a number or percentage specified for merger in the partnership agreement; and

(2) in the case of a limited partnership that is a party to the merger, by the vote required for approval of a merger by the law of the State or foreign jurisdiction in which the limited partnership is organized and, in the absence of such a specifically applicable law, by all of the partners, notwithstanding a provision to the contrary in the partnership agreement.

(d) After a plan of merger is approved and before the merger takes effect, the plan may be amended or abandoned as provided in the plan.

(e) The merger takes effect on the later of:

(1) the approval of the plan of merger by all parties to the merger, as provided in subsection (c);

(2) the filing of all documents required by law to be filed as a condition to the effectiveness of the merger; or

(3) any effective date specified in the plan of merger.

§ 906. Effect of Merger

(a) When a merger takes effect:

(1) the separate existence of every partnership or limited partnership that is a party to the merger, other than the surviving entity, ceases;

(2) all property owned by each of the merged partnerships or limited partnerships vests in the surviving entity;

(3) all obligations of every partnership or limited partnership that is a party to the merger become the obligations of the surviving entity; and

(4) an action or proceeding pending against a partnership or limited partnership that is a party to the merger may be continued as if the merger had not occurred, or the surviving entity may be substituted as a party to the action or proceeding.

(b) The [Secretary of State] of this State is the agent for service of process in an action or proceeding against a surviving foreign partnership or limited partnership to enforce an obligation of a domestic partnership or limited partnership that is a party to a merger. The surviving entity shall promptly notify the [Secretary of State] of the mailing address of its chief executive office and of any change of address. Upon receipt of process, the [Secretary of State] shall mail a copy of the process to the surviving foreign partnership or limited partnership.

(c) A partner of the surviving partnership or limited partnership is liable for:

(1) all obligations of a party to the merger for which the partner was personally liable before the merger;

(2) all other obligations of the surviving entity incurred before the merger by a party to the merger, but those obligations may be satisfied only out of property of the entity; and

(3) Except as otherwise provided in Section 306, all obligations of the surviving entity incurred after the merger takes effect, but those obligations may be satisfied only out of property of the entity if the partner is a limited partner.

(d) If the obligations incurred before the merger by a party to the merger are not satisfied out of the property of the surviving partnership or limited partnership, the general partners of that party immediately before the effective date of the merger shall contribute the amount necessary to satisfy that party's obligations to the surviving entity, in the manner provided in Section 807 or in the [Limited Partnership Act] of the jurisdiction in which the party was formed, as the case may be, as if the merged party were dissolved.

(e) A partner of a party to a merger who does not become a partner of the surviving partnership or limited partnership is dissociated from the entity, of which that partner was a partner, as of the date the merger takes effect. The surviving entity shall cause the partner's interest in the entity to be purchased under Section 701 or another statute specifically applicable to that partner's interest with respect to a merger. The surviving entity is bound under Section 702 by an act of a general partner dissociated under this subsection, and the partner is liable under Section 703 for transactions entered into by the surviving entity after the merger takes effect.

§ 907. Statement of Merger

(a) After a merger, the surviving partnership or limited partnership may file a statement that one or more partnerships or limited partnerships have merged into the surviving entity.

(b) A statement of merger must contain:

(1) the name of each partnership or limited partnership that is a party to the merger;

(2) the name of the surviving entity into which the other partnerships or limited partnership were merged;

(3) the street address of the surviving entity's chief executive office and of an office in this State, if any; and

(4) whether the surviving entity is a partnership or a limited partnership.

(c) Except as otherwise provided in subsection (d), for the purposes of Section 302, property of the surviving partnership or limited partnership which before the merger was held in the name of another party to the merger is property held in the name of the surviving entity upon filing a statement of merger.

(d) For the purposes of Section 302 real property of the surviving partnership or limited partnership which before the merger was held in the name of another party to the merger is property held in the name of the surviving entity upon recording a certified copy of the statement of merger in the office for recording transfers of that real property.

(e) A filed and, if appropriate, recorded statement of merger, executed and declared to be accurate pursuant to Section 105(c), stating the name of a partnership or limited partnership that is a party to the merger in whose name property was held before the merger and the name of the surviving entity, but not containing all of the other information required by subsection (b), operates with respect to the partnerships or limited partnerships named to the extent provided in subsections (c) and (d).

§ 908. Nonexclusive

This [article] is not exclusive. Partnerships or limited partnerships may be converted or merged in any other manner provided by law.

[ARTICLE] 10

LIMITED LIABILITY PARTNERSHIP

§ 1001. Statement of Qualification.

(a) A partnership may become a limited liability partnership pursuant to this section.

(b) The terms and conditions on which a partnership becomes a limited liability partnership must be approved by the vote necessary to amend the partnership agreement except, in the case of a partnership agreement that expressly considers contribution obligations, the vote necessary to amend those provisions.

(c) After the approval required by subsection (b), a partnership may become a limited liability partnership by filing a statement of qualification. The statement must contain:

(1) the name of the partnership;

(2) the street address of the partnership's chief executive office and, if different, the street address of an office in this State, if any;

(3) if there is no office in this State, the name and street address of the partnership's agent for service of process who must be an individual resident of this State or any other person authorized to do business in this State;

(4) a statement that the partnership elects to be a limited liability partnership; and

(5) a deferred effective date, if any.

(d) The status of a partnership as a limited liability partnership is effective on the later of the filing of the statement or a date specified in the statement. The status remains effective, regardless of changes in the partnership, until it is canceled pursuant to Section 105(d) or revoked pursuant to Section 1003.

(e) The status of a partnership as a limited liability partnership and the liability of its partners is not affected by errors or later changes in the information required to be contained in the statement of qualification under subsection (c).

(f) The filing of a statement of qualification establishes that a partnership has satisfied all conditions precedent to the qualification of the partnership as a limited liability partnership.

(g) An amendment or cancellation of a statement of qualification is effective when it is filed or on a deferred effective date specified in the amendment or cancellation.

§ 1002. Name.

The name of a limited liability partnership must end with "Registered Limited Liability Partnership", "Limited Liability Partnership", "R.L.L.P.", "L.L.P.", "RLLP", or "LLP".

§ 1003. Annual Report.

(a) A limited liability partnership, and a foreign limited liability partnership authorized to transact business in this State, shall file an annual report in the office of the [Secretary of State] which contains:

(1) the name of the limited liability partnership and the State or other jurisdiction under whose laws the foreign limited liability partnership is formed;

(2) the current street address of the partnership's chief executive office and, if different, the current street address of an office in this State, if any; and

(3) if there is no current office in this State, the name and street address of the partnership's current agent for service of process who must be an individual resident of this State or any other person authorized to do business in this State.

(b) An annual report must be filed between [January 1 and April 1] of each year following the calendar year in which a partnership files a statement of qualification or a foreign partnership becomes authorized to transact business in this State.

(c) The [Secretary of State] may administratively revoke the statement of qualification of a partnership that fails to file an annual report when due or to pay the required filing fee. The [Secretary of State] shall provide the partnership at least 60 days' written notice of intent to revoke the statement. The notice must be mailed to the partnership at its chief executive office set forth in the last filed statement of qualification or annual report. The notice must specify the annual report that has not been filed, the fee that has not been paid, and the effective date of the revocation. The revocation is not effective if the annual report is filed and the fee is paid before the effective date of the revocation.

(d) A revocation under subsection (c) only affects a partnership's status as a limited liability partnership and is not an event of dissolution of the partnership.

(e) A partnership whose statement of qualification has been administratively revoked may apply to the [Secretary of State] for reinstatement within two years after the effective date of the revocation. The application must state:

(1) the name of the partnership and the effective date of the revocation; and

(2) that the ground for revocation either did not exist or has been corrected.

(f) A reinstatement under subsection (e) relates back to and takes effect as of the effective date of the revocation, and the partnership's status as a limited liability partnership continues as if the revocation had never occurred.

[ARTICLE] 11

FOREIGN LIMITED LIABILITY PARTNERSHIP

§ 1101. Law Governing Foreign Limited Liability Partnership.

(a) The laws under which a foreign limited liability partnership is formed govern relations among the partners and between the partners and the partnership and the liability of partners for obligations of the partnership.

(b) A foreign limited liability partnership may not be denied a statement of foreign qualification by reason of any difference between the laws under which the partnership was formed and the laws of this State.

(c) A statement of foreign qualification does not authorize a foreign limited liability partnership to engage in any business or exercise any power that a partnership may not engage in or exercise in this State as a limited liability partnership.

§ 1102. Statement of Foreign Qualification.

(a) Before transacting business in this State, a foreign limited liability partnership must file a statement of foreign qualification. The statement must contain:

(1) the name of the foreign limited liability partnership which satisfies the requirements of the State or other jurisdiction under whose laws it is formed and ends with "Registered Limited Liability Partnership", "Limited Liability Partnership", "R.L.L.P.", "L.L.P.", "RLLP", or "LLP";

(2) the street address of the partnership's chief executive office and, if different, the street address of an office in this State, if any;

(3) if there is no office in this State, the name and street address of the partnership's agent for service of process; and

(4) a deferred effective date, if any.

(b) The agent of a foreign limited liability partnership for service of process must be an individual who is a resident of this State or other person authorized to do business in this State.

(c) The status of a partnership as a foreign limited liability partnership is effective on the later of the filing of the statement of foreign qualification or a date specified in the statement. The status remains effective, regardless of changes in the partnership, until it is canceled pursuant to Section 105(d) or revoked pursuant to Section 1003.

(d) An amendment or cancellation of a statement of foreign qualification is effective when it is filed or on a deferred effective date specified in the amendment or cancellation.

§ 1103. Effect of Failure to Qualify.

(a) A foreign limited liability partnership transacting business in this State may not maintain an action or proceeding in this State unless it has in effect a statement of foreign qualification.

(b) The failure of a foreign limited liability partnership to have in effect a statement of foreign qualification does not impair the validity of a contract or act of the foreign limited liability partnership or preclude it from defending an action or proceeding in this State.

(c) Limitations on personal liability of partners are not waived solely by transacting business in this State without a statement of foreign qualification.

(d) If a foreign limited liability partnership transacts business in this State without a statement of foreign qualification, the [Secretary of State] is its agent for service of process with respect to [claims for relief] arising out of the transaction of business in this State.

§ 1104. Activities Not Constituting Transacting Business.

(a) Activities of a foreign limited liability partnership which do not constitute transacting business within the meaning of this [article] include:

(1) maintaining, defending, or settling an action or proceeding;

(2) holding meetings of its partners or carrying on any other activity concerning its internal affairs;

(3) maintaining bank accounts;

(4) maintaining offices or agencies for the transfer, exchange, and registration of the partnership's own securities or maintaining trustees or depositories with respect to those securities;

(5) selling through independent contractors;

(6) soliciting or obtaining orders, whether by mail or through employees or agents or otherwise, if the orders require acceptance outside this State before they become contracts;

(7) creating or acquiring indebtedness, mortgages, or security interests in real or personal property;

(8) securing or collecting debts or foreclosing mortgages or other security interests in property securing the debts, and holding, protecting, and maintaining property so acquired;

(9) conducting an isolated transaction that is completed within 30 days and is not one in the course of similar transactions of like nature; and

(10) transacting business in interstate commerce.

(b) For purposes of this [article], the ownership in this State of income-producing real property or tangible personal property, other than property excluded under subsection (a), constitutes transacting business in this State.

(c) This section does not apply in determining the contacts or activities that may subject a foreign limited liability partnership to service of process, taxation, or regulation under any other law of this State.

§ 1105. Action by [Attorney General].

The [Attorney General] may maintain an action to restrain a foreign limited liability partnership from transacting business in this State in violation of this [article].

[ARTICLE] 12

MISCELLANEOUS PROVISIONS

§ 1201. Uniformity of Application and Construction

This [Act] shall be applied and construed to effectuate its general purpose to make uniform the law with respect to the subject of this [Act] among States enacting it.

§ 1202. Short Title

This [Act] may be cited as the Uniform Partnership Act (1997).

§ 1203. Severability Clause

If any provision of this [Act] or its application to any person or circumstance is held invalid, the invalidity does not affect other provisions or applications of this [Act] which can be given effect without the invalid provision or application, and to this end the provisions of this [Act] are severable.

§ 1204. Effective Date

This [Act] takes effect. . . .

§ 1205. Repeals

Effective January 1, 199__, the following acts and parts of acts are repeated: [the State Partnership Act as amended and in effect immediately before the effective date of this Act].

§ 1206. Applicability

(a) Before January 1, 199__, this [Act] governs only a partnership formed:

(1) after the effective date of this [Act], unless that partnership is continuing the business of a dissolved partnership under [Section 41 of the prior Uniform Partnership Act]; and

(2) before the effective date of this [Act], that elects, as provided by subsection (c), to be governed by this [Act].

(b) After January 1, 199__, this [Act] governs all partnerships.

(c) Before January 1, 199__, a partnership voluntarily may elect, in the manner provided in its partnership agreement or by law for amending the partnership agreement, to be governed by this [Act]. The provisions of this [Act] relating to the liability of the partnership's partners to third parties apply to limit those partners' liability to a third party who had done business with the partnership within one year preceding the partnership's election to be governed by this [Act], only if the third party knows or has received a notification of the partnership's election to be governed by this [Act].

§ 1207. Savings Clause

This [Act] does not affect an action or proceeding commenced or right accrued before this [Act] takes effect.

§ 1208. Effective Date

These [Amendments] take effect . . . .

§ 1209. Repeals

Effective January 1, 199_, the following acts and parts of acts are repealed: [the Limited Liability Partnership amendments to the State Partnership Act as amended and in effect immediately before the effective date of these [Amendments]].

§ 1210. Applicability

(a) Before January 1, 199_, these [Amendments] govern only a limited liability partnership formed:

(1) on or after the effective date of these [Amendments], unless that partnership is continuing the business of a dissolved limited liability partnership; and

(2) before the effective date of these [Amendments], that elects, as provided by subsection (c), to be governed by these |Amendments].

(b) On and after January 1, 199_, these [Amendments] govern all partnerships.

(c) Before January 1, 199_, a partnership voluntarily may elect, in the manner provided in its partnership agreement or by law for amending the partnership agreement, to be governed by these [Amendments]. The provisions of these [Amendments] relating to the liability of the partnership's partners to third parties apply to limit those partners' liability to a third party who had done business with the partnership within one year preceding the partnership's election to be governed by these [Amendments], only if the third party knows or has received a notification of the partnership's election to be governed by these [Amendments].

(d) The existing provisions for execution and filing a statement of qualification of a limited liability partnership continue until either the limited liability partnership elects to have this [Act] apply or January 1, 199_.

§ 1211. Savings Clause

These [Amendments] do not affect an action or proceeding commenced or right accrued before these [Amendments] take effect.

APPENDIX D

UNIFORM LIMITED LIABILITY COMPANY ACT (1995)

Editor's note: The Uniform Limited Liability Company Act (1995)(ULLCA) is contained in volume 6A of Uniform Laws Annotated (1995). The version of ULLCA reproduced below incorporates the amendments made to it in response to the check-the-box regulations adopted by the Internal Revenue Service. The data on adoptions contained below is based on the 2000 Cumulative Annual Pocket Part to volume 6A, as updated through August 2000 by information supplied by the National Conference of Commissioners on Uniform State Laws (NCCUSL) at www.nccusl.org. The date set forth immediately after each jurisdiction is the effective date of the Act.

The following jurisdictions have adopted ULLCA: Alabama (1998), Florida (1999), Hawaii (1997), Illinois (1999), Montana (1999), South Carolina (1996), South Dakota (1998), Vermont (1996), Virgin Islands (1999), and West Virginia (1996). In addition, a number of other states have redrafted their limited liability company acts to incorporate provisions from ULLCA.

[ARTICLE] 6

MEMBER'S DISSOCIATION

[ARTICLE] 7

MEMBER'S DISSOCIATION WHEN BUSINESS NOT WOUND UP

[ARTICLE] 8

WINDING UP COMPANY'S BUSINESS

[ARTICLE]   12

MISCELLANEOUS PROVISIONS

[ARTICLE]   1

GENERAL PROVISIONS

§ 101. Definitions.

In this [Act]:

(1) "Articles of organization" means initial, amended, and restated articles of organization and articles of merger. In the case of a foreign limited liability company, the term includes all records serving a similar function required to be filed in the office of the [Secretary of State] or other official having custody of company records in the State or country under whose law it is organized.

(2) "At-will company" means a limited liability company other than a term company.

(3) "Business" includes every trade, occupation, profession, and other lawful purpose, whether or not carried on for profit.

(4) "Debtor in bankruptcy" means a person who is the subject of an order for relief under Title 11 of the United States Code or a comparable order under a successor statute of general application or a comparable order under federal, state, or foreign law governing insolvency.

(5) "Distribution" means a transfer of money, property, or other benefit from a limited liability company to a member in the member's capacity as a member or to a transferee of the member's distributional interest.

(6) "Distributional interest" means all of a member's interest in distributions by the limited liability company.

(7) "Entity" means a person other than an individual.

(8) "Foreign limited liability company" means an unincorporated entity organized under laws other than the laws of this State which afford limited liability to its owners comparable to the liability under Section 303 and is not required to obtain a certificate of authority to transact business under any law of this State other than this [Act].

(9) "Limited liability company" means a limited liability company organized under this [Act].

(10) "Manager" means a person, whether or not a member of a manager-managed company, who is vested with authority under Section 301.

(11) "Manager-managed company" means a limited liability company which is so designated in its articles of organization.

(12) "Member-managed company" means a limited liability company other than a manager-managed company.

(13) "Operating agreement" means the agreement under Section 103 concerning the relations among the members, managers, and limited liability company. The term includes amendments to the agreement.

(14) "Person" means an individual, corporation, business trust, estate, trust, partnership, limited liability company, association, joint venture, government, governmental subdivision, agency, or instrumentality, or any other legal or commercial entity.

(15) "Principal office" means the office, whether or not in this State, where the principal executive office of a domestic or foreign limited liability company is located.

(16) "Record" means information that is inscribed on a tangible medium or that is stored in an electronic or other medium and is retrievable in perceivable form.

(17) "Sign" means to identify a record by means of a signature, mark, or other symbol, with intent to authenticate it.

(18) "State" means a State of the United States, the District of Columbia, the Commonwealth of Puerto Rico, or any territory or insular possession subject to the jurisdiction of the United States.

(19) "Term company" means a limited liability company in which its members have agreed to re-

main members until the expiration of a term specified in the articles of organization.

(20) "Transfer" includes an assignment, conveyance, deed, bill of sale, lease, mortgage, security interest, encumbrance, and gift.

§ 102. Knowledge and Notice

(a) A person knows a fact if the person has actual knowledge of it.

(b) A person has notice of a fact if the person:

(1) knows the fact;

(2) has received a notification of the fact; or

(3) has reason to know the fact exists from all of the facts known to the person at the time in question.

(c) A person notifies or gives a notification of a fact to another by taking steps reasonably required to inform the other person in ordinary course, whether or not the other person knows the fact.

(d) A person receives a notification when the notification:

(1) comes to the person's attention; or

(2) is duly delivered at the person's place of business or at any other place held out by the person as a place for receiving communications.

(e) An entity knows, has notice, or receives a notification of a fact for purposes of a particular transaction when the individual conducting the transaction for the entity knows, has notice, or receives a notification of the fact, or in any event when the fact would have been brought to the individual's attention had the entity exercised reasonable diligence. An entity exercises reasonable diligence if it maintains reasonable routines for communicating significant information to the individual conducting the transaction for the entity and there is reasonable compliance with the routines. Reasonable diligence does not require an individual acting for the entity to communicate information unless the communication is part of the individual's regular duties or the individual has reason to know of the transaction and that the transaction would be materially affected by the information.

§ 103. Effect of Operating Agreement; Non-waivable Provisions

(a) Except as otherwise provided in subsection (b), all members of a limited liability company may enter into an operating agreement, which need not be in writing, to regulate the affairs of the company and the conduct of its business, and to govern relations among the members, managers, and company. To the extent the operating agreement does not otherwise provide, this [Act] governs relations among the members, managers, and company.

(b) The operating agreement may not:

(1) unreasonably restrict a right to information or access to records under Section 408;

(2) eliminate the duty of loyalty under Section 409(b) or 603(b)(3), but the agreement may:

(i) identify specific types or categories of activities that do not violate the duty of loyalty, if not manifestly unreasonable; and

(ii) specify the number or percentage of members or disinterested managers that may authorize or ratify, after full disclosure of all material facts, a specific act or transaction that otherwise would violate the duty of loyalty;

(3) unreasonably reduce the duty of care under Section 409(c) or 603(b)(3);

(4) eliminate the obligation of good faith and fair dealing under Section 409(d), but the operating agreement may determine the standards by which the performance of the obligation is to be measured, if the standards are not manifestly unreasonable;

(5) vary the right to expel a member in an event specified in Section 601(6);

(6) vary the requirement to wind up the limited liability company's business in a case specified in Section 801(3) or (4); or

(7) restrict rights of a person, other than a manager, member, and transferee of a member's distributional interest, under this [Act].

§ 104. Supplemental Principles of Law

(a) Unless displaced by particular provisions of this [Act], the principles of law and equity supplement this [Act].

(b) If an obligation to pay interest arises under this [Act] and the rate is not specified, the rate is that specified in [applicable statute].

§ 105. Name

(a) The name of a limited liability company must contain "limited liability company" or "limited company" or the abbreviation "L.L.C.", "LLC", "L.C.", or "LC". "Limited" may be abbreviated as "Ltd.", and "company" may be abbreviated as "Co.".

(b) Except as authorized by subsections (c) and (d), the name of a limited liability company must be distinguishable upon the records of the [Secretary of State] from:

(1) the name of any corporation, limited partnership, or company incorporated, organized or authorized to transact business, in this State;

(2) a name reserved or registered under Section 106 or 107;

(3) a fictitious name approved under Section 1005 for a foreign company authorized to transact business in this State because its real name is unavailable.

(c) A limited liability company may apply to the [Secretary of State] for authorization to use a name that is not distinguishable upon the records of the [Secretary of State] from one or more of the names described in subsection (b). The [Secretary of State] shall authorize use of the name applied for if:

(1) the present user, registrant, or owner of a reserved name consents to the use in a record and submits an undertaking in form satisfactory to the [Secretary of State] to change the name to a name that is distinguishable upon the records of the [Secretary of State] from the name applied for; or

(2) the applicant delivers to the [Secretary of State] a certified copy of the final judgment of a court of competent jurisdiction establishing the applicant's right to use the name applied for in this State.

(d) A limited liability company may use the name, including a fictitious name, of another domestic or foreign company which is used in this State if the other company is organized or authorized to transact business in this State and the company proposing to use the name has:

(1) merged with the other company;

(2) been formed by reorganization with the other company; or

(3) acquired substantially all of the assets, including the name, of the other company.

§ 106. Reserved Name

(a) A person may reserve the exclusive use of the name of a limited liability company, including a fictitious name for a foreign company whose name is not available, by delivering an application to the [Secretary of State] for filing. The application must set forth the name and address of the applicant and the name proposed to be reserved. If the [Secretary of State] finds that the name applied for is available, it must be reserved for the applicant's exclusive use for a nonrenewable 120–day period.

(b) The owner of a name reserved for a limited liability company may transfer the reservation to another person by delivering to the [Secretary of State] a signed notice of the transfer which states the name and address of the transferee.

§ 107. Registered Name

(a) A foreign limited liability company may register its name subject to the requirements of Section 1005, if the name is distinguishable upon the records of the [Secretary of State] from names that are not available under Section 105(b).

(b) A foreign limited liability company registers its name, or its name with any addition required by Section 1005, by delivering to the [Secretary of State] for filing an application:

(1) setting forth its name, or its name with any addition required by Section 1005, the State or country and date of its organization, and a brief description of the nature of the business in which it is engaged; and

(2) accompanied by a certificate of existence, or a record of similar import, from the State or country of organization.

(c) A foreign limited liability company whose registration is effective may renew it for successive years by delivering for filing in the office of the

[Secretary of State] a renewal application complying with subsection (b) between October 1 and December 31 of the preceding year. The renewal application renews the registration for the following calendar year.

(d) A foreign limited liability company whose registration is effective may qualify as a foreign company under its name or consent in writing to the use of its name by a limited liability company later organized under this [Act] or by another foreign company later authorized to transact business in this State. The registered name terminates when the limited liability company is organized or the foreign company qualifies or consents to the qualification of another foreign company under the registered name.

§ 108.   Designated Office and Agent for Service of Process

(a) A limited liability company and a foreign limited liability company authorized to do business in this State shall designate and continuously maintain in this State:

(1) an office, which need not be a place of its business in this State; and

(2) an agent and street address of the agent for service of process on the company.

(b) An agent must be an individual resident of this State, a domestic corporation, another limited liability company, or a foreign corporation or foreign company authorized to do business in this State.

§ 109. Change of Designated Office or Agent for Service of Process

A limited liability company may change its designated office or agent for service of process by delivering to the [Secretary of State] for filing a statement of change which sets forth:

(1) the name of the company;

(2) the street address of its current designated office;

(3) if the current designated office is to be changed, the street address of the new designated office;

(4) the name and address of its current agent for service of process; and

(5) if the current agent for service of process or street address of that agent is to be changed, the new address or the name and street address of the new agent for service of process.

§ 110. Resignation of Agent for Service of Process

(a) An agent for service of process of a limited liability company may resign by delivering to the [Secretary of State] for filing a record of the statement of resignation.

(b) After filing a statement of resignation, the [Secretary of State] shall mail a copy to the designated office and another copy to the limited liability company at its principal office.

(c) An agency is terminated on the 31st day after the statement is filed in the office of the [Secretary of State].

§ 111. Service of Process

(a) An agent for service of process appointed by a limited liability company or a foreign limited liability company is an agent of the company for service of any process, notice, or demand required or permitted by law to be served upon the company.

(b) If a limited liability company or foreign limited liability company fails to appoint or maintain an agent for service of process in this State or the agent for service of process cannot with reasonable diligence be found at the agent's address, the [Secretary of State] is an agent of the company upon whom process, notice, or demand may be served.

(c) Service of any process, notice, or demand on the [Secretary of State] may be made by delivering to and leaving with the [Secretary of State], the [Assistant Secretary of State], or clerk having charge of the limited liability company department of the [Secretary of State's] office duplicate copies of the process, notice, or demand. If the process, notice, or demand is served on the [Secretary of State], the [Secretary of State] shall forward one of the copies by registered or certified mail, return receipt requested, to the company at its designated office. Service is effected under this subsection at the earliest of:

(1) the date the company receives the process, notice, or demand;

(2) the date shown on the return receipt, if signed on behalf of the company; or

(3) five days after its deposit in the mail, if mailed postpaid and correctly addressed.

(d) The [Secretary of State] shall keep a record of all processes, notices, and demands served pursuant to this section and record the time of and the action taken regarding the service.

(e) This section does not affect the right to serve process, notice, or demand in any manner otherwise provided by law.

§ 112. Nature of Business and Powers

(a) A limited liability company may be organized under this [Act] for any lawful purpose, subject to any law of this State governing or regulating business.

(b) Unless its articles of organization provide otherwise, a limited liability company has the same powers as an individual to do all things necessary or convenient to carry on its business or affairs, including power to:

(1) sue and be sued, and defend in its name;

(2) purchase, receive, lease, or otherwise acquire, and own, hold, improve, use, and otherwise deal with real or personal property, or any legal

or equitable interest in property, wherever located;

(3) sell, convey, mortgage, grant a security interest in, lease, exchange, and otherwise encumber or dispose of all or any part of its property;

(4) purchase, receive, subscribe for, or otherwise acquire, own, hold, vote, use, sell, mortgage, lend, grant a security interest in, or otherwise dispose of and deal in and with, shares or other interests in or obligations of any other entity;

(5) make contracts and guarantees, incur liabilities, borrow money, issue its notes, bonds, and other obligations, which may be convertible into or include the option to purchase other securities of the limited liability company, and secure any of its obligations by a mortgage on or a security interest in any of its property, franchises, or income;

(6) lend money, invest and reinvest its funds, and receive and hold real and personal property as security for repayment;

(7) be a promoter, partner, member, associate, or manager of any partnership, joint venture, trust, or other entity;

(8) conduct its business, locate offices, and exercise the powers granted by this [Act] within or without this State;

(9) elect managers and appoint officers, employees, and agents of the limited liability compa-

ny, define their duties, fix their compensation, and lend them money and credit;

(10) pay pensions and establish pension plans, pension trusts, profit sharing plans, bonus plans, option plans, and benefit or incentive plans for any or all of its current or former members, managers, officers, employees, and agents;

(11) make donations for the public welfare or for charitable, scientific, or educational purposes; and

(12) make payments or donations, or do any other act, not inconsistent with law, that furthers the business of the limited liability company.

[ARTICLE] 2

ORGANIZATION

§ 201. Limited Liability Company as Legal Entity

A limited liability company is a legal entity distinct from its members.

§ 202. Organization

(a) One or more persons may organize a limited liability company, consisting of one or more members, by delivering articles of organization to the office of the [Secretary of State] for filing.

(b) Unless a delayed effective date is specified, the existence of a limited liability company begins when the articles of organization are filed.

(c) The filing of the articles of organization by the [Secretary of State] is conclusive proof that the organizers satisfied all conditions precedent to the creation of a limited liability company.

§ 203. Articles of Organization

(a) Articles of organization of a limited liability company must set forth:

(1) the name of the company;

(2) the address of the initial designated office;

(3) the name and street address of the initial agent for service of process;

(4) the name and address of each organizer;

(5) whether the company is to be a term company and, if so, the term specified;

(6) whether the company is to be manager-managed, and, if so, the name and address of each initial manager; and

(7) whether one or more of the members of the company are to be liable for its debts and obligations under Section 303(c).

(b) Articles of organization of a limited liability company may set forth:

(1) provisions permitted to be set forth in an operating agreement; or

(2) other matters not inconsistent with law.

(c) Articles of organization of a limited liability company may not vary the nonwaivable provisions of Section 103(b). As to all other matters, if any provision of an operating agreement is inconsistent with the articles of organization:

(1) the operating agreement controls as to managers, members, and members' transferees; and

(2) the articles of organization control as to persons, other than managers, members and their transferees, who reasonably rely on the articles to their detriment.

§ 204. Amendment or Restatement of Articles of Organization

(a) Articles of organization of a limited liability company may be amended at any time by delivering articles of amendment to the [Secretary of State] for filing. The articles of amendment must set forth the:

(1) name of the limited liability company;

(2) date of filing of the articles of organization; and

(3) amendment to the articles.

(b) A limited liability company may restate its articles of organization at any time. Restated articles of organization must be signed and filed in the same manner as articles of amendment. Restated articles of organization must be designated as such in the heading and state in the heading or in an introductory paragraph the limited liability company's present name and, if it has been changed, all of its former names and the date of the filing of its initial articles of organization.

§ 205. Signing of Records

(a) Except as otherwise provided in this [Act], a record to be filed by or on behalf of a limited liability company in the office of the [Secretary of State] must be signed in the name of the company by a:

(1) manager of a manager-managed company;

(2) member of a member-managed company;

(3) person organizing the company, if the company has not been formed; or

(4) fiduciary, if the company is in the hands of a receiver, trustee, or other court-appointed fiduciary.

(b) A record signed under subsection (a) must state adjacent to the signature the name and capacity of the signer.

(c) Any person may sign a record to be filed under subsection (a) by an attorney-in-fact. Powers of attorney relating to the signing of records to be filed under subsection (a) by an attorney-in-fact need not be filed in the office of the [Secretary of State] as evidence of authority by the person filing but must be retained by the company.

§ 206. Filing in Office of [Secretary of State]

(a) Articles of organization or any other record authorized to be filed under this [Act] must be in a medium permitted by the [Secretary of State] and must be delivered to the office of the [Secretary of State]. Unless the [Secretary of State] determines that a record fails to comply as to form with the filing requirements of this [Act], and if all filing fees have been paid, the [Secretary of State] shall file the record and send a receipt for the record and the fees to the limited liability company or its representative.

(b) Upon request and payment of a fee, the [Secretary of State] shall send to the requester a certified copy of the requested record.

(c) Except as otherwise provided in subsection (d) and Section 207(c), a record accepted for filing by the [Secretary of State] is effective:

(1) at the time of filing on the date it is filed, as evidenced by the [Secretary of State's] date and time endorsement on the original record; or

(2) at the time specified in the record as its effective time on the date it is filed.

(d) A record may specify a delayed effective time and date, and if it does so the record becomes effective at the time and date specified. If a delayed effective date but no time is specified, the record is effective at the close of business on that date. If a delayed effective date is later than the 90th day after the record is filed, the record is effective on the 90th day.

§ 207. Correcting Filed Record

(a) A limited liability company or foreign limited liability company may correct a record filed by the

[Secretary of State] if the record contains a false or erroneous statement or was defectively signed.

(b) A record is corrected:

(1) by preparing articles of correction that:

(i) describe the record, including its filing date, or attach a copy of it to the articles of correction;

(ii) specify the incorrect statement and the reason it is incorrect or the manner in which the signing was defective; and

(iii) correct the incorrect statement or defective signing; and

(2) by delivering the corrected record to the [Secretary of State] for filing.

(c) Articles of correction are effective retroactively on the effective date of the record they correct except as to persons relying on the uncorrected record and adversely affected by the correction. As to those persons, articles of correction are effective when filed.

§ 208. Certificate of Existence or Authorization

(a) A person may request the [Secretary of State] to furnish a certificate of existence for a limited liability company or a certificate of authorization for a foreign limited liability company.

(b) A certificate of existence for a limited liability company must set forth:

(1) the company's name;

(2) that it is duly organized under the laws of this State, the date of organization, whether its duration is at-will or for a specified term, and, if the latter, the period specified;

(3) if payment is reflected in the records of the [Secretary of State] and if nonpayment affects the existence of the company, that all fees, taxes, and penalties owed to this State have been paid;

(4) whether its most recent annual report required by Section 211 has been filed with the [Secretary of State];

(5) that articles of termination have not been filed; and

(6) other facts of record in the office of the [Secretary of State] which may be requested by the applicant.

(c) A certificate of authorization for a foreign limited liability company must set forth:

(1) the company's name used in this State;

(2) that it is authorized to transact business in this State;

(3) if payment is reflected in the records of the [Secretary of State] and if nonpayment affects the authorization of the company, that all fees, taxes, and penalties owed to this State have been paid;

(4) whether its most recent annual report required by Section 211 has been filed with the [Secretary of State];

(5) that a certificate of cancellation has not been filed; and

(6) other facts of record in the office of the [Secretary of State] which may be requested by the applicant.

(d) Subject to any qualification stated in the certificate, a certificate of existence or authorization issued by the [Secretary of State] may be relied upon as conclusive evidence that the domestic or foreign limited liability company is in existence or is authorized to transact business in this State.

§ 209. Liability for False Statement in Filed Record

If a record authorized or required to be filed under this [Act] contains a false statement, one who suffers loss by reliance on the statement may recover damages for the loss from a person who signed the record or caused another to sign it on the person's behalf and knew the statement to be false at the time the record was signed.

§ 210. Filing by Judicial Act

If a person required by Section 205 to sign any record fails or refuses to do so, any other person who is adversely affected by the failure or refusal may petition the [designate the appropriate court] to direct the signing of the record. If the court finds that it is proper for the record to be signed and that a person so designated has failed or refused to sign the record, it shall order the [Secretary of State] to sign and file an appropriate record.

§ 211. Annual Report for [Secretary of State]

(a) A limited liability company, and a foreign limited liability company authorized to transact business in this State, shall deliver to the [Secretary of State] for filing an annual report that sets forth:

(1) the name of the company and the State or country under whose law it is organized;

(2) the address of its designated office and the name and address of its agent for service of process in this State;

(3) the address of its principal office; and

(4) the names and business addresses of any managers.

(b) Information in an annual report must be current as of the date the annual report is signed on behalf of the limited liability company.

(c) The first annual report must be delivered to the [Secretary of State] between [January 1 and April 1] of the year following the calendar year in which a limited liability company was organized or a foreign company was authorized to transact business. Subsequent annual reports must be delivered to the [Secretary of State] between [January 1 and April 1] of the ensuing calendar years.

(d) If an annual report does not contain the information required in subsection (a), the [Secretary of State] shall promptly notify the reporting limited liability company or foreign limited liability company and return the report to it for correction. If the report is corrected to contain the information required in subsection (a) and delivered to the [Secretary of State] within 30 days after the effective date of the notice, it is timely filed.

[ARTICLE] 3

RELATIONS OF MEMBERS AND MANAGERS TO PERSONS DEALING WITH LIMITED LIABILITY COMPANY

§ 301. Agency of Members and Managers

(a) Subject to subsections (b) and (c):

(1) Each member is an agent of the limited liability company for the purpose of its business, and an act of a member, including the signing of an instrument in the company's name, for apparently carrying on in the ordinary course the company's business or business of the kind carried on by the company binds the company, unless the member had no authority to act for the company in the particular matter and the person with whom the member was dealing knew or had notice that the member lacked authority.

(2) An act of a member which is not apparently for carrying on in the ordinary course the company's business or business of the kind carried on by the company binds the company only if the act was authorized by the other members.

(b) Subject to subsection (c), in a manager-managed company:

(1) A member is not an agent of the company for the purpose of its business solely by reason of

being a member. Each manager is an agent of the company for the purpose of its business, and an act of a manager, including the signing of an instrument in the company's name, for apparently carrying on in the ordinary course the company's business or business of the kind carried on by the company binds the company, unless the manager had no authority to act for the company in the particular matter and the person with whom the manager was dealing knew or had notice that the manager lacked authority.

(2) An act of a manager which is not apparently for carrying on in the ordinary course the company's business or business of the kind carried on by the company binds the company only if the act was authorized under Section 404.

(c) Unless the articles of organization limit their authority, any member of a member-managed company or manager of a manager-managed company may sign and deliver any instrument transferring or affecting the company's interest in real property. The instrument is conclusive in favor of a person who gives value without knowledge of the lack of the authority of the person signing and delivering the instrument.

§ 302. Limited Liability Company Liable for Member's or Manager's Actionable Conduct

A limited liability company is liable for loss or injury caused to a person, or for a penalty incurred, as a result of a wrongful act or omission, or other actionable conduct, of a member or manager acting in the ordinary course of business of the company or with authority of the company.

§ 303. Liability of Members and Managers

(a) Except as otherwise provided in subsection (c), the debts, obligations, and liabilities of a limited liability company, whether arising in contract, tort, or otherwise, are solely the debts, obligations, and liabilities of the company. A member or manager is not personally liable for a debt, obligation, or liability of the company solely by reason of being or acting as a member or manager.

(b) The failure of a limited liability company to observe the usual company formalities or requirements relating to the exercise of its company powers or management of its business is not a ground for imposing personal liability on the members or managers for liabilities of the company.

(c) All or specified members of a limited liability company are liable in their capacity as members for all or specified debts, obligations, or liabilities of the company if:

(1) a provision to that effect is contained in the articles of organization; and

(2) a member so liable has consented in writing to the adoption of the provision or to be bound by the provision.

[ARTICLE]   4

RELATIONS OF MEMBERS TO EACH OTHER AND TO LIMITED LIABILITY COMPANY

§ 401.   Form of Contribution

A contribution of a member of a limited liability company may consist of tangible or intangible property or other benefit to the company, including money, promissory notes, services performed, or other agreements to contribute cash or property, or contracts for services to be performed.

§ 402.   Member's Liability for Contributions

(a) A member's obligation to contribute money, property, or other benefit to, or to perform services for, a limited liability company is not excused by the member's death, disability, or other inability to perform personally. If a member does not make the required contribution of property or services, the member is obligated at the option of the company to contribute money equal to the value of that portion of the stated contribution which has not been made.

(b) A creditor of a limited liability company who extends credit or otherwise acts in reliance on an obligation described in subsection (a), and without notice of any compromise under Section 404(c)(5), may enforce the original obligation.

§ 403. Member's and Manager's Rights to Payments and Reimbursement

(a) A limited liability company shall reimburse a member or manager for payments made and indemnify a member or manager for liabilities incurred by the member or manager in the ordinary course of the business of the company or for the preservation of its business or property.

(b) A limited liability company shall reimburse a member for an advance to the company beyond the amount of contribution the member agreed to make.

(c) A payment or advance made by a member which gives rise to an obligation of a limited liability company under subsection (a) or (b) constitutes a loan to the company upon which interest accrues from the date of the payment or advance.

(d) A member is not entitled to remuneration for services performed for a limited liability company, except for reasonable compensation for services rendered in winding up the business of the company.

§ 404. Management of Limited Liability Company

(a) In a member-managed company:

(1) each member has equal rights in the management and conduct of the company's business; and

(2) except as otherwise provided in subsection (c) or in Section 801(b)(3)(i), any matter relating

to the business of the company may be decided by a majority of the members.

(b) In a manager-managed company:

(1) each manager has equal rights in the management and conduct of the company's business;

(2) except as otherwise provided in subsection (c) or in Section 801(b)(3)(i), any matter relating to the business of the company may be exclusively decided by the manager or, if there is more than one manager, by a majority of the managers; and

(3) a manager:

(i) must be designated, appointed, elected, removed, or replaced by a vote, approval, or consent of a majority of the members; and

(ii) holds office until a successor has been elected and qualified, unless the manager sooner resigns or is removed.

(c) The only matters of a member or manager-managed company's business requiring the consent of all of the members are:

(1) the amendment of the operating agreement under Section 103;

(2) the authorization or ratification of acts or transactions under Section 103(b)(2)(ii) which would otherwise violate the duty of loyalty;

(3) an amendment to the articles of organization under Section 204;

(4) the compromise of an obligation to make a contribution under Section 402(b);

(5) the compromise, as among members, of an obligation of a member to make a contribution or return money or other property paid or distributed in violation of this [Act];

(6) the making of interim distributions under Section 405(a), including the redemption of an interest;

(7) the admission of a new member;

(8) the use of the company's property to redeem an interest subject to a charging order;

(9) the consent to dissolve the company under Section 801(b)(2);

(10) a waiver of the right to have the company's business wound up and the company terminated under Section 802(b);

(11) the consent of members to merge with another entity under Section 904(c)(1); and

(12) the sale, lease, exchange, or other disposal of all, or substantially all, of the company's property with or without goodwill.

(d) Action requiring the consent of members or managers under this [Act] may be taken without a meeting.

(e) A member or manager may appoint a proxy to vote or otherwise act for the member or manager by signing an appointment instrument, either personally or by the member's or manager's attorney-in-fact.

§ 405. Sharing of and Right to Distributions

(a) Any distributions made by a limited liability company before its dissolution and winding up must be in equal shares.

(b) A member has no right to receive, and may not be required to accept, a distribution in kind.

(c) If a member becomes entitled to receive a distribution, the member has the status of, and is entitled to all remedies available to, a creditor of the limited liability company with respect to the distribution.

§ 406. Limitations on Distributions

(a) A distribution may not be made if:

(1) the limited liability company would not be able to pay its debts as they become due in the ordinary course of business; or

(2) the company's total assets would be less than the sum of its total liabilities plus the amount that would be needed, if the company were to be dissolved, wound up, and terminated at the time of the distribution to satisfy the preferential rights upon dissolution, winding up, and termination of members whose preferential rights are superior to those receiving the distribution.

(b) A limited liability company may base a determination that a distribution is not prohibited under subsection (a) on financial statements prepared on the basis of accounting practices and principles that are reasonable in the circumstances or on a fair valuation or other method that is reasonable in the circumstances.

(c) Except as otherwise provided in subsection (e), the effect of a distribution under subsection (a) is measured:

(1) in the case of distribution by purchase, redemption, or other acquisition of a distributional interest in a limited liability company, as of the date money or other property is transferred or debt incurred by the company; and

(2) in all other cases, as of the date the:

(i) distribution is authorized if the payment occurs within 120 days after the date of authorization; or

(ii) payment is made if it occurs more than 120 days after the date of authorization.

(d) A limited liability company's indebtedness to a member incurred by reason of a distribution made in accordance with this section is at parity with the company's indebtedness to its general, unsecured creditors.

(e) Indebtedness of a limited liability company, including indebtedness issued in connection with or as part of a distribution, is not considered a liability for purposes of determinations under subsection (a) if its terms provide that payment of principal and interest are made only if and to the extent that payment of a distribution to members could then be made under this section. If the indebtedness is issued as a distribution, each payment of principal or interest on the indebtedness is treated as a distribution, the effect of which is measured on the date the payment is made.

§ 407. Liability for Unlawful Distributions

(a) A member of a member-managed company or a member or manager of a manager-managed company who votes for or assents to a distribution made in violation of Section 406, the articles of organization, or the operating agreement is personally liable to the company for the amount of the distribution which exceeds the amount that could have been distributed without violating Section 406, the articles of organization, or the operating agreement if it is established that the member or manager did not perform the member's or manager's duties in compliance with Section 409.

(b) A member of a manager-managed company who knew a distribution was made in violation of Section 406, the articles of organization, or the operating agreement is personally liable to the company, but only to the extent that the distribution received by the member exceeded the amount that could have been properly paid under Section 406.

(c) A member or manager against whom an action is brought under this section may implead in the action all:

(1) other members or managers who voted for or assented to the distribution in violation of

subsection (a) and may compel contribution from them; and

(2) members who received a distribution in violation of subsection (b) and may compel contribution from the member in the amount received in violation of subsection (b).

(d) A proceeding under this section is barred unless it is commenced within two years after the distribution.

§ 408. Member's Right to Information

(a) A limited liability company shall provide members and their agents and attorneys access to its records, if any, at the company's principal office or other reasonable locations specified in the operating agreement. The company shall provide former members and their agents and attorneys access for proper purposes to records pertaining to the period during which they were members. The right of access provides the opportunity to inspect and copy records during ordinary business hours. The company may impose a reasonable charge, limited to the costs of labor and material, for copies of records furnished.

(b) A limited liability company shall furnish to a member, and to the legal representative of a deceased member or member under legal disability:

(1) without demand, information concerning the company's business or affairs reasonably required for the proper exercise of the member's

rights and performance of the member's duties under the operating agreement or this [Act]; and

(2) on demand, other information concerning the company's business or affairs, except to the extent the demand or the information demanded is unreasonable or otherwise improper under the circumstances.

(c) A member has the right upon written demand given to the limited liability company to obtain at the company's expense a copy of any written operating agreement.

§ 409. General Standards of Member's and Manager's Conduct

(a) The only fiduciary duties a member owes to a member-managed company and its other members are the duty of loyalty and the duty of care imposed by subsections (b) and (c).

(b) A member's duty of loyalty to a member-managed company and its other members is limited to the following:

(1) to account to the company and to hold as trustee for it any property, profit, or benefit derived by the member in the conduct or winding up of the company's business or derived from a use by the member of the company's property, including the appropriation of a company's opportunity;

(2) to refrain from dealing with the company in the conduct or winding up of the company's busi-

ness as or on behalf of a party having an interest adverse to the company; and

(3) to refrain from competing with the company in the conduct of the company's business before the dissolution of the company.

(c) A member's duty of care to a member-managed company and its other members in the conduct of and winding up of the company's business is limited to refraining from engaging in grossly negligent or reckless conduct, intentional misconduct, or a knowing violation of law.

(d) A member shall discharge the duties to a member-managed company and its other members under this [Act] or under the operating agreement and exercise any rights consistently with the obligation of good faith and fair dealing.

(e) A member of a member-managed company does not violate a duty or obligation under this [Act] or under the operating agreement merely because the member's conduct furthers the member's own interest.

(f) A member of a member-managed company may lend money to and transact other business with the company. As to each loan or transaction, the rights and obligations of the member are the same as those of a person who is not a member, subject to other applicable law.

(g) This section applies to a person winding up the limited liability company's business as the personal or legal representative of the last surviving member as if the person were a member.

(h) In a manager-managed company:

(1) a member who is not also a manager owes no duties to the company or to the other members solely by reason of being a member;

(2) a manager is held to the same standards of conduct prescribed for members in subsections (b) through (f);

(3) a member who pursuant to the operating agreement exercises some or all of the rights of a manager in the management and conduct of the company's business is held to the standards of conduct in subsections (b) through (f) to the extent that the member exercises the managerial authority vested in a manager by this [Act]; and

(4) a manager is relieved of liability imposed by law for violation of the standards prescribed by subsections (b) through (f) to the extent of the managerial authority delegated to the members by the operating agreement.

§ 410. Actions by Members

(a) A member may maintain an action against a limited liability company or another member for legal or equitable relief, with or without an accounting as to the company's business, to enforce:

(1) the member's rights under the operating agreement;

(2) the member's rights under this [Act]; and

(3) the rights and otherwise protect the interests of the member, including rights and interests

arising independently of the member's relationship to the company.

(b) The accrual, and any time limited for the assertion, of a right of action for a remedy under this section is governed by other law. A right to an accounting upon a dissolution and winding up does not revive a claim barred by law.

§ 411. Continuation of Term Company After Expiration of Specified Term

(a) If a term company is continued after the expiration of the specified term, the rights and duties of the members and managers remain the same as they were at the expiration of the term except to the extent inconsistent with rights and duties of members and managers of an at-will company.

(b) If the members in a member-managed company or the managers in a manager-managed company continue the business without any winding up of the business of the company, it continues as an at-will company.

[ARTICLE] 5

TRANSFEREES AND CREDITORS OF MEMBER

§ 501. Member's Distributional Interest

(a) A member is not a co-owner of, and has no transferable interest in, property of a limited liability company.

(b) A distributional interest in a limited liability company is personal property and, subject to Sections 502 and 503, may be transferred in whole or in part.

(c) An operating agreement may provide that a distributional interest may be evidenced by a certificate of the interest issued by the limited liability company and, subject to Section 503, may also provide for the transfer of any interest represented by the certificate.

§ 502. Transfer of Distributional Interest

A transfer of a distributional interest does not entitle the transferee to become or to exercise any rights of a member. A transfer entitles the transferee to receive, to the extent transferred, only the distributions to which the transferor would be entitled.

§ 503. Rights of Transferee

(a) A transferee of a distributional interest may become a member of a limited liability company if and to the extent that the transferor gives the transferee the right in accordance with authority described in the operating agreement or all other members consent.

(b) A transferee who has become a member, to the extent transferred, has the rights and powers, and is subject to the restrictions and liabilities, of a member under the operating agreement of a limited liability company and this [Act]. A transferee who becomes a member also is liable for the transferor member's obligations to make contributions under Section 402 and for obligations under Section 407 to return unlawful distributions, but the transferee is not obligated for the transferor member's liabilities unknown to the transferee at the time the transferee becomes a member.

(c) Whether or not a transferee of a distributional interest becomes a member under subsection (a), the transferor is not released from liability to the limited liability company under the operating agreement or this [Act].

(d) A transferee who does not become a member is not entitled to participate in the management or conduct of the limited liability company's business, require access to information concerning the company's transactions, or inspect or copy any of the company's records.

(e) A transferee who does not become a member is entitled to:

(1) receive, in accordance with the transfer, distributions to which the transferor would otherwise be entitled;

(2) receive, upon dissolution and winding up of the limited liability company's business:

(i) in accordance with the transfer, the net amount otherwise distributable to the transferor;

(ii) a statement of account only from the date of the latest statement of account agreed to by all the members;

(3) seek under Section 801(5) a judicial determination that it is equitable to dissolve and wind up the company's business.

(f) A limited liability company need not give effect to a transfer until it has notice of the transfer.

§ 504. Rights of Creditor

(a) On application by a judgment creditor of a member of a limited liability company or of a member's transferee, a court having jurisdiction may charge the distributional interest of the judgment debtor to satisfy the judgment. The court may appoint a receiver of the share of the distributions due or to become due to the judgment debtor and make all other orders, directions, accounts, and inquiries the judgment debtor might have made or which the circumstances may require to give effect to the charging order.

(b) A charging order constitutes a lien on the judgment debtor's distributional interest. The court may order a foreclosure of a lien on a distributional interest subject to the charging order at any time. A purchaser at the foreclosure sale has the rights of a transferee.

(c) At any time before foreclosure, a distributional interest in a limited liability company which is charged may be redeemed:

(1) by the judgment debtor;

(2) with property other than the company's property, by one or more of the other members; or

(3) with the company's property, but only if permitted by the operating agreement.

(d) This [Act] does not affect a member's right under exemption laws with respect to the member's distributional interest in a limited liability company.

(e) This section provides the exclusive remedy by which a judgment creditor of a member or a transferee may satisfy a judgment out of the judgment debtor's distributional interest in a limited liability company.

[ARTICLE] 6

MEMBER'S DISSOCIATION

§ 601. Events Causing Member's Dissociation

A member is dissociated from a limited liability company upon the occurrence of any of the following events:

(1) the company's having notice of the member's express will to withdraw upon the date of notice or on a later date specified by the member;

(2) an event agreed to in the operating agreement as causing the member's dissociation;

(3) upon transfer of all of a member's distributional interest, other than a transfer for security purposes or a court order charging the member's distributional interest which has not been foreclosed;

(4) the member's expulsion pursuant to the operating agreement;

(5) the member's expulsion by unanimous vote of the other members if:

(i) it is unlawful to carry on the company's business with the member;

(ii) there has been a transfer of substantially all of the member's distributional interest, other than a transfer for security purposes or a court order charging the member's distributional interest which has not been foreclosed;

(iii) within 90 days after the company notifies a corporate member that it will be expelled because it has filed a certificate of dissolution or the equivalent, its charter has been revoked, or its right to conduct business has been suspended by the jurisdiction of its incorporation, the member fails to obtain a revocation of the certificate of dissolution or a reinstatement of its charter or its right to conduct business; or

(iv) a partnership or a limited liability company that is a member has been dissolved and its business is being wound up;

(6) on application by the company or another member, the member's expulsion by judicial determination because the member:

(i) engaged in wrongful conduct that adversely and materially affected the company's business;

(ii) willfully or persistently committed a material breach of the operating agreement or of a duty owed to the company or the other members under Section 409; or

(iii) engaged in conduct relating to the company's business which makes it not reasonably practicable to carry on the business with the member;

(7) the member's:

(i) becoming a debtor in bankruptcy;

(ii) executing an assignment for the benefit of creditors;

(iii) seeking, consenting to, or acquiescing in the appointment of a trustee, receiver, or liquidator of the member or of all or substantially all of the member's property; or

(iv) failing, within 90 days after the appointment, to have vacated or stayed the appointment of a trustee, receiver, or liquidator of the member or of all or substantially all of the member's property obtained without the member's consent or acquiescence, or failing within 90 days after the expiration of a stay to have the appointment vacated;

(8) in the case of a member who is an individual:

(i) the member's death;

(ii) the appointment of a guardian or general conservator for the member; or

(iii) a judicial determination that the member has otherwise become incapable of performing the member's duties under the operating agreement;

(9) in the case of a member that is a trust or is acting as a member by virtue of being a trustee of a trust, distribution of the trust's entire rights to receive distributions from the company, but not merely by reason of the substitution of a successor trustee;

(10) in the case of a member that is an estate or is acting as a member by virtue of being a personal representative of an estate, distribution of the estate's entire rights to receive distributions from the company, but not merely the substitution of a successor personal representative; or

(11) termination of the existence of a member if the member is not an individual, estate, or trust other than a business trust.

§ 602. Member's Power to Dissociate; Wrongful Dissociation

(a) Unless otherwise provided in the operating agreement, a member has the power to dissociate from a limited liability company at any time, rightfully or wrongfully, by express will pursuant to Section 601(1).

(b) If the operating agreement has not eliminated a member's power to dissociate, the member's dissociation from a limited liability company is wrongful only if:

(1) it is in breach of an express provision of the agreement; or

(2) before the expiration of the specified term of a term company:

(i) the member withdraws by express will;

(ii) the member is expelled by judicial determination under Section 601(6);

(iii) the member is dissociated by becoming a debtor in bankruptcy; or

(iv) in the case of a member who is not an individual, trust other than a business trust, or estate, the member is expelled or otherwise dissociated because it willfully dissolved or terminated its existence.

(c) A member who wrongfully dissociates from a limited liability company is liable to the company and to the other members for damages caused by the dissociation. The liability is in addition to any other obligation of the member to the company or to the other members.

(d) If a limited liability company does not dissolve and wind up its business as a result of a member's wrongful dissociation under subsection (b), damages sustained by the company for the wrongful dissociation must be offset against distributions otherwise due the member after the dissociation.

§ 603. Effect of Member's Dissociation

(a) Upon a member's dissociation:

(1) in an at-will company, the company must cause the dissociated member's distributional interest to be purchased under [Article] 7; and

(2) in a term company:

(i) if the company dissolves and winds up its business on or before the expiration of its specified term, [Article] 8 applies to determine the dissociated member's rights to distributions; and

(ii) if the company does not dissolve and wind up its business on or before the expiration of its specified term, the company must cause the dissociated member's distributional interest to be purchased under [Article] 7 on the date of the expiration of the term specified at the time of the member's dissociation.

(b) Upon a member's dissociation from a limited liability company:

(1) the member's right to participate in the management and conduct of the company's business terminates, except as otherwise provided in Section 803, and the member ceases to be a member and is treated the same as a transferee of a member;

(2) the member's duty of loyalty under Section 409(b)(3) terminates; and

(3) the member's duty of loyalty under Section 409(b)(1) and (2) and duty of care under Section 409(c) continue only with regard to matters arising and events occurring before the member's dissociation, unless the member participates in winding up the company's business pursuant to Section 803.

[ARTICLE]   7

MEMBER'S DISSOCIATION WHEN BUSINESS NOT WOUND UP

§ 701. Company Purchase of Distributional Interest

(a) A limited liability company shall purchase a distributional interest of a:

(1) member of an at-will company for its fair value determined as of the date of the member's dissociation if the member's dissociation does not result in a dissolution and winding up of the company's business under Section 801; or

(2) member of a term company for its fair value determined as of the date of the expiration of the specified term that existed on the date of the member's dissociation if the expiration of the specified term does not result in a dissolution and winding up of the company's business under Section 801.

(b) A limited liability company must deliver a purchase offer to the dissociated member whose distributional interest is entitled to be purchased not later than 30 days after the date determined under subsection (a). The purchase offer must be accompanied by:

(1) a statement of the company's assets and liabilities as of the date determined under subsection (a);

(2) the latest available balance sheet and income statement, if any; and

(3) an explanation of how the estimated amount of the payment was calculated.

(c) If the price and other terms of a purchase of a distributional interest are fixed or are to be determined by the operating agreement, the price and terms so fixed or determined govern the purchase unless the purchaser defaults. If a default occurs, the dissociated member is entitled to commence a proceeding to have the company dissolved under Section 801(4)(iv).

(d) If an agreement to purchase the distributional interest is not made within 120 days after the date determined under subsection (a), the dissociated member, within another 120 days, may commence a proceeding against the limited liability company to enforce the purchase. The company at its expense shall notify in writing all of the remaining members, and any other person the court directs, of the commencement of the proceeding. The jurisdiction of the court in which the proceeding is commenced under this subsection is plenary and exclusive.

(e) The court shall determine the fair value of the distributional interest in accordance with the standards set forth in Section 702 together with the terms for the purchase. Upon making these determinations, the court shall order the limited liability company to purchase or cause the purchase of the interest.

(f) Damages for wrongful dissociation under Section 602(b), and all other amounts owing, whether or not currently due, from the dissociated member to a limited liability company, must be offset against the purchase price.

§ 702. Court Action to Determine Fair Value of Distributional Interest

(a) In an action brought to determine the fair value of a distributional interest in a limited liability company, the court shall:

(1) determine the fair value of the interest, considering among other relevant evidence the going concern value of the company, any agreement among some or all of the members fixing the price or specifying a formula for determining value of distributional interests for any other purpose, the recommendations of any appraiser appointed by the court, and any legal constraints on the company's ability to purchase the interest;

(2) specify the terms of the purchase, including, if appropriate, terms for installment payments, subordination of the purchase obligation to the rights of the company's other creditors, security for a deferred purchase price, and a covenant not to compete or other restriction on a dissociated member; and

(3) require the dissociated member to deliver an assignment of the interest to the purchaser upon receipt of the purchase price or the first installment of the purchase price.

(b) After the dissociated member delivers the assignment, the dissociated member has no further claim against the company, its members, officers, or managers, if any, other than a claim to any unpaid balance of the purchase price and a claim under any agreement with the company or the remaining members that is not terminated by the court.

(c) If the purchase is not completed in accordance with the specified terms, the company is to be dissolved upon application under Section 801(4)(iv). If a limited liability company is so dissolved, the dissociated member has the same rights and priorities in the company's assets as if the sale had not been ordered.

(d) If the court finds that a party to the proceeding acted arbitrarily, vexatiously, or not in good faith, it may award one or more other parties their reasonable expenses, including attorney's fees and the expenses of appraisers or other experts, incurred in the proceeding. The finding may be based on the company's failure to make an offer to pay or to comply with Section 701(b).

(e) Interest must be paid on the amount awarded from the date determined under Section 701(a) to the date of payment.

§ 703.   Dissociated Member's Power to Bind Limited Liability Company

For two years after a member dissociates without the dissociation resulting in a dissolution and winding up of a limited liability company's business, the company, including a surviving company under [Article] 9, is bound by an act of the dissociated member which would have bound the company under

Section 301 before dissociation only if at the time of entering into the transaction the other party:

(1) reasonably believed that the dissociated member was then a member;

(2) did not have notice of the member's dissociation; and

(3) is not deemed to have had notice under Section 704.

§ 704. Statement of Dissociation

(a) A dissociated member or a limited liability company may file in the office of the [Secretary of State] a statement of dissociation stating the name of the company and that the member is dissociated from the company.

(b) For the purposes of Sections 301 and 703, a person not a member is deemed to have notice of the dissociation 90 days after the statement of dissociation is filed.

[ARTICLE] 8

WINDING UP COMPANY'S BUSINESS

§ 801. Events Causing Dissolution and Winding Up of Company's Business

A limited liability company is dissolved, and its business must be wound up, upon the occurrence of any of the following events:

(1) an event specified in the operating agreement;

(2) consent of the number or percentage of members specified in the operating agreement;

(3) an event that makes it unlawful for all or substantially all of the business of the company to be continued, but any cure of illegality within 90 days after notice to the company of the event is effective retroactively to the date of the event for purposes of this section;

(4) on application by a member or a dissociated member, upon entry of a judicial decree that:

(i) the economic purpose of the company is likely to be unreasonably frustrated;

(ii) another member has engaged in conduct relating to the company's business that makes it not reasonably practicable to carry on the company's business with that member;

(iii) it is not otherwise reasonably practicable to carry on the company's business in conformity with the articles of organization and the operating agreement;

(iv) the company failed to purchase the petitioner's distributional interest as required by Section 701; or

(v) the managers or members in control of the company have acted, are acting, or will act in a manner that is illegal, oppressive, fraudulent, or unfairly prejudicial to the petitioner; or

(5) on application by a transferee of a member's interest, a judicial determination that it is equitable to wind up the company's business:

(i) after the expiration of the specified term, if the company was for a specified term at the time the applicant became a transferee by member dissociation, transfer, or entry of a charging order that gave rise to the transfer; or

(ii) at any time, if the company was at will at the time the applicant became a transferee by member dissociation, transfer, or entry of a charging order that gave rise to the transfer.

§ 802. Limited Liability Company Continues After Dissolution

(a) Subject to subsection (b), a limited liability company continues after dissolution only for the purpose of winding up its business.

(b) At any time after the dissolution of a limited liability company and before the winding up of its business is completed, the members, including a dissociated member whose dissociation caused the dissolution, may unanimously waive the right to have the company's business wound up and the company terminated. In that case:

(1) the limited liability company resumes carrying on its business as if dissolution had never occurred and any liability incurred by the company or a member after the dissolution and before the waiver is determined as if the dissolution had never occurred; and

(2) the rights of a third party accruing under Section 804(a) or arising out of conduct in reliance on the dissolution before the third party knew or received a notification of the waiver are not adversely affected.

§ 803. Right to Wind Up Limited Liability Company's Business

(a) After dissolution, a member who has not wrongfully dissociated may participate in winding up a limited liability company's business, but on application of any member, member's legal representative, or transferee, the [designate the appropriate court], for good cause shown, may order judicial supervision of the winding up.

(b) A legal representative of the last surviving member may wind up a limited liability company's business.

(c) A person winding up a limited liability company's business may preserve the company's business or property as a going concern for a reasonable time, prosecute and defend actions and proceedings, whether civil, criminal, or administrative, settle and close the company's business, dispose of and transfer the company's property, discharge the company's liabilities, distribute the assets of the company pursuant to Section 806, settle disputes by mediation or arbitration, and perform other necessary acts.

§ 804. Member's or Manager's Power and Liability as Agent After Dissolution

(a) A limited liability company is bound by a member's or manager's act after dissolution that:

(1) is appropriate for winding up the company's business; or

(2) would have bound the company under Section 301 before dissolution, if the other party to the transaction did not have notice of the dissolution.

(b) A member or manager who, with knowledge of the dissolution, subjects a limited liability company to liability by an act that is not appropriate for winding up the company's business is liable to the company for any damage caused to the company arising from the liability.

§ 805. Articles of Termination

(a) At any time after dissolution and winding up, a limited liability company may terminate its existence by filing with the [Secretary of State] articles of termination stating:

(1) the name of the company;

(2) the date of the dissolution; and

(3) that the company's business has been wound up and the legal existence of the company has been terminated.

(b) The existence of a limited liability company is terminated upon the filing of the articles of termination, or upon a later effective date, if specified in the articles of termination.

§ 806. Distribution of Assets in Winding Up Limited Liability Company's Business

(a) In winding up a limited liability company's business, the assets of the company must be applied to discharge its obligations to creditors, including members who are creditors. Any surplus must be applied to pay in money the net amount distributable to members in accordance with their right to distributions under subsection (b).

(b) Each member is entitled to a distribution upon the winding up of the limited liability company's business consisting of a return of all contributions which have not previously been returned and a distribution of any remainder in equal shares.

§ 807. Known Claims Against Dissolved Limited Liability Company

(a) A dissolved limited liability company may dispose of the known claims against it by following the procedure described in this section.

(b) A dissolved limited liability company shall notify its known claimants in writing of the dissolution. The notice must:

(1) specify the information required to be included in a claim;

(2) provide a mailing address where the claim is to be sent;

(3) state the deadline for receipt of the claim, which may not be less than 120 days after the date the written notice is received by the claimant; and

(4) state that the claim will be barred if not received by the deadline.

(c) A claim against a dissolved limited liability company is barred if the requirements of subsection (b) are met, and:

(1) the claim is not received by the specified deadline; or

(2) in the case of a claim that is timely received but rejected by the dissolved company, the claimant does not commence a proceeding to enforce the claim within 90 days after the receipt of the notice of the rejection.

(d) For purposes of this section, "claim" does not include a contingent liability or a claim based on an event occurring after the effective date of dissolution.

§ 808. Other Claims Against Dissolved Limited Liability Company

(a) A dissolved limited liability company may publish notice of its dissolution and request persons having claims against the company to present them in accordance with the notice.

(b) The notice must:

(1) be published at least once in a newspaper of general circulation in the [county] in which the dissolved limited liability company's principal office is located or, if none in this State, in which its designated office is or was last located;

(2) describe the information required to be contained in a claim and provide a mailing address where the claim is to be sent; and

(3) state that a claim against the limited liability company is barred unless a proceeding to enforce the claim is commenced within five years after publication of the notice.

(c) If a dissolved limited liability company publishes a notice in accordance with subsection (b), the claim of each of the following claimants is barred unless the claimant commences a proceeding to enforce the claim against the dissolved company within five years after the publication date of the notice:

(1) a claimant who did not receive written notice under Section 807;

(2) a claimant whose claim was timely sent to the dissolved company but not acted on; and

(3) a claimant whose claim is contingent or based on an event occurring after the effective date of dissolution.

(d) A claim not barred under this section may be enforced:

(1) against the dissolved limited liability company, to the extent of its undistributed assets; or

(2) if the assets have been distributed in liquidation, against a member of the dissolved company to the extent of the member's proportionate share of the claim or the company's assets distributed to the member in liquidation, whichever is less, but a member's total liability for all claims under this section may not exceed the total amount of assets distributed to the member.

§ 809. Grounds for Administrative Dissolution

The [Secretary of State] may commence a proceeding to dissolve a limited liability company administratively if the company does not:

(1) pay any fees, taxes, or penalties imposed by this [Act] or other law within 60 days after they are due; or

(2) deliver its annual report to the [Secretary of State] within 60 days after it is due.

§ 810. Procedure for and Effect of Administrative Dissolution

(a) If the [Secretary of State] determines that a ground exists for administratively dissolving a limited liability company, the [Secretary of State] shall enter a record of the determination and serve the company with a copy of the record.

(b) If the company does not correct each ground for dissolution or demonstrate to the reasonable satisfaction of the [Secretary of State] that each ground determined by the [Secretary of State] does not exist within 60 days after service of the notice, the [Secretary of State] shall administratively dissolve the company by signing a certification of the dissolution that recites the ground for dissolution and its effective date. The [Secretary of State] shall file the original of the certificate and serve the company with a copy of the certificate.

(c) A company administratively dissolved continues its existence but may carry on only business necessary to wind up and liquidate its business and affairs under Section 802 and to notify claimants under Sections 807 and 808.

(d) The administrative dissolution of a company does not terminate the authority of its agent for service of process.

§ 811. Reinstatement Following Administrative Dissolution

(a) A limited liability company administratively dissolved may apply to the [Secretary of State] for reinstatement within two years after the effective date of dissolution. The application must:

(1) recite the name of the company and the effective date of its administrative dissolution;

(2) state that the ground for dissolution either did not exist or have [sic] been eliminated;

(3) state that the company's name satisfies the requirements of Section 105; and

(4) contain a certificate from the [taxing authority] reciting that all taxes owed by the company have been paid.

(b) If the [Secretary of State] determines that the application contains the information required by subsection (a) and that the information is correct, the [Secretary of State] shall cancel the certificate of dissolution and prepare a certificate of reinstatement that recites this determination and the effective date of reinstatement, file the original of the certificate, and serve the company with a copy of the certificate.

(c) When reinstatement is effective, it relates back to and takes effect as of the effective date of the administrative dissolution and the company may resume its business as if the administrative dissolution had never occurred.

§ 812. Appeal From Denial of Reinstatement

(a) If the [Secretary of State] denies a limited liability company's application for reinstatement following administrative dissolution, the [Secretary of State] shall serve the company with a record that explains the reason or reasons for denial.

(b) The company may appeal the denial of reinstatement to the [name appropriate] court within 30 days after service of the notice of denial is perfected. The company appeals by petitioning the court to set aside the dissolution and attaching to the petition copies of the [Secretary of State's] certificate of dissolution, the company's application for reinstatement, and the [Secretary of State's] notice of denial.

(c) The court may summarily order the [Secretary of State] to reinstate the dissolved company or may take other action the court considers appropriate.

(d) The court's final decision may be appealed as in other civil proceedings.

[ARTICLE] 9

CONVERSIONS AND MERGERS

§ 901. Definitions

In this [article]:

(1) "Corporation" means a corporation under [the State Corporation Act], a predecessor law, or comparable law of another jurisdiction.

(2) "General partner" means a partner in a partnership and a general partner in a limited partnership.

(3) "Limited partner" means a limited partner in a limited partnership.

(4) "Limited partnership" means a limited partnership created under [the State Limited Partnership Act], a predecessor law, or comparable law of another jurisdiction.

(5) "Partner" includes a general partner and a limited partner.

(6) "Partnership" means a general partnership under [the State Partnership Act], a predecessor law, or comparable law of another jurisdiction.

(7) "Partnership agreement" means an agreement among the partners concerning the partnership or limited partnership.

(8) "Shareholder" means a shareholder in a corporation.

§ 902. Conversion of Partnership or Limited Partnership to Limited Liability Company

(a) A partnership or limited partnership may be converted to a limited liability company pursuant to this section.

(b) The terms and conditions of a conversion of a partnership or limited partnership to a limited liability company must be approved by all of the partners or by a number or percentage of the partners required for conversion in the partnership agreement.

(c) An agreement of conversion must set forth the terms and conditions of the conversion of the interests of partners of a partnership or of a limited partnership, as the case may be, into interests in the converted limited liability company or the cash or other consideration to be paid or delivered as a result of the conversion of the interests of the partners, or a combination thereof.

(d) After a conversion is approved under subsection (b), the partnership or limited partnership shall file articles of organization in the office of the [Secretary of State] which satisfy the requirements of Section 203 and contain:

(1) a statement that the partnership or limited partnership was converted to a limited liability company from a partnership or limited partnership, as the case may be;

(2) its former name;

(3) a statement of the number of votes cast by the partners entitled to vote for and against the conversion and, if the vote is less than unanimous, the number or percentage required to approve the conversion under subsection (b); and

(4) in the case of a limited partnership, a statement that the certificate of limited partnership is to be canceled as of the date the conversion took effect.

(e) In the case of a limited partnership, the filing of articles of organization under subsection (d) cancels its certificate of limited partnership as of the date the conversion took effect.

(f) A conversion takes effect when the articles of organization are filed in the office of the [Secretary of State] or at any later date specified in the articles of organization.

(g) A general partner who becomes a member of a limited liability company as a result of a conversion remains liable as a partner for an obligation incurred by the partnership or limited partnership before the conversion takes effect.

(h) A general partner's liability for all obligations of the limited liability company incurred after the conversion takes effect is that of a member of the company. A limited partner who becomes a member as a result of a conversion remains liable only to the extent the limited partner was liable for an obligation incurred by the limited partnership before the conversion takes effect.

§ 903. Effect of Conversion; Entity Unchanged

(a) A partnership or limited partnership that has been converted pursuant to this [article] is for all purposes the same entity that existed before the conversion.

(b) When a conversion takes effect:

(1) all property owned by the converting partnership or limited partnership vests in the limited liability company;

(2) all debts, liabilities, and other obligations of the converting partnership or limited partnership continue as obligations of the limited liability company;

(3) an action or proceeding pending by or against the converting partnership or limited partnership may be continued as if the conversion had not occurred;

(4) except as prohibited by other law, all of the rights, privileges, immunities, powers, and purposes of the converting partnership or limited partnership vest in the limited liability company; and

(5) except as otherwise provided in the agreement of conversion under Section 902(c), all of the partners of the converting partnership continue as members of the limited liability company.

§ 904. Merger of Entities

(a) Pursuant to a plan of merger approved under subsection (c), a limited liability company may be merged with or into one or more limited liability companies, foreign limited liability companies, corporations, foreign corporations, partnerships, foreign partnerships, limited partnerships, foreign limited partnerships, or other domestic or foreign entities.

(b) A plan of merger must set forth:

(1) the name of each entity that is a party to the merger;

(2) the name of the surviving entity into which the other entities will merge;

(3) the type of organization of the surviving entity;

(4) the terms and conditions of the merger;

(5) the manner and basis for converting the interests of each party to the merger into interests or obligations of the surviving entity, or into money or other property in whole or in part; and

(6) the street address of the surviving entity's principal place of business.

(c) A plan of merger must be approved:

(1) in the case of a limited liability company that is a party to the merger, by all of the members or by a number or percentage of members specified in the operating agreement;

(2) in the case of a foreign limited liability company that is a party to the merger, by the vote required for approval of a merger by the law

of the State or foreign jurisdiction in which the foreign limited liability company is organized;

(3) in the case of a partnership or domestic limited partnership that is a party to the merger, by the vote required for approval of a conversion under Section 902(b); and

(4) in the case of any other entities that are parties to the merger, by the vote required for approval of a merger by the law of this State or of the State or foreign jurisdiction in which the entity is organized and, in the absence of such a requirement, by all the owners of interests in the entity.

(d) After a plan of merger is approved and before the merger takes effect, the plan may be amended or abandoned as provided in the plan.

(e) The merger is effective upon the filing of the articles of merger with the [Secretary of State], or at such later date as the articles may provide.

§ 905. Articles of Merger

(a) After approval of the plan of merger under Section 904(c), unless the merger is abandoned under Section 904(d), articles of merger must be signed on behalf of each limited liability company and other entity that is a party to the merger and delivered to the [Secretary of State] for filing. The articles must set forth:

(1) the name and jurisdiction of formation or organization of each of the limited liability com-

panies and other entities that are parties to the merger;

(2) for each limited liability company that is to merge, the date its articles of organization were filed with the [Secretary of State];

(3) that a plan of merger has been approved and signed by each limited liability company and other entity that is to merge;

(4) the name and address of the surviving limited liability company or other surviving entity;

(5) the effective date of the merger;

(6) if a limited liability company is the surviving entity, such changes in its articles of organization as are necessary by reason of the merger;

(7) if a party to a merger is a foreign limited liability company, the jurisdiction and date of filing of its initial articles of organization and the date when its application for authority was filed by the [Secretary of State] or, if an application has not been filed, a statement to that effect; and

(8) if the surviving entity is not a limited liability company, an agreement that the surviving entity may be served with process in this State and is subject to liability in any action or proceeding for the enforcement of any liability or obligation of any limited liability company previously subject to suit in this State which is to merge, and for the enforcement, as provided in this [Act], of the right of members of any limited liability

company to receive payment for their interest against the surviving entity.

(b) If a foreign limited liability company is the surviving entity of a merger, it may not do business in this State until an application for that authority is filed with the [Secretary of State].

(c) The surviving limited liability company or other entity shall furnish a copy of the plan of merger, on request and without cost, to any member of any limited liability company or any person holding an interest in any other entity that is to merge.

(d) Articles of merger operate as an amendment to the limited liability company's articles of organization.

§ 906. Effect of Merger

(a) When a merger takes effect:

(1) the separate existence of each limited liability company and other entity that is a party to the merger, other than the surviving entity, terminates;

(2) all property owned by each of the limited liability companies and other entities that are party to the merger vests in the surviving entity;

(3) all debts, liabilities, and other obligations of each limited liability company and other entity that is party to the merger become the obligations of the surviving entity;

(4) an action or proceeding pending by or against a limited liability company or other party to a merger may be continued as if the merger had not occurred or the surviving entity may be substituted as a party to the action or proceeding; and

(5) except as prohibited by other law, all the rights, privileges, immunities, powers, and purposes of every limited liability company and other entity that is a party to a merger vest in the surviving entity.

(b) The [Secretary of State] is an agent for service of process in an action or proceeding against the surviving foreign entity to enforce an obligation of any party to a merger if the surviving foreign entity fails to appoint or maintain an agent designated for service of process in this State or the agent for service of process cannot with reasonable diligence be found at the designated office. Upon receipt of process, the [Secretary of State] shall send a copy of the process by registered or certified mail, return receipt requested, to the surviving entity at the address set forth in the articles of merger. Service is effected under this subsection at the earliest of:

(1) the date the company receives the process, notice, or demand;

(2) the date shown on the return receipt, if signed on behalf of the company; or

(3) five days after its deposit in the mail, if mailed postpaid and correctly addressed.

(c) A member of the surviving limited liability company is liable for all obligations of a party to the merger for which the member was personally liable before the merger.

(d) Unless otherwise agreed, a merger of a limited liability company that is not the surviving entity in the merger does not require the limited liability company to wind up its business under this [Act] or pay its liabilities and distribute its assets pursuant to this [Act].

(e) Articles of merger serve as articles of dissolution for a limited liability company that is not the surviving entity in the merger.

§ 907.   [Article] Not Exclusive

This [article] does not preclude an entity from being converted or merged under other law.

[ARTICLE]   10

FOREIGN LIMITED LIABILITY COMPANIES

§ 1001.   Law Governing Foreign Limited Liability Companies

(a) The laws of the State or other jurisdiction under which a foreign limited liability company is organized govern its organization and internal affairs and the liability of its managers, members, and their transferees.

(b) A foreign limited liability company may not be denied a certificate of authority by reason of any difference between the laws of another jurisdiction under which the foreign company is organized and the laws of this State.

(c) A certificate of authority does not authorize a foreign limited liability company to engage in any business or exercise any power that a limited liability company may not engage in or exercise in this State.

§ 1002. Application For Certificate of Authority

(a) A foreign limited liability company may apply for a certificate of authority to transact business in this State by delivering an application to the [Secretary of State] for filing. The application must set forth:

(1) the name of the foreign company or, if its name is unavailable for use in this State, a name that satisfies the requirements of Section 1005;

(2) the name of the State or country under whose law it is organized;

(3) the street address of its principal office;

(4) the address of its initial designated office in this State;

(5) the name and street address of its initial agent for service of process in this State;

(6) whether the duration of the company is for a specified term and, if so, the period specified;

(7) whether the company is manager-managed, and, if so, the name and address of each initial manager; and

(8) whether the members of the company are to be liable for its debts and obligations under a provision similar to Section 303(c).

(b) A foreign limited liability company shall deliver with the completed application a certificate of existence or a record of similar import authenticated by the secretary of state or other official having custody of company records in the State or country under whose law it is organized.

§ 1003. Activities Not Constituting Transacting Business

(a) Activities of a foreign limited liability company that do not constitute transacting business in this State within the meaning of this [article] include:

(1) maintaining, defending, or settling an action or proceeding;

(2) holding meetings of its members or managers or carrying on any other activity concerning its internal affairs;

(3) maintaining bank accounts;

(4) maintaining offices or agencies for the transfer, exchange, and registration of the foreign company's own securities or maintaining trustees or depositories with respect to those securities;

(5) selling through independent contractors;

(6) soliciting or obtaining orders, whether by mail or through employees or agents or otherwise, if the orders require acceptance outside this State before they become contracts;

(7) creating or acquiring indebtedness, mortgages, or security interests in real or personal property;

(8) securing or collecting debts or enforcing mortgages or other security interests in property securing the debts, and holding, protecting, and maintaining property so acquired;

(9) conducting an isolated transaction that is completed within 30 days and is not one in the course of similar transactions of a like manner; and

(10) transacting business in interstate commerce.

(b) For purposes of this [article], the ownership in this State of income-producing real property or tangible personal property, other than property excluded under subsection (a), constitutes transacting business in this State.

(c) This section does not apply in determining the contacts or activities that may subject a foreign limited liability company to service of process, taxation, or regulation under any other law of this State.

§ 1004. Issuance of Certificate of Authority

Unless the [Secretary of State] determines that an application for a certificate of authority fails to comply as to form with the filing requirements of this [Act], the [Secretary of State], upon payment of all filing fees, shall file the application and send a receipt for it and the fees to the limited liability company or its representative.

§ 1005. Name of Foreign Limited Liability Company

(a) If the name of a foreign limited liability company does not satisfy the requirements of Section 105, the company, to obtain or maintain a certificate of authority to transact business in this State, must use a fictitious name to transact business in this State if its real name is unavailable and it delivers to the [Secretary of State] for filing a copy of the resolution of its managers, in the case of a manager-managed company, or of its members, in the case of a member-managed company, adopting the fictitious name.

(b) Except as authorized by subsections (c) and (d), the name, including a fictitious name to be used to transact business in this State, of a foreign limited liability company must be distinguishable upon the records of the [Secretary of State] from:

(1) the name of any corporation, limited partnership, or company incorporated, organized, or authorized to transact business in this State;

(2) a name reserved or registered under Section 106 or 107; and

(3) the fictitious name of another foreign limited liability company authorized to transact business in this State.

(c) A foreign limited liability company may apply to the [Secretary of State] for authority to use in this State a name that is not distinguishable upon the records of the [Secretary of State] from a name described in subsection (b). The [Secretary of State] shall authorize use of the name applied for if:

(1) the present user, registrant, or owner of a reserved name consents to the use in a record and submits an undertaking in form satisfactory to the [Secretary of State] to change its name to a name that is distinguishable upon the records of the [Secretary of State] from the name of the foreign applying limited liability company; or

(2) the applicant delivers to the [Secretary of State] a certified copy of a final judgment of a court establishing the applicant's right to use the name applied for in this State.

(d) A foreign limited liability company may use in this State the name, including the fictitious name, of another domestic or foreign entity that is used in this State if the other entity is incorporated, organized, or authorized to transact business in this State and the foreign limited liability company:

(1) has merged with the other entity;

(2) has been formed by reorganization of the other entity; or

(3) has acquired all or substantially all of the assets, including the name, of the other entity.

(e) If a foreign limited liability company authorized to transact business in this State changes its name to one that does not satisfy the requirements of Section 105, it may not transact business in this

State under the name as changed until it adopts a name satisfying the requirements of Section 105 and obtains an amended certificate of authority.

§ 1006.   Revocation of Certificate of Authority

(a) A certificate of authority of a foreign limited liability company to transact business in this State may be revoked by the [Secretary of State] in the manner provided in subsection (b) if:

(1) the company fails to:

(i) pay any fees, taxes, and penalties owed to this State;

(ii) deliver its annual report required under Section 211 to the [Secretary of State] within 60 days after it is due;

(iii) appoint and maintain an agent for service of process as required by this [article]; or

(iv) file a statement of a change in the name or business address of the agent as required by this [article]; or

(2) a misrepresentation has been made of any material matter in any application, report, affidavit, or other record submitted by the company pursuant to this [article].

(b) The [Secretary of State] may not revoke a certificate of authority of a foreign limited liability company unless the [Secretary of State] sends the company notice of the revocation, at least 60 days before its effective date, by a record addressed to its agent for service of process in this State, or if the company fails to appoint and maintain a proper agent in this State, addressed to the office required to be maintained by Section 108. The notice must specify the cause for the revocation of the certificate of authority. The authority of the company to transact business in this State ceases on the effective date of the revocation unless the foreign limited liability company cures the failure before that date.

§ 1007. Cancellation of Authority

A foreign limited liability company may cancel its authority to transact business in this State by filing in the office of the [Secretary of State] a certificate of cancellation. Cancellation does not terminate the authority of the [Secretary of State] to accept service of process on the company for [claims for relief] arising out of the transactions of business in this State.

§ 1008. Effect of Failure to Obtain Certificate of Authority

(a) A foreign limited liability company transacting business in this State may not maintain an action or proceeding in this State unless it has a certificate of authority to transact business in this State.

(b) The failure of a foreign limited liability company to have a certificate of authority to transact business in this State does not impair the validity of a contract or act of the company or prevent the foreign limited liability company from defending an action or proceeding in this State.

(c) Limitations on personal liability of managers, members, and their transferees are not waived solely by transacting business in this State without a certificate of authority.

(d) If a foreign limited liability company transacts business in this State without a certificate of authority, it appoints the [Secretary of State] as its agent for service of process for [claims for relief] arising out of the transaction of business in this State.

§ 1009. Action by [Attorney General]

The [Attorney General] may maintain an action to restrain a foreign limited liability company from transacting business in this State in violation of this [article].

[ARTICLE]   11
DERIVATIVE ACTIONS

§ 1101. Right of Action

A member of a limited liability company may maintain an action in the right of the company if the members or managers having authority to do so have refused to commence the action or an effort to cause those members or managers to commence the action is not likely to succeed.

§ 1102. Proper Plaintiff

In a derivative action for a limited liability company, the plaintiff must be a member of the company when the action is commenced; and:

(1) must have been a member at the time of the transaction of which the plaintiff complains; or

(2) the plaintiff's status as a member must have devolved upon the plaintiff by operation of law or pursuant to the terms of the operating agreement from a person who was a member at the time of the transaction.

§ 1103. Pleading

In a derivative action for a limited liability company, the complaint must set forth with particularity the effort of the plaintiff to secure initiation of the action by a member or manager or the reasons for not making the effort.

§ 1104. Expenses

If a derivative action for a limited liability company is successful, in whole or in part, or if anything is received by the plaintiff as a result of a judgment, compromise, or settlement of an action or claim, the court may award the plaintiff reasonable expenses, including reasonable attorney's fees, and shall direct the plaintiff to remit to the limited liability company the remainder of the proceeds received.

[ARTICLE] 12

MISCELLANEOUS PROVISIONS

§ 1201. Uniformity of Application and Construction

This [Act] shall be applied and construed to effectuate its general purpose to make uniform the law with respect to the subject of this [Act] among States enacting it.

§ 1202. Short Title

This [Act] may be cited as the Uniform Limited Liability Company Act (1995).

§ 1203. Severability Clause

If any provision of this [Act] or its application to any person or circumstance is held invalid, the invalidity does not affect other provisions or applications of this [Act] which can be given effect without the invalid provision or application, and to this end the provisions of this [Act] are severable.

§ 1204. Effective Date

This [Act] takes effect [_____].

§ 1205. Transitional Provisions

(a) Before January 1, 199__, this [Act] governs only a limited liability company organized:

(1) after the effective date of this [Act], unless the company is continuing the business of a dissolved limited liability company under [Section of the existing Limited Liability Company Act]; and

(2) before the effective date of this [Act], which elects, as provided by subsection (c), to be governed by this [Act].

(b) On and after January 1, 199__, this [Act] governs all limited liability companies.

(c) Before January 1, 199___, a limited liability company voluntarily may elect, in the manner provided in its operating agreement or by law for amending the operating agreement, to be governed by this [Act].

§ 1206. Savings Clause

This [Act] does not affect an action or proceeding commenced or right accrued before the effective date of this [Act].

INDEX

References are to Pages

545

†